DICTIONARY OF POPULAR CULTURE

About the author

Tony Thorne is the author of the highly acclaimed *Bloomsbury Dictionary of Contemporary Slang*. He has published a number of books, contributed to best-selling dictionaries and lectured and broadcast worldwide on issues of language and culture. He currently teaches at King's College, University of London.

DICTIONARY OF POPULAR CULTURE

Fads, Fashions & Cults

*From Acid House to Zoot Suit – via Existentialism
and Political Correctness – the definitive guide to
(post-) modern culture*

Tony Thorne

BLOOMSBURY

To the Class of '68

First published 1993 as *Fads, Fashions & Cults*
by Bloomsbury Publishing Limited,
2 Soho Square, London W1V 5DE

This paperback edition published in 1994

Copyright © 1993 by Tony Thorne

The moral right of the author has been asserted

A CIP record for this book is available upon request
from the British Library

ISBN 0 7475 1457 7

Typeset by Hewer Text Composition Services, Edinburgh
Printed and bound by Cox and Wyman Ltd, Reading

Acknowledgements

Any errors of fact and all contentious opinions contained in this book are entirely the responsibility of the compiler. A number of individuals and organizations helped with advice and information, and thanks are due to them, as well as the many commentators whose words have been quoted in the text. Particular thanks go to Ray Granger and Iona Opie for access to their archives; to James Park, Henry Boxer, Nick Myers, Annabel Edwards and Professor John Newson for comments and suggestions; to my daughter Alexandra Thorne for tips on pre-teen fads; and to Julian Alexander, Kathy Rooney, Tracey Smith, Kate Newman, Caroline Johnson and Louise Speller for seeing the project into print.

Preface

In reviewing the six months since the first edition of this book was published it is interesting to consider both the new fads and fashions which have surfaced and the change, if any, in public attitudes towards them.

Novelties there have certainly been, but what is striking is how few have been truly original: the evolution of eccentric sports has thrown up HUMAN TENPIN BOWLING, people enclosed in steel spheres and rolled against giant pins; the SURFBOARD and SKATEBOARD, have mutated into the Snowboard (see SNOW SURFING), have given rise to the SNAKEBOARD – dual footplates allowing a sinuous acrobatic motion across the ground.

In the field of music and youth culture GRUNGE grew from a scruffy marginal fad into a fully-fledged cult. Promoted by Seattle record companies and absorbing a look (sixties' tat plus seventies' bad taste) and a lifestyle (deadpan, indolent, insolent), Grunge made it from the street to the catwalk and back in disgrace to the street in less than a year. At the same time the cold, electronic DISCO-based HOUSE and TECHNO music seemed to merge further into ROCK-inspired INDIE POP, while the RIOT GIRLS movement, spreading from the US to Britain in early 1993, combined FEMINISM with the latest manifestation of PUNK attitude.

In the 'higher reaches' of progressive culture the backlash against the DECONSTRUCTION movement and the POST-STRUCTURALISM of the 1960s' French intellectuals has proceeded apace; not unconnected is the reaction on both sides of the Atlantic to PC and all its strictures.

Out on the NEW AGE fringes, TREE-SNIFFING developed into TREE-HUGGING, and the discredited CROP CIRCLES refused to go away. In the design shops LAVA LAMPS languished unsold while the younger generation added erotic HIGH-TEC Japanese MANGA COMICS to their repertoire of VIDEO GAMES, SKATEBOARDING and GRAFFITI.

Tony Thorne
London 1994

Introduction

Fads and fashions are by definition ephemeral things. A cursory look at the years since 1945 reveals a fascinating succession of transient crazes, vogues and trends, most visible in what is called pop-culture, but also discernible in the 'higher' cultural reaches of literature, the graphic and plastic arts, philosophy and politics. It may be timely then, in the run-up to the millenium, to record these phenomena, so that those who lived through them and those who came after them can try to make sense of the minutiae of modern history. What were the HULA-HOOP, the ANGRY YOUNG MEN, the BEAUTIFUL PEOPLE? Why does the name DAVY CROCKETT figure large in the memories of forty-something-year-olds? Where does the concept of NEW AGE come from? Or for that matter the much-touted NEW MAN? Standard reference works give only half the answers; encyclopedias and dictionaries of philosophy and thought treat only high culture; journalistic reports are usually in close-up and omit the context; sociological textbooks are full of generalizations and obfuscations. There is a need for a dispassionate compendium of the modes and mores of postwar Anglo-Saxon culture and this book is an attempt to provide just that. It is meant for the casual browser as much as for the serious student: for those wanting to decode a difficult term, or for those with the patience to trace the crosscurrents of fashion through a string of cross-references.

Fads and fashions are not isolated occurrences. The network of connections linking the entries in this book points to their deeper significance. In some cases the links are obvious: TALKOVER and TOASTING evolved via DUB into RAP, which together with BREAK DANCING and BODY POPPING formed the adolescent HIP HOP subculture which spread worldwide from its New York origins. There are also underlying tendencies which realize themselves in different surface forms at different times. PIRATE RADIO, CB RADIO, FANZINES, INDIE labels and HACKERS, for instance, all represent an attempt to empower the consumer by taking back control of the electronic media. In some cases the components of a fashion may be tangled or obscure: did the YUPPIE create the Enterprise Culture of the 1980s or vice versa? Did the Yuppie embody the progressive self-awareness of the HIPPIE wedded to capitalism, as American commentators have suggested, or in Britain was he or she not a blend of resurrected MOD and déclassé SLOANE RANGER?

In the 1980s, the following of fashion became thoroughly self-conscious: fashions were relentlessly recycled, parodied and pastiched, with the full complicity of the mass media and the more specialized style magazines. In clothing, music, architecture and design the accumulated ideas and images of preceding generations were appropriated and stripped of their meanings: the notion of MODERNISM – the idea of linear progress led by an aesthetic élite – finally submerged in a new reality dictated by high-technology and competing consumer whims. This book takes a Post-Modernist stance, giving equal weight to the frivolous, the banal, and the grandiose, on the assumption that they all have something important to tell us about the real, pluralist, cosmopolitan environment we now live in. It does not imply, as Modernism did, that difficulty and inaccessibility are a precondition of art and it considers that a quintessentially trivial craze such as the HULA-HOOP is as inherently interesting as an economic fad such as MONETARISM.

In looking back it is astonishing how long many of these ideas and images took to penetrate public consciousness; the SLOANE RANGER took twenty years to acquire a name; the seminal STRUCTURALISTS and SEMIOLOGISTS writing in French in the 1950s and 1960s were often not translated for a decade, taking even longer to come to the attention of academe and the media. As well as bringing the reader up to date, this book may serve a secondary purpose in rehabilitating marginalized or lost ideas; it may also subvert the assumptions sometimes made by those who were not there or did not see.

The scope of this book is suggested by its title. Each of the words actually chosen seemed to have a special resonance which matched the various categories contained herein. The jaunty pejorative 'fad' (definable as 'a short-lived practice or interest, usually pursued with exaggerated zeal') is of unknown origin, but probably comes from a dialect term related to 'fiddle-faddle'; it seems to define perfectly such things as SUSHI or BROOMBALL. 'Fashion', suggesting respectable modishness, fits such entries as ZOOT SUIT, EARTH SHOES or the NEW LOOK. The word 'cult' is defined in Hugh Rawson's *Dictionary of Invective* as 'an organised group of people, religious or not, with whom you disagree'; for me this describes the MOONIES or WICCA.

In fact, of course, there are no strict definitions of the words above, and the criteria for inclusion are largely subjective. I have chosen not to include gadgets like the mobile telephone or the compact disc, as their appearance seems an inevitable result of technological advance. Changing concepts in politics and education do not appear unless they have made an impact, as THATCHERISM certainly did, on other areas of culture. Cults of personality like the necrophiliac interest surrounding Marilyn Monroe, James Dean and Elvis Presley have been exhaustively covered elsewhere, and genres which were firmly established before the starting point of 1945 (opera or classical music, for instance) are not included. The entries in *Fads, Fashions & Cults* almost all concern the English-speaking world, except when a notion or movement from elsewhere such as EXISTENTIALISM and ORGANIC ARCHITECTURE has penetrated Anglo-Saxon parochialism.

Reference works usually affect omniscience and objectivity; neither is remotely possible in this case, where the subject matter is so firmly bound up with taste, opinion and controversy. I am sure that many will disagree with the choice of entries, the interpretations given and the judgements inevitably implied in certain cases. Another danger in attempting to grasp the transitory is that one's comments will quickly be outstripped by events, that the book will succumb to obsolescence. Even as the manuscript is delivered for typesetting a report confirms that BAR FLY JUMPING has progressed from a minority craze to a multi-million-pound success, spinning off more and more novelty sports (like the self-explanatory Pole-Jousting and Bouncy-Boxing) which are too recent to be explained here. Simultaneously the anti-FEMINIST backlash has taken a new turn in the UK with the publication of Neil Lyndon's acerbic *No More Sex War* and ensuing vitriolic counterblasts from his former wife among others. Only time will tell if these events merit more than a passing reference.

Finally, a word on how to judge the text. A book today should not be a frozen monologue delivered to the reader, but a dialogue in which the reader may join in, pose questions and answer back. Comments, criticisms and elucidations will be gratefully received and acknowledged.

ABSTRACT EXPRESSIONISM

The dominant movement in painting in the 1950s, Abstract
Expressionism's main exponents formed the so-called New York
School, comprising Jackson Pollock, Willem de Kooning, Franz
Kline and Mark Rothko, although the phrase had first been applied
to the Russian-German-French painter Wassily Kandinsky and the
Armenian-American Arshile Gorky. Working from the mid-1940s
in non-figurative and semi-figurative modes, the American artists
practised unrestrained brushwork and use of colour to produce
direct expressions of feelings and forms, typically on large canvases.
Although this tendency institutionalized radical innovation, it
never transcended either the traditional format canvas or the
standard modes of gallery exhibition. Some of its exponents,
such as Pollock, tended towards free-form fragmentation, while
others, such as Rothko, favoured the cooler, so-called Colour Field
painting. The style and execution of the former was intensely
individualistic, gestural and often frenzied, lending itself to criticisms
of self-indulgence and phoniness, and to caricature in the popular
media, but the fact that most Abstract Expressionist art was not
susceptible to non-expert criticism led to its rapid endorsement by
the international art market, which it continued to dominate until
the 1990s.

In painting, Abstract Expressionism and other forms of abstraction
(particularly POST-PAINTERLY and HARD EDGE) continued to be
influential throughout the 1960s, but their subjectivity and lack of
a social or communal dimension gradually weakened their hold
on progressive aesthetic opinion in favour of POP ART, while the
movement's most dynamic approach, ACTION PAINTING, was to
some extent incorporated into PERFORMANCE ART. In the late 1980s,
however, the cult New York painter Julian Schnabel was still able to
attract attention by briefly reprising its techniques. Historically, the

Abstract Expressionist movement established the postwar leadership of the USA, and New York in particular, in the field of modern art. This led, somewhat bizarrely, to it being promoted by the CIA as a cultural weapon in the Cold War.

- *Postwar US art communicates the exhilaration, panic and despair engendered by a chaotic urban environment. It breathes the kind of hyperactivity that presages premature death – Jackson Pollock's alcoholic car crash, Mark Rothko's suicide . . .*

  Geraldine Norman and Edward Lucie-Smith,
  Independent, *August 1990*

ABSURD

See THEATRE OF THE ABSURD.

ACID HOUSE

Not to be confused with the ACID ROCK of a previous generation, the Acid House cult began in 1987 with the coming together in dance clubs of HOUSE music and the euphoric hallucinogenic drug ECSTASY (MDMA), known by the generic name of 'acid' (a term also applied by a previous generation to LSD). In Britain, clubs established to re-create the atmosphere of the discothèques and large-scale impromptu parties of Ibiza (a favourite rendezvous for DANCEFLOOR enthusiasts from all over Western Europe) generated a youth movement that incorporated garishly quasi-PSYCHEDELIC BAGGY surf (see SURFING), beach and leisure clothing, ecstatic non-stop en *masse* dancing, an egalitarian and multiracial ethos of apolitical hedonism, and electronic BALEARIC BEAT music that included Eurodisco, DUB, RAP and even ROCK, as well as House. Adherents of this style displayed 'Smiley' logos, chanted the slogan 'A-c-e-e-d!', and advocated a return to the values of 'peace and love' promoted in the late 1960s.

Forgoing the élitism of early 1980s club culture, Acid House took off in the summer of 1988 – known as the second 'Summer of Love', the first having been in 1967 – and spread across Britain via RAVES or WAREHOUSE parties. These were organized gatherings held in warehouses, hangars or other empty buildings that were publicized through underground networks. Celebrants would pay to attend, usually in very large numbers, and the parties could last for several nights if not prevented by police raids. By 1991, however, the term Acid House was out of favour with the younger generation and the musical repertoire had extended to include TECHNO, but the movement had developed into an influential Dancefloor culture with its own anti-ideology and graphics (influenced by GRAFFITI and NEO-FAUVISM), and a thriving network of clubs, pirate radio stations (see PIRATE BROADCASTING), record labels and sellers of clothes and accessories. Existing in parallel with Rap and INDIE POP, Acid House illustrates the triumph of the heirs of DISCO, rather than of Rock 'n' Roll, as the dominant youth cult of the Eighties. In 1992 large numbers of Acid House devotees joined forces for the first time with TRAVELLERS and CRUSTIES on the summer free-festival circuit and there were signs of a fusion of lifestyles and musical genres.

- *Acid House reinvented the '60s hippy explosion but on its terms; via clubs not albums, using DJs' club runners, producers and personalities, as opposed to traditional band units.*
  Paolo Hewitt, NME, *December 1988*

- *Acid House, a movement with one idea, simply patted itself on the head and danced itself to a standstill. Its only achievement was to resurrect the facile self-satisfaction of Sixties hedonism.*
  Jon Wilde, Esquire, *Winter 1991*

ACID ROCK

A synonym for the PSYCHEDELIC electric ROCK music that accompanied the HIPPIE culture of the late 1960s, and which contributed to HARD ROCK, COCK ROCK and HEAVY METAL. The label was applied particularly to loud American bands such as Blue Cheer, Moby Grape, Steppenwolf and the 13th Floor Elevators, but (strangely) rarely to the more authentic evokers of drug experiences such as Country Joe and the Fish and Captain Beefheart.

ACTION PAINTING

The term Action Painting was coined in 1952 by the critic Harold Rosenberg to describe the most physical manifestations of ABSTRACT EXPRESSIONISM. Compositions were created by splashing, spattering, smearing or dripping paint on to a canvas, transforming action into vision not by description but by result. The term was applied to de

Kooning, Motherwell and others, but became associated in popular perception with Jackson Pollock in particular. Later practitioners focused even more strongly on the staging of the act of painting by riding bicycles across canvases and attaching explosive paint sacs to canvases, for example, thus pushing Action Painting into the arena of PERFORMANCE ART. The novelty and shock value of Action Painting naturally dwindled, and by the 1970s its main significance was as an educational and therapeutic technique.

ACUPUNCTURE

During the 1970s the ancient Chinese medical practice of acupuncture – the strategic placing of needles into the human body – was slowly admitted into the repertoire of mainstream Western healing techniques. The treatment is based on the assumption that a network of lines of energy runs throughout the human body, and that penetrating one or more of the 1000 designated points along these 'meridians' will restore the flow of the life-force. Orthodox science does not accept the body-as-microcosm notion behind acupuncture, nor has it fully explained the neural relationships that allow the technique to be used, for example, to anaesthetize patients. Nevertheless, acupuncture is now an accepted form of complementary medicine, as well as being the inspiration in HOLISTIC therapy for a number of other 'alternative' practices, such as acupressure, REFLEXOLOGY and SHIATSU.

ADAM

See ECSTASY.

AEROBICS

Aerobics is the generic term for fashionable keep-fit exercises usually performed in groups and to accompanying rhythmic music; it is a blend of the earlier fads of jogging and dance therapy. The word is formed from the prefix aero- (from the Greek aer, meaning air) and bios, the Greek for life, and strictly speaking refers to any rigorous exercise that speeds up breathing and oxygenates the bloodstream. Aerobics classes involving group workouts to DISCO music began in California at the end of the 1970s and by 1983 had spread to the

UK, accompanying the new emphasis on self-improvement through physical fitness, and assisted by propagation on video cassette and television and by a booming market in clothing accessories. Fanciful claims have been made for aerobics as a modern form of 'tribal group-bonding', whilst in marketing terms the mainstream adoption of self-reinvention through health disciplines (originally pioneered by the COUNTERCULTURE) is an example of CONSUMERISM of the third stage (the first involves consumption of goods, the second of services, and the third of experience). Like previous cults such as the HULA-HOOP and the TWIST, aerobics has lent itself to marathons: in Britain in May 1992, 14,000 people worked out for twenty minutes for charity, setting a new world record. A year earlier, the VIDEO GAMES company Nintendo introduced the 'Nintendo Mat' on which computer aerobics could be practised.

AEROBIE

The trademark name for a flat plastic ring which is thrown in the same way as its forerunner, the FRISBEE, for fun or in competition. The Aerobie, which appeared in 1986, is more aerodynamically efficient than the Frisbee and can travel further, but is less suited to hovering aerobatics and has not become the centre of a cult or culture like its predecessor. The same manufacturers subsequently produced the pyramid-shaped Orbiter.

AFGHAN COATS

These UNISEX sheepskin coats were adopted from Afghani shepherds by some of the first travellers on the so-called 'HIPPIE trail' – the overland route from Europe to India and Nepal. The coats, which were usually three-quarter length or in the form of sleeveless jerkins, were made of part-treated undyed skins worn with the wool on the inside, forming ruffs at the wrists, neck and hem. Later versions often featured coloured embroidery. Their smell, along with that of PATCHOULI OIL, became an integral part of the ambience of antique markets, pop festivals and MACROBIOTIC cafés during the late Sixties and early Seventies. The Afghan was actually high fashion in progressive circles only in 1967 and 1968, before being imported in bulk and becoming identified, like LOON PANTS, with a Hippie stereotype. After 1973 the style virtually disappeared except among precursors of the later NEW AGE TRAVELLERS. Among the fashion-conscious young the Afghan featured in parody revivals such as the neo-PSYCHEDELIA of the 1980s and the THEME DISCO craze of the early Nineties.

AFRO

The natural result of the convergence of long hair and Afro-Caribbean hair texture, the Afro (a shortening of 'Afro-American') became an emblematic expression of black pride in 1967. Until that time most black militants of both sexes had worn short or medium-length hairstyles indistinguishable from those of conformist black society (in which the imitation of white styles by straightening and bleaching was also widespread). Allowing hair to grow and then teasing it into a mass of tight curls produced a spectacular anti-Establishment symbol that quickly spread from the street and campuses to the music and fashion industries. Among white HIPPIES, both male and female, and particularly in Britain, the style became detached from its political overtones and was adopted as the hair fad of the moment in the winter of 1967–8, necessitating backcombing or perming. Afro wigs were also worn by those forbidden to grow their hair, such as American prison inmates, and by those who were willing to make only a part-time fashion statement. The Afro was never African (it was banned in Tanzania as a symbol of neo-colonialism), it was rejected by RASTAFARIANS, and by about 1973 was mainly limited to the visual repertoire of unfashionable black FUNK music groups.

- *The Afro wig worn by Black Panther George Jackson in San Quentin provided the guards there with the perfect reason for shooting him in 1971. They claimed he had a 9mm automatic pistol beneath it.*

    Dylan Jones, Haircults, 1990

- *Lord Lichfield's fashionable 'Afro' hairdo inspired Adel Rootstein to use him as the model for one of her shop-window dummies.*

    Vogue *retrospective on the 1970s, June 1991*

AFRO MUSIC

The name given to dance music played by such groups as Osibisa and Assagai in the early Seventies. Afro music was influenced by

West African HIGH LIFE and East African KWELA; it was an early component in what came to be known as ethnic music and in the 1980s as WORLD MUSIC.

AIR GUITAR

This refers to the practice by HEAVY METAL fans in which part of the ecstatic reaction to the music (along with HEAD-BANGING and MOSHING) is to mime the frantic playing of an imaginary guitar. Some fans even constructed cardboard guitars for much-ridiculed performances, but these were usually reserved for solitary listening at home.

- *There are three or four hundred people gathered here for a five-band, death-metal bonanza. And I'm the only one who can't play air guitar.*
  Zoë Heller, Independent on Sunday, 6 September 1992

AIRPORT STYLE

See FESTIVAL STYLE.

A-LINE

The A-line was the more austere silhouette introduced by Christian Dior in 1955 as the successor to *haute couture's* NEW LOOK. The triangular shape (severely cut jacket above flared, often pleated skirt) continued to dominate women's fashion until the PENCIL SKIRT of the early 1960s. The Fifties vogue for novelty in high-fashion silhouettes ran the gamut of the H-line, the trapeze line, the tulip line, the oval line, the profile line, the princess line, the sinuous line, the umbrella line, the horseshoe line and the scissor line. The term A-Line continued to be used for the standard triangular skirt shape into the 1990s.

ALTERNATIVE COMEDY

Alternative comedy evolved in the USA and Britain in the mid-1970s from the realization that the audiences and venues for ROCK music would be receptive to other forms of entertainment.

In North America, gong shows, in which members of the public are given an opportunity to perform onstage until jeered off, became popular on campuses and in bars and led to the establishment of the Comedy Store in Los Angeles. In Britain PUB ROCK had by 1979 bred a pub cabaret network in which stand-up comedians, often influenced by PUNK values and RANTING poetry, were usually the star attractions. London's own Comedy Store opened in Leicester Square in 1980, providing a showcase for many of the cult comedians of the next decade. Some, such as Alexei Sayle and the members of the Comic Strip repertory, quickly transferred to television, while others, particularly those from the 'second wave' such as Jeremy Hardy, Jo Brand and John Hegley, for example, continued to work in the flourishing pub/club/festival circuit. Alternative comedy was characterized by its rejection of the sexist and sometimes racist values of traditional club comedians and of the apolitical complacency of mainstream televised humour. Alternative comedians added the frenetic style of delivery and the nihilism of Punk to the existing strain of irreverence and SATIRE in British TV. The trend promoted women as performers and ridiculed male stereotypes and coincidentally tapped into the huge youth audience for comedy, which, unlike the highly fragmented, partisan music scene, is relatively uncritical and homogenous.

- *Ben Elton is now about as 'alternative' as June Whitfield, and the Comic Strip movies were so gratuitously unfunny as to defy belief. Part of the problem was that the 1980s saw the young adopt comedy as part of their culture, along with pop and pizza.*
  Bryan Appleyard, Sunday Times, September 1990

- *On stage was a rancid ranting autopilot megaphone gobshite alternative comedian. His act certainly was an alternative to comedy. As abrasive as crushed velvet, and like a psychiatric case-history come to life . . .*
  Bruce Thomas, The Big Wheel, 1990

ALTERNATIVE SOCIETY

A synonym for the COUNTERCULTURE of the 1960s and early 1970s, the alternative society is a concept embodied in the Marxist idea of a dialectic. By synthesis an alternative society is said to be constantly in formation.

- *... the Oxford Creative Workshop is holding a three-day talk-in on the alternative society in Oxford. To be discussed: How can a commune keep out of debt without compromising? How can spontaneity of vision be preserved in a switched-off world?*
  Advertisement in Oz magazine, May 1969

ALTERNATIVE MEDICINE

See HOLISTIC MEDICINE: NEW AGE.

AMBIENT MUSIC

See REPETITIVE MUSIC.

ANGRY BRIGADE

Britain's only equivalent to the urban guerrillas active in Europe and the USA in the late 1960s and early 1970s, the Angry Brigade was a small cell of libertarian Marxist activists. The group coalesced around a core of members of the 'Red Engine' group active in Essex University in 1968; their aim was the destabilizing of bourgeois society on behalf of an indifferent proletariat by means of sabotage. Between the summer of 1967 and the end of 1971 they were responsible for a series of attacks, including the machine-gunning of the façade of the US Embassy in London, the bombing of the home of the Conservative Minister of Employment, Robert Carr, and the fire-bombing of the Biba department store. In 1972 police raided a communal household in Stoke Newington, north London, and arrested the ringleaders, including Jake Prescott, Ian Purdie, Angie Weir and Hilary Creek, who were subsequently imprisoned. Despite achieving unprecedented publicity, the Angry Brigade failed to mobilize support for violent direct action among either the orthodox left or the hedonist COUNTERCULTURE in Britain. (At least two other groups were also involved in minor bombing campaigns in 1970 and 1971, but were unreported by the mass-circulation press.) In its stance, the Angry Brigade anticipated the approach of later anti-Establishment groups such as CLASS WAR, and single-issue campaigners such as some ANIMAL RIGHTS supporters.

● *Jake [Prescott] has been further charged with bombing a BBC van at the Miss World Contest on November 20, and the Department of Employment and Productivity on December 9.*

IT *magazine, May 1971*

ANGRY YOUNG MEN

The term 'Angry Young Man' became a buzz word for the late 1950s after being applied in 1956 to the authors and fictional heroes of a genre of British writing that included work by John Osborne, Kingsley Amis and Colin Wilson. John Waine, John Braine, Allan Sillitoe and Keith Waterhouse were also often included. The phrase itself was first used in 1951 as the title of the Irish writer Leslie Paul's autobiography, and was later appropriated by the publicist of the Royal Court Theatre for the première of John Osborne's play *Look Back in Anger*. The real Angry Young Men were lower-middle-class critics of the snobberies, hypocrisies and frustrations then prevalent in British society; their fictional leading men (there were no female equivalents) were outsiders railing against or mocking the Establishment. The tone of voice employed communicated impotent protest and a yearning for self-advancement rather than any suggestion of an ALTERNATIVE SOCIETY; in retrospect the 'movement' appears provincial and unfocused, paralysed by class envy and cultural stereotypes, especially in comparison with its Continental predecessor EXISTENTIALISM, and its American contemporary, the BEAT MOVEMENT. It did, however, introduce the note of dissent into popular culture that contributed to the KITCHEN SINK school of drama, the SATIRE boom, and subsequent Sixties subversions

ANIMAL RIGHTS

The animal rights movement began in the mid-1970s on the basis that, according to natural law, other species should be as entitled to enjoy their rights as the oppressed black, female and gay (see GAY LIBERATION) members of the human species. At first the tendency, without a name or particular focus, was opposed to such things as the fur trade and factory farming, as well as to vivisection, which had been campaigned against in the UK for decades. By the end of the 1970s, however, the question had been radicalized and publicized by the activities of extremists such as the Animal Liberation Front.

This movement, founded by hunt saboteurs (see SABBING), has no membership as such, but exists as a loose confederation of cells operating a central underground 'post office'. It favours direct action in the form of 'economic sabotage' (the releasing of animals from farming and research facilities, and the destruction of such properties). It has disowned bomb attacks and death threats against individuals made in its name, but organizations such as the RSPCA, LYNX, Beauty Without Cruelty and the Anti-Vivisection Society have rejected its tactics. Nevertheless, the extremists do enjoy the active or tacit support of many leftists, anarchists, student activists and radical environmentalists and between 1985 and 1991 at least 400 significant attacks were carried out by animal rights campaigners in Britain and Northern Ireland, many going un- or under-reported by the press in order to minimize public anxiety. In conjunction with less radical campaigning on the issues of cosmetics and fur, the animal rights movement had by 1990 succeeded in reducing the number of animals used in experimentation in the UK from four million to three million, and in putting the scientific Establishment on the defensive.

- *There will be injuries and possibly deaths on both sides . . . before our ultimate victory for animal liberation is achieved. This is sad but certain.*

  Ronnie Lee, imprisoned founder of the ALF

ANORAKS

See INDIE POP.

ANTHROPIC PRINCIPLE

The anthropic principle – from the Greek *anthropikos*, relating to Man or humanity – is a matrix of ideas in the field of physics and cosmology sometimes known as the NEW SCIENCE that aroused interest in the scientific community in the early 1980s, and which by around 1986 was beginning to intrigue non-specialists in the same way as such notions as the UNCERTAINTY PRINCIPLE and CHAOS THEORY. Put very simply, the weak anthropic principle implies that the human presence in the universe is not merely accidental, and that human observation of the cosmos itself determines such things as probability in physical laws. The strong anthropic principle goes further by implying that our role in the universe may in some way be essential in order to bring phenomena into being and assist the evolution of matter. The ideas generated by these theories, although imperfectly understood in many cases, have attracted both revisionists and conservatives who wish to re-establish humanity at the centre of creation, as well as progressives who imagine humans as actively participating in the information processing that sustains space/time.

ANTI-NAZI LEAGUE
See ROCK AGAINST RACISM.

ANTI-PSYCHIATRY
Anti-psychiatry, promoted by Thomas Szasz in the USA and by R. D. Laing and David Cooper in the UK, was a radical rejection of orthodox psychiatry's definitions of mental illness and its treatment of supposed sufferers. In *The Myth of Mental Illness*, published in 1960, the Hungarian-American analyst Szasz claimed that schizophrenia was a label invented by the psychiatric Establishment in order to exercise social control over disturbed individuals. Laing ascribed psychiatric problems to contradictions imposed on individuals by the family and society, and opposed the incarceration and drugging of the mentally disturbed. (A parallel though more abstract challenge to Establishment thinking in this area was launched in France by Felix Guattari and Gilles Deleuze). The alternative explanations advanced and therapies practised by anti-psychiatrists became fashionable in the later 1960s and remained influential, although recent evidence of the electro-chemical basis for behaviour has called into question many of their claims.

APPROPRIATIONISM
In the era of POP ART, painters and sculptors following the pre-war lead of Duchamp and the Surrealists began to incorporate images and artefacts designed by others into their own work. From the 1970s onwards it also became commonplace for graphic designers and advertisers to appropriate ready-made visuals for their own ends. In the field of music, although cross-reference was common, plagiarism

was more problematical, as demonstrated by the litigation against George Harrison over his song 'My Sweet Lord' by the holders of the rights to the Chiffons' 'He's So Fine'. The musical situation was confused by the advent of SAMPLING in the early Eighties.

The question of authorship and originality in fine art has always been vexed. In addition to using second-hand visual devices, many gallery artists, particularly of the avant-garde, delegated the actual execution of their ideas to (usually anonymous) minions. The American Elaine Sturtevant was probably the first so-called Appropriationist − a non-pejorative label for an avowed copyist − producing imitations of canvases by Frank Stella, Andy Warhol and Claes Oldenburg. Other copyists included Mike Bidlo, Sherry Levine and, most controversially, Jeff Koons. Koons, already more notorious as the lover (later husband) of the Italian-Hungarian porn-star MP La Cicciolina than as a sculptor, was sued in 1992 by the photographer Art Rogers, whose 'Puppies' postcard had been used by Koons as the basis of a KITSCH assemblage. Appropriationism, also known as Simulationism, highlighted the POST-MODERN disdain for originality, ownership of signs and messages, and traditional artistic conventions. The debate was between those who defended plagiarism as a knowing gesture and those who considered it a pretentious cloak for cynical exploitation.

ARGENTINE DUCKTAIL

The greased-back hairstyle worn by Mexican-American youths in the 1940s and associated with the ZOOT SUIT. It was inspired by the styles worn by tango dancers (hence the Argentine reference) and itself inspired the later DA.

AROMATHERAPY

A form of NEW AGE treatment providing body-toning and stress-reduction through massage with natural essential oils. It was readily assimilated into mainstream health and beauty techniques from about 1979. The practice is based on the assumption that blends of oils − composed according to the patient's physical and emotional condition − will be absorbed in small quantities through the skin while body 'meridians' and pressure points are manipulated.

- *Placing a 'tally' from the patient in the centre of a dowsing disc – a lock of hair or a handwriting sample – the therapist will dowse to find the most suitable oil and then the best method of treatment.*
  Brian Inglis and Ruth West, The Alternative Health Guide, 1983

ART BRUT
See OUTSIDER ART.

ARTS LABS
A phenomenon of the later 1960s, the 'Arts Laboratory' was born of the trend for mixed-media events, group activities, open access and audience participation. The original Arts Lab was established in Drury Lane in London's Covent Garden by Jim Haynes in 1967. It consisted of spaces (without seating) devoted at different times to exhibitions, films, dance, music and theatre, as well as a kitchen and a bookshop. It was famous for, among other things, providing a setting for some of England's first regular LIGHT SHOWS and for the first progressive use of video. The all-night London centre was forced to close in 1969, by which time it was being used as a 'crash-pad' as well as a focus for the COUNTERCULTURE. Fifty other Arts Labs were begun within a year elsewhere in the UK and although the name ceased to be used after about 1973, the pioneering concept influenced community art centres in the following decade.

AUTEURISM
The notion of the 'auteur' was developed by critics writing in the French film magazine Les Cahiers du Cinéma in the late 1950s and early 1960s. These critics chose to elevate the status of certain directors by characterizing their films as expressions of their continuing themes and concerns, rather than simply as one-off collaborations with producers, scriptwriters, cinematographers, etc., or as the product of a studio. These directors were thus credited with almost total creative responsibility for their work in the same way as a literary author (auteur in French). The term was applied by French enthusiasts to such Hollywood directors as John Ford, Howard Hawks, Nicholas Ray and Alfred Hitchcock (who was bemused by the idea), and later to the self-conscious proponents of the nouvelle

vague (see NEW WAVE). From 1962, auteur became a buzz word
of Anglo-American film theory, and by the 1980s it was being
applied in pretentious circles to areas beyond film such as music
(producers or arrangers being promoted at the expense of composers
or performers), advertising and fashion. In spite of protests by
screenwriters and an increased awareness of the roles of technicians
and producers in the making of films, auteur theory seems to have
consolidated and legitimated the supremacy of the director.

B

BADGES

Apart from their recurrent popularity as part of school-playground crazes, ready-made pin lapel badges have featured as youth fashion accessories three times in Britain during postwar years, presaged by the artist Peter Blake's *Self-Portrait with Badges* painted in 1961. The first was in 1966 during the late-MOD predilection for dressing in imitation of POP ART, when the military regalia (including medals) of the previous year gave way to primary colours, flags and a profusion of badges. From 1968 to 1972 there was a second wave of badges, typically bearing PSYCHEDELIC graphics and anti-war slogans, which were worn by HIPPIES. In 1977 and 1978 badges were again used to signal PUNK allegiance; slogans included the well-known 'No Future', 'I'm a Mess' and 'Get Out of My Way'. In the 1980s RAP and HIP HOP fans stole Volkswagen emblems to wear as badges or medallions, while ACID HOUSE enthusiasts wore badges featuring the 'Smiley' logo.

BAGGY TENDENCY

'Baggy' became a key word in the late 1980s in denoting the anti-designer fashions of the followers of ACID HOUSE and INDIE POP music. The deliberately unstructured look favoured after 1986 consisted of baggy jeans or shorts worn with loose-fitting sweatshirts or Hawaiian shirts. One of the options in this repertoire was the Bermuda shorts known as 'baggies' and worn by surfers (see SURFING) since the 1960s (although, confusingly, the same word was used in the USA in the 1970s to refer to Oxford bags). Baggy came to mean not only the clothes worn, but the overall look and attitude portrayed by pudding-basin hairstyles, shambling posture and a cultivated amiable vacuity.

- *'I've got all the good baggy records – all five of them,' admits Chris. 'After baggy you were looking round for what to buy . . . I think things are so shite because people's expectations are low.'*
  NME, *January 1992*

BALD LOOK

See SKINHEADS.

BALDRICKS

The ephemeral nickname applied to a subset of youths in the Manchester area who from 1986 pioneered a neo-PSYCHEDELIC/ACID HOUSE look consisting of flared trousers, BAGGY, often floral, shirts worn with pudding-basin hairstyles and, typically, a mock-vacuous manner reminiscent of the scruffy, obtuse character of the manservant Baldrick in the TV comedy series *Blackadder*. The look, but not the name, was given wider currency by groups such as the Stone Roses and the Inspiral Carpets, and relates to the Liverpool SCALLIES and the primarily Scottish SHAMBLING tendency.

BALEARIC BEAT

The catch-all title originally applied in DANCEFLOOR culture to the varied genres of music that were played in the discos, clubs and parties of Ibiza and Formentera in the late 1980s, and which gave rise to the British ACID HOUSE cult. The word Balearic is an Anglicization of the Spanish 'Islas Baleares'. In the early 1990s the term was still being used, usually referring to clubs and DJs in Britain playing an eclectic selection of music that included a high proportion of European, as opposed to British and American, sounds. By the early Nineties, Rimini and Antwerp were rivalling London and Ibiza as centres of dance culture.

BAND AID

After watching a television report by Michael Buerk on the famine in Ethiopia, Bob Geldof, singer with Dublin NEW WAVE group the Boomtown Rats, spent ten days cajoling friends and acquaintances in the music industry into organizing a Christmas single for charity.

On 25 November 1984, the song 'Do They Know It's Christmas?' was recorded under the collective name Band Aid (a pun playing on the fact that representatives of Britain's top bands were involved and on the trademark name of medical adhesive plasters). The record sold 3.6 million copies, the highest-selling Christmas number one ever. Charity records and concerts, including George Harrison and Ravi Shankar's concert for Bangladesh, had been attempted in the 1970s, but Band Aid triggered the first concerted attempt to harness for humanitarian purposes the earning power of pop and ROCK with their attendant technology and promotional networks. Band Aid was followed by the Live Aid concert in July 1985, broadcast worldwide from London and Philadelphia simultaneously, using satellite links; subsequent charity promotions included Sport Aid, Fashion Aid and Comic Relief.

The Band Aid phenomenon demonstrated how direct action, using the tools of the so-called 'enterprise culture' (free use of the media, credit-card donations, telephone pledging and sponsoring) could successfully intervene in geopolitical issues. Among some professionals in the 1990s a 'band-aid solution' came to be a pejorative term, implying well-publicized stopgap hand-outs as against long-term reform. On the other hand, some cultural commentators hailed Band Aid as the arrival of Marshall McLuhan's (see MCLUHANISM) concept of the GLOBAL VILLAGE.

- *'Bob was pretty direct. You couldn't say no. All he said was: "Let's get some money and send it to these people, because we've got loads."'*
  Trevor Horn, record producer, reminiscing in 1991

BAR FLY JUMPING

A novelty bar-room entertainment in the tradition of mechanical bucking broncos, DWARF-THROWING and KARAOKE, bar fly jumping originated in Australia and New Zealand and was imported into the UK in 1991. The 'sport' consists of dressing in a Velcro-covered boiler suit and bouncing from a miniature trampoline against a padded Velcro-covered wall supported by scaffolding. The object of competitive bar fly jumping is to perform acrobatic jumps and/or to stick to the wall as high up as possible. The fact that equipment is expensive, a degree of physical fitness is necessary (participants have to sign a disclaimer before jumping), and that the activity is not actually conducive to heavy drinking, all militate against it catching on, although by 1992 it had been taken up by party planners on the upper-class charity-ball circuit and by some serious sports enthusiasts operating in traditional leisure centres and gymnasia.

- *'It's just crazy,' enthused Alistair Choat, one of the bar fly promoters, who, with his line in video CVs and karaoke machines, makes Loadsamoney look like a charity worker.*
  Sunday Times, *September 1991*

BASE-JUMPING

An amateur dangerous sport appearing in the 1980s, base-jumping is the name given to parachuting from tall buildings or other structures such as bridges. This spectacular and extremely risky activity was discouraged by parachutist associations and clubs; nevertheless daredevils jumped successfully from the Eiffel Tower in 1984. In 1992 a two-man jump from the Hilton Hotel in London resulted in one fatality.

B-BOYS

The male devotees of HIP HOP and RAP culture. The nickname (the 'B' stands for beat) was first used by black BREAK DANCERS and BODY POPPERS in New York at the end of the 1970s, later spreading to their associates and fans. By the early 1980s it was in use among other ethnic groups and in the UK; the female counterpart was the B-girl or more fashionable FLYGIRL. B-boy style, epitomized by the group Run DMC and imitated by white Rappers the Beastie Boys, consisted of flying jackets, labelled sports clothes and TRAINERS, baseball caps and metal jewellery. The heyday of the B-boy was defined by the *New Musical Express* as one transitional phase in the evolution of Hip Hop, lasting from 1982 to 1985.

BEAT BOOM

A press and music-industry coinage to describe the explosion of guitar-based pop-music combos originating in Liverpool after 1961. Groups and singers from Liverpool and the surrounding area were categorized as part of the MERSEY BOOM or Mersey Sound, but the fashion for ROCK and R & B-based ballads sung with minimum orchestration and British intonation quickly gathered momentum in other provincial cities (represented by the Searchers and the Hollies, for example) as well as in the London area (the Kinks and the Zombies). These musicians were known generically as beat groups to distinguish them from the dance bands who operated in many of the same venues. The term fell into disuse around the end of 1965.

BEATLE BOOTS
See CHELSEA BOOTS.

BEAT MOVEMENT
First used by the American writer Jack Kerouac to refer to the disaffected among his generation in postwar America, 'beat' had the sense of beaten, downtrodden or poor, later also playing on the coincidental aptness of 'beatitude'. The term was first quoted in John Clellon Holmes' novel *Go*, published in 1952. Coined in imitation of earlier literary groups such as the Lost Generation of the 1920s, the phrase 'the Beat Generation' originally applied to a small number of writers, artists and Bohemians of the late 1940s and early 1950s whose activities and beliefs were minutely chronicled in autobiographical, mystical and experimental prose and poetry; these included, among others, Kerouac, Holmes, Gregory Corso, William Burroughs and Allen Ginsberg. The members of this coterie had in common a notion of individual enlightenment through the rejection of bourgeois society and the embracing of a rootless lifestyle, literary romanticism and experimentalism, elements of Eastern religions, and in many cases the use of drugs and alcohol. As writers they were influenced by a variety of forerunners, including Walt Whitman, Thomas Wolfe, Henry Miller, Baudelaire, Verlaine and, particularly, Rimbaud. Kerouac was additionally inspired by images of the Buddhist mendicant searcher for truth, and the frontiersman/hobo as personified by his friend and mentor, Neal Cassady.

When these components were distilled into Kerouac's novel *On the Road* in 1957, it became an instant success and inspired many young people to call themselves 'Beats' and adopt the values of the book's heroes. To the outward trappings of the beat lifestyle were added elements of the EXISTENTIALISM café society of Europe, as well as an identification with modern jazz and modern art. In 1958 the San Francisco newspaper columnist Herb Caen coined the word Beatnik (the '-nik' suffix is a familiar and derogatory form in Slavonic and Yiddish) to refer disparagingly to the beret- and sandal-wearing members of what had become a subculture based on his own city and New York (where older exponents were calling themselves HIPSTERS). Lawrence Ferlinghetti's City Lights bookshop and publishing company helped to disseminate the Beat message from San Francisco, and by the end of the 1950s it was established among an avant-garde élite in Britain. From 1960 to 1965 the Beats formed a distinct, mainly middle-class youth cult in the UK, based on art schools, CND, modern and TRAD jazz clubs, FOLK clubs and coffee bars, and coexisting with MODS and ROCKERS. In the summer of 1965 Ginsberg and Corso joined Alexander Trocchi, Jeff Nuttall, Michael Horovitz and many others in London for a poetry reading at the Albert Hall (filmed under the title *Wholly Communion*), which in retrospect can be seen as the moment at which the American and European COUNTERCULTURES coalesced and became aware of the radical potential that gave birth to the HIPPIE movement the following year.

Of the original Beats, Cassady died of exposure, Kerouac suffered an alcoholic decline before dying in 1969 and Burroughs went into self-imposed exile in Tangier with Brion Gysin, the originator of CUT-UPS, while continuing his psycho-sexual literary experiments. (He later returned to a barricaded existence in the US.) Ginsberg and Corso continued to write and perform into the 1990s.

- *The most beautifully executed, the clearest and most important utterance yet made by the generation Kerouac himself named years ago as 'beat', and whose principal avatar he is.*
  Gilbert Millstein, reviewing On the Road, *New York Times,*
  5 September 1957

- *A petition signed by 2321 residents and holidaymakers at St Ives, Cornwall, was handed to the mayor, Ald. Archie Knight, during the weekend. It calls for tighter vagrancy laws to rid the town of beatniks.*
  Daily Telegraph, *21 July 1969*

BEAUTIFUL PEOPLE

The Beautiful People were the international élite of the HIPPIE era,
the flamboyant and narcissistic ROCK musicians, photographers and
models, etc. First used in the USA at the beginning of 1965 in all
seriousness, the expression was later invariably used ironically, as in
the 1967 Beatles single 'Baby You're a Rich Man'.

- *'When the mode of the music changes, the walls of the city shake'
  shimmers the occasional message in* International Times. *And it's a
  message that maybe we should stand by to receive because it reflects
  an attitude very prevalent among the Beautiful People who are
  dropping out and shaking walls in most of England's cities.*

  Melody Maker, *19 August 1967*

BEEHIVE

Also known in the USA as the B-52 (after the giant bulbous
Second World War bomber plane), the beehive-shaped hairdo was
emblematic of working-class chic in the early 1960s. The style
originated in the USA in 1958 as one of a variety of elaborately
teased and lacquered versions of BIG HAIR that mutated from earlier
pageboy and bouffant styles. It was adopted in Britain shortly after,
typically worn with pastel colours, taffeta and stilettos. By the mid-
1960s the beehive was out of fashion, but probably subconsciously
influenced the later more modest conical cuts and bouffants worn
by MOD girls. The beehive has continued to fascinate connoisseurs
and revivalists of 1960s KITSCH. It was resurrected by the B-52s, an
avant-garde post-PUNK pop group from Macon, Georgia, in 1978,
and again by British *chanteuse* Mari Wilson in 1980, also featuring
in John Waters' 1988 cult film, *Hairspray*. An updated 'wraparound'
beehive was favoured by the socialite Ivana Trump in 1990 and 1991.

- *In the space of a few minutes, I count twenty-six girls all with
  identical beehives, with twenty-six identical velvet bows in them.*
  Eric Newby, Town *magazine, September 1963*

- *. . . many American girls became hairhoppers, continually
  altering their massive beehives, strolling around like Empire State
  humans . . .*
  Dylan Jones, Haircults, *1990*

BHAGWAN SHREE RAJNEESH

See ORANGE PEOPLE.

BHANGRA

Bhangra – also known as Bhangra Beat – is the dominant version of Indian pop music played in the UK, and as such has been a focus for specifically Asian youth culture. The music originated in the late 1970s, when traditional Punjabi celebratory folk music began to be played with electronic instruments. Asian discos were established, followed by record companies, a visual style (involving traditional Indian colours and materials combined with Western leisure and DISCO fashions) and its own shops and publications. Bhangra spans teenage disco culture and an older generation's dance music; it remains male-dominated and oriented strongly towards the Punjabi-speaking community, except in its offshoot forms of Asian RAP (also known as Bhangramuffin) and Bhangra HOUSE, which appeared in the late 1980s. The influence of other Anglo-Asian collaborations, such as the joke-PUNK band the Four Kings and the Asian pop sound of Monsoon, was short-lived and minimal in comparison with the huge record sales and increasing media exposure of Bhangra, which gained a regular late-night television slot in 1991.

BIG BANG

The grandiose nickname inspired by the theoretical birth of the cosmos (Wall Street high-flyers had already been referring to themselves as 'Masters of the Universe') and conferred on the deregulation of the London Stock Exchange on 27 October 1986. Only a few years earlier the Stock Exchange had been fiercely resisting any government intervention in its working, continuing to operate as a closed and arcane system, largely without the benefit of modern technology. The switching-on of the computerized SEAQ (Stock Exchange Automated Quotation) system marked the opening-up of Stock Exchange membership to outsiders, as well as the plugging-in of London to the international securities market. This was the apotheosis of the YUPPIE, but it was immediately followed by the temporary breakdown of the overloaded SEAQ, and one year later by 'Black Monday', Britain's share in the global market crash.

- *The prize within the City's grasp is the leading position in the European time zone in a seamless market extending around the world.*

  Financial Times, *27 October 1986*

BIG HAIR

A slang term in American English denoting the exaggeratedly teased and lacquered bouffant hairstyles fashionable in the USA in the mid-Fifties. Big Hair survived into the 1980s as a symbol of the KITSCH culture of trailer parks, blue-collar bars and country music singers.

BIKERS

See HELL'S ANGELS; ROCKERS.

BIMBOS

The journalistic buzz word of 1986, bimbo defines a young, glamorous but empty-headed and usually grasping woman, typically a would-be model or actress. The word was first revived in the United States, before being seized upon by British journalists eager to discover a new sociological category, particularly one applicable to a current *cause célèbre*. This was the dalliance of the model Fiona Wright with the chairman of the Burton menswear group, Sir Ralph Halpern, and her later kiss-and-tell revelations and lawsuit against a second model (the so-called 'battle of the bimbos') to recover her diaries. The bimbo was a phenomenon of the time in two ways: she epitomized the mercenary, non-cerebral semi-celebrity being promoted by gossip columns and the Sunday tabloids, and she provided a female counterpart to the contemporary male discovery, the 'toyboy'. She was an amalgam of gold-digger, kept woman, starlet, and the dolly bird of the 1960s.

The word chosen to epitomize this new version almost certainly derives from *bambino*, Italian for baby, when shortened into a nickname. The epithet originally denoted a male, especially a big, unintelligent and aggressive male or dupe, in the American slang of the early 1900s. By the 1920s the same word was being applied to women, particularly by popular crime-fiction writers, and it was this usage that was revived in the mid-1980s. Bimbo gave rise to derivations such as the diminutive 'bimbette', the noun 'bimbetude', and the short-lived 'bimboy' and 'himbo' for the male equivalent.

- *Darryl Hannah plays an interior designer and Gekko's part-time mistress who turns her attention to Bud Fox's apartment and bed. She's meant to be a rich man's bimbo.*
  American film director Oliver Stone describing the film
  Wall Street, Sunday Times, February 1988

- *Charlotte Greig has a message for fools such as I . . . Not all women in pop are . . . brainless bimbos lured into Lurex by cynical rock business shitheads . . .*
  Ms London magazine, 4 September 1989

BIOFEEDBACK

By monitoring the electric impulses within one's own body it is possible to regulate physical functions that are normally involuntary or prompted by the unconscious. The subject is linked to a machine such as an oscilloscope, which displays signals emanating from the body. Once training has been received, electrical activity, chemical levels and the autonomic nervous system can all be partially controlled by concentration or relaxation techniques. Although widely used by practitioners of alternative THERAPIES, biofeedback techniques have been an accepted tool of mainstream medical practice since the late 1960s.

- *New Biofeedback devices for learning and control. The Relaxometer uses an audio signal showing changes in nervous activity and encouraging self-awareness. The Alpha Sensor helps train brain wave activity associated with meditative trance and a special state of passive awareness.*
  Advertisement in Private Eye, 19 September 1975

BLACK PANTHERS

The Black Panthers were a combination of community self-help group, armed self-defence force and revolutionary political party. Founded in 1966 by Bobby Seale and Huey Newton, they took their name from the symbol of Stokely Carmichael's Student Non-violent Coordinating Committee (SNCC), forming the most visible extremist manifestation of BLACK POWER. Newton proclaimed himself their

'Prime Minister', while Eldridge Cleaver, author of *Soul on Ice*, became 'Minister of Information'. In spite of humanitarian and welfare schemes for the poor, the Panthers alienated moderate opinion by proclaiming the violent overthrow of 'fascist' American society, employing Marxist-Leninist terminology and associating themselves with the criminal and HIPPIE subcultures. From 1967 to 1972 they were engaged in a nonstop confrontation with the police and FBI that ended with the death and imprisonment of many of their members. Newton survived until 1989, when he was murdered in Oakland, California.

The Black Panthers never succeeded in mobilizing significant support beyond the ghetto, but contributed a potent mythology to the continuing movement for black rights. White sympathizers and admirers of the Panther movement ranged from John Sinclair's WHITE PANTHERS to the dilettante BEAUTIFUL PEOPLE of New York and London, as described in Tom Wolfe's *Radical Chic & Mau-Mauing the Flak Catchers*. In 1990 militant RAP devotees in New York and California began to disseminate Panther tracts and to revive interest in the movement as evidence of the FBI's covert campaign to destroy the Panthers at all costs began to re-emerge.

- *Cleaver was one of a number of Panthers arrested following an encounter with members of the Oakland police department in which Cleaver was wounded and 17-year-old Bobby Hutton was killed.*
  IT magazine, March 1969

- *... Black Panthers' brilliant (and humane) national campaign to provide breakfasts for undernourished children so they can learn better ('we must survive this evil government so we can build a new one') is outlined in the April 27 issue of their paper ...*
  John Wilcock, Oz magazine, July 1969

BLACK POWER

The loose term 'Black Power' encompasses the many strands of the struggle for black rights beginning in the United States in the latter part of the 1960s. The phrase itself was a slogan coined by the black activist Stokely Carmichael, whose SNCC (Student Non-violent Coordinating Committee) was a successor to the anti-segregation and civil rights movements of the early 1960s. By 1966 black consciousness had become radicalized, urbanized and was espousing revolutionary philosophies, including black nationalism, Marxist-Leninism (embraced by the BLACK PANTHERS) and Islam (propounded since the 1950s by Elijah Mohammad and Malcolm X's Nation of Islam, the so-called 'Black Muslims'). Other prominent figures in the Black Power movement were Angela Davis, the communist university lecturer tried for conspiracy, kidnap and murder in 1970, and George Jackson, author of the *Soledad Brother* diaries, who died in prison in 1971. The cause of black liberation, however it was slanted, provided the inspiration for the FEMINIST and GAY rights movements that followed. In spite of mobilizing support and raising awareness among liberals and leftists worldwide, it failed to influence the existing power structures. Black Power itself subsided with the general reversal of progressive tendencies in the mid-1970s, but was revived in the early 1980s under different names by the moderate Jesse Jackson, the more controversial Louis D. Farrakhan, and elements of the RAP and HIP HOP movements. In Britain during the late Sixties the nascent Black Power movement in London and Reading was largely discredited by the activities of Michael X (later executed in Trinidad for murder), although initiatives such as Black Theatre survived.

- *Is Black Power dead? There are people who now say it never really existed. It was a meaningless flash. Some thoughtful, hopeful people say it was a 'good thing' really, but the guys then fuck it up – they make it a hustle.*
  Desmond Quammie, IT *magazine, April 1969*

BLANK GENERATION

Applied by the PUNK movement to itself, the epithet 'Blank Generation' referred to the pose of absolute nihilism enshrined in the Punk slogan 'No Future'. 'Blank Generation', recalling the Lost Generation and the BEAT Generation, was the title of a song by Richard Hell and the Voidoids, written in New York in 1975. The notion was later echoed by the Sex Pistols in their 'Pretty Vacant'. In the early Nineties the phrase was briefly resurrected to describe the aimless 'twenty-somethings' also dubbed the new GENERATION X.

- *'Blank Generation' laid out the attractions of vacancy: not just being or looking bored, but the deeper vacancy of the subconscious.*
  Jon Savage, England's Dreaming, *1991*

BLITZ KIDS

More or less a synonym for the NEW ROMANTICS or the CULT WITH NO
NAME, the Blitz Kids originally referred to the clientele of the Blitz
nightclub operated in 1980 and 1981 by Steve Strange and Rusty
Egan in Holborn, London. The Tuesday-night sessions attracted
former PUNKS, underground DISCO habitués and students from
St Martin's School of Art, who created a coterie that influenced
youth styles and music for the next decade. Boy George O'Dowd,
later an international singing star, was in charge of the cloakroom;
Marilyn, briefly a transvestite singing sensation, was the cigarette
'girl'; Spandau Ballet was the resident band, and style arbiters
such as David Bowie, Malcolm McLaren and Vivienne Westwood
visited. Other regular attenders, then unknown, went on to express
themselves through fashion design, music video and journalism.
The Blitz Kids had no coherent identifiable look; their ethos was
an indiscriminate camp romanticism with style replacing ideology.
Gender distinctions were blurred (see GENDER-BENDERS), clothing
was a free-for-all theatrical parody and music was middle-of-the-road
ELECTRO pop. In this sense the Blitz Kids reprised the values of the
GLAM ROCK era and in 1980 already embodied the fragmentation of
youth culture following PUNK, as well as the rise of the club and
DANCEFLOOR entrepreneurism and design obsession that characterized
the rest of the Eighties. One of the many style magazines of that
era was named after the club, which closed in 1981; the magazine
survived until 1991.

- *All the kids who were beaten up at school for being weird came
  together in one place . . . Your yob couldn't work out what we
  were, we weren't even punks. So they gave us a kicking anyway, just
  in case.*

  Fashion designer Stephen Linard, reminiscing in the
  Sunday Times, August 1990

BLUEBEAT

A variety of Jamaican dance music based on a heavy, shuffling
simplified blues rhythm that coexisted with the very similar SKA and
ROCKSTEADY music of the late 1960s as an immediate forerunner of
REGGAE. Bluebeat was a favourite with British MODS and the revivalist
TWO TONE movement of 1979.

BMX BIKES

A craze among older pre-teens and young teenagers that flourished between 1984 and 1988, BMXing, (the initials denote 'Bicycle Motocross') required thick-tyred, strengthened-frame bikes. These had originated in the 1960s as home-CUSTOMIZED versions of standard touring or racing bikes. In the early 1980s manufactured BMX bikes replaced the street chopper (itself based on American motorcycle styles) as the young cyclist's favourite. Acrobatic, competitive BMXing was accompanied by its own magazines, accessories and cinema films. (A British INDIE POP band also took the name BMX Bandits after the films.) The popularity of BMXing waned somewhat in the late 1980s, perhaps due to the revival of SKATEBOARDING and the appeal of MOUNTAIN BIKES to older cyclists.

BOBBYSOXERS

Bobby socks were white cotton, almost calf-length socks usually worn folded down over the shoes by female teenagers and college students in the USA. The socks, typically teamed with saddle shoes or sneakers, long pleated skirts, sweaters and PONYTAILS, gave their name to a look that endured until the mid-1960s. The look in turn accompanied a conformist white middle-class adolescent lifestyle based on high-school rituals, JITTERBUGGING, the sobbing ballads of Johnny Ray and later ROCK 'N' ROLL, chewing gum, milk shakes, drive-ins, and dating. The term was specifically applied to girls in their early teens, and although aspects of their uniform were picked up elsewhere (by, among others, British Teddy Girls (see TEDDY BOYS) and Australian WIDGIES in the late 1950s, and Eastern Europeans in the late 1960s), the name was confined to North Americans.

BODGIES

Bodgies were the male members of an Australian youth cult of the 1950s that was the equivalent of the British TEDDY BOY phenomenon. They typically wore drape jackets, brightly coloured shirts, tight trousers and crêpe-soled shoes known as brothel creepers. The origin of the name 'bodgie' is disputed; it is said by some to be an American slang term of the 1930s denoting a JITTERBUG dance fanatic. Others derive it more convincingly from the British and Australian 'bodge' (meaning to botch or mess up) and 'bodger' (a lazy or worthless individual). Bodgies, who flourished between 1952 and 1960, had their female counterparts, known as WIDGIES.

BODY POPPING

The highly stylized jerking dance movements of body popping were performed to heavily rhythmic FUNK or ELECTRO pop and later to HIP HOP music. The style imitated the motions of a robot, and was perhaps first inspired by mime routines common among street performers in the USA. Strictly speaking, body popping was a blend of two styles of the late Seventies: the free-form electric boogie practised in the South Bronx, New York, birthplace of Hip Hop culture, and the stricter, more balletic popping which began in California. Popularized by Jeffrey Daniels of the pop group Shalamar in 1980, body popping caught on in discothèques and clubs as well as on urban pavements, where it formed part of the repertoire of BREAK DANCING. No longer a recognizable style by the late 1980s, body popping was absorbed into the JACKING of Hip Hop, HOUSE and other DANCEFLOOR genres.

BONEHEADS

See SKINHEADS.

BOVVER BOOTS

Originally heavy army-issue laced ankle boots or industrial steel-capped footwear, bovver boots (so called from the London working-class pronunciation of 'bother' as a menacing euphemism for violence) were the most notorious part of the uniform of the original SKINHEADS or Bovver Boys. Popular from 1967 to 1971, bovver boots were later replaced by the more flexible DMS.

BOVVER BOYS

See SKINHEADS.

BRAIDS

Less radical than DREADLOCKS, braided hair was a fashion that began in the Afro-Caribbean community and was picked up by subcultures in the late 1970s and by mainstream fashion in the 1980s. Early elaborations included the use of beads, whilst in the Eighties artificial strands of (sometimes brightly coloured) hair were woven into braided locks.

BREAK DANCING

An authentic product of ghetto street culture, break dancing spread from the black urban youth scene of New York, where teenagers performed horizontal acrobatics on sidewalks to the sound of heavily rhythmic music played on so-called GHETTO-BLASTERS (also known as 'beat boxes' or 'boogie boxes'). The dance moves, which were typically combined with upright BODY POPPING, were imitated by Hispanic, Asian and white performers and formed, along with RAPPING and SCRATCHING, one of the mainstays of the HIP HOP culture that spread worldwide between 1979 and 1985.

BROOMBALL

A novelty sport of the early Nineties, broomball consists of using a broomstick to hit a ball across an ice rink. The game, ostensibly for fun and competition, but allowing rowdiness, is played by two teams with players wearing soft shoes. Popular among YUPPIES, a league was formed in the City of London for members of financial institutions.

BROTHEL CREEPERS

See TEDDY BOYS; BODGIES.

BRUTALISM

See NEW BRUTALISM.

BUMBAGS

So-called bumbags first became a fashion accessory in avant-garde circles in 1976 when PUNKS supplemented their bondage and fetish clothing with kilts, substituting colostomy bags for sporrans or handbags. Specially manufactured low-slung rubber or PVC bags then became part of the stereotype Punk uniform. When sports paraphernalia, particularly that derived from jogging, windsurfing and mountain-biking, was carried over into youth fashion in the 1980s, it included a second type of bumbag: the zipped or Velcro-fastening pouch shaped to fit against waist or hips.

● *Wallets are in – but don't be seen dead in a bumbag.*
                              Sunday Times *magazine, 26 April 1992*

BUNGY-JUMPING

One of many spectacular dangerous sports appearing since 1980, bungy-jumping involves leaping from a high place, typically a suspension bridge, while attached by a strong elastic link. The name for this activity is formed from 'bungy' or 'bunjie', the 1930s British public-school slang meaning eraser or rubber. Also spelt bungie or bungee, the spelling is sometimes modified to 'bungi-jumping', perhaps for the sake of exoticism, or on the mistaken assumption that it derives from a non-European language. By 1991 bungy-jumping had caught on in Australia and the USA. In Britain it had become a popular fund-raising activity. Sponsored jumps were staged from a crane on the Brighton seafront, and the UK's first permanent bungy site was inaugurated in the summer of 1992.

BUNGY-RUNNING

A variation of BUNGY-JUMPING invented in Australia in 1991, bungy-running is a safer, horizontal form of that activity in which contestants or performers are attached to a padded wall by an elastic line. The object is to run from the wall, stretching the line as far as one's strength will allow, before bouncing back. Along with BAR FLY JUMPING, bungy-running is in a tradition of high-technology novelty bar-room sports.

CABBAGE PATCH DOLLS

The craze for Cabbage Patch dolls was a manufactured fad
appealing to young children. Appearing in the early 1980s, the
dolls were presented as orphans to be 'adopted' by the child.
An adoption certificate was included in the price. The gimmick
of personalizing toys became widespread and in Hong Kong the
dolls inspired at least one imitation – a doll with a coveted British
passport allowing emigration. The 'Cabbage Patch Kid' label was
invented by Xavier Roberts, who derived it from the American
tradition of telling young children that babies were found in the
cabbage patch.

CALYPSO

See SOCA.

CAMRA

A successful British consumer pressure group, the Campaign for
Real Ale, or CAMRA, was started in the early 1970s in protest at
the imminent disappearance of traditionally brewed ales in favour
of gaseous, low-strength, 'top-pressured' keg beers. The six major
brewery combines, created by merger and takeover during the 1960s
and enjoying a near-monopoly, had embarked on a rationalization
programme involving the modernizing of traditional pubs, the closure
of small local breweries and the promotion of varieties of sterile (as
opposed to fermenting) beer, some of which could have been sold
in the USA under Prohibition. The private individuals involved in
the campaign formed local volunteer groups and organized protest
marches, demonstrations and alternative beer tastings and festivals,
as well as press-based publicity campaigns and the publication of

an annual *Good Beer Guide* that identified those pubs serving cask-conditioned 'Real Ale'. CAMRA had unprecedented success in forcing a radical change in the policies of the major brewers, who in the mid-1970s reintroduced traditional-style beers and amended their closure and refurbishment programmes. It also succeeded in promoting and safeguarding the remaining small independent breweries. Although the purpose of the original campaign was largely accomplished by the early 1980s, CAMRA continued to agitate against monopoly in the beer trade and against the spread of low-quality lagers. It was significant as a model of a grass-roots pressure group that appealed to a relatively militant, articulate and affluent constituency (its membership reached 30,000 at the end of the 1970s) and it turned the techniques of media and marketing against the commercial Establishment.

CASUALS

Similar in some ways to the SUEDEHEADS of the early 1970s and distinguished from the SKINHEADS by their less radical appearance, the Casuals (also known initially as PRINGLES after the brand of cashmere pullovers they favoured) were an urban working-class youth subculture formed around football tribalism and hooliganism. Appearing at the end of the 1970s and surviving until about 1987, the movement adopted a conformist and label-obsessed look for both sexes based on expensive pastel-coloured sports- and leisurewear of the sort normally associated with *nouveau-riche* adult suburbanites and golfers. (Female Casuals actually based their styles mainly on male clothing such as cardigans and 'slacks'). Most Casuals came from the skilled upper working class, as opposed to the often disadvantaged and unemployed Skinheads, and combined a conservative and materialist ethos with a predisposition to organized violence. Unlike most youth tribes, the Casuals were not identified with any particular musical style, preferring mainstream DISCO. By the later 1980s the activities of their territorial gangs, known as 'Firms' or 'Crews', had attracted the attention of the mass media, although the name Casual remained relatively obscure. A late version of this culture provided the model for the comedian Harry Enfield's 'Loadsamoney' character, a demon of bigoted affluence who achieved cult status in 1988. By the following year Casuals as a self-consciously distinct group were disappearing, many

of them attracted by the hedonistic, generally non-violent ACID
HOUSE cult.

● *For those stuck in boring jobs or still at school, casual was a great
escape . . . They enjoyed the characters, the top boys, the tales.
They enjoyed a different brand name each month, a new word each
Saturday, and a different posture every minute.*
Gavin Hills, The Face, *December 1991*

CATASTROPHE THEORY

An element of the NEW SCIENCE which has been borrowed by non-
scientific fields, catastrophe theory is a mathematical explanation of
dramatic 'singularities' – moments at which systems erupt or become
wildly unpredictable. The theory was developed by the French
mathematician René Thom and first posited in 1968; it enables stages
in a process to be geometrically mapped, showing how minor changes
and stimuli can produce disproportionate results. Catastrophe theory
has been applied, often controversially, to phenomena in biology,
economics and business, as well as to social conflict.

CB RADIO

A semi-underground rural subculture based on Citizens' Band Radio
grew up in the United States from about 1974 before spreading to
Britain, where it became a working-class fad in the later 1970s,
although the two-way radio transceivers were not licensed for UK
non-specialists until 1981. In the US, the so-called Citizens' Band
frequency had been available since 1958, but it was the accessibility
of cheap new technology that triggered the movement among truck
drivers, later spreading to other private users of all age groups.
The attraction of CB radio over and above its practical usefulness
on American highways was that it gave individuals access to
and personal control of a communications system (on 27 MHz or
934 MHz, with a normal range of five miles) that allowed social
networking and the occasional outwitting of the authorities. The
broadcasting generated its own clandestine code of nicknames, or
'handles', and slang or jargon terms, such as 'smokey bears' (the
police), 'rubber duck' (the number-one vehicle in a convoy). In the
USA, CB enthusiasts were celebrated in feature films such as Convoy,

TV series such as *The Dukes of Hazzard*, and in Country music records; in the UK the fad was frustrated by congested roads, police disapproval and media indifference.

CEREALOGY
See CROP CIRCLES.

CHAOS THEORY

Chaos theory is an aspect of the NEW SCIENCE that attracted the attention of non-scientists in the 1980s in the same way as such notions as the ANTHROPIC PRINCIPLE and the UNCERTAINTY PRINCIPLE. It is based on the attempt to measure, control or replicate mathematically unpredictable behaviour in systems or phenomena. The so-called 'chaotic' processes can be observed in weather patterns or in turbulence in mobile liquids or gases where barely perceptible interferences in initial conditions give rise to significant changes in resulting movement. Extrapolating from this led to such romantic images as the movement of a butterfly wing in Africa affecting global climatic patterns, tying in with the NEW AGE vision of a unified reality, as in the GAIA HYPOTHESIS. The US management guru Peter Drucker claimed that chaos theory rendered outdated and invalid most previous thinking on the economics and organization of the business world. A more frivolous application of the theory has been in the generating of fractals – computerized PSYCHEDELIC patterns used in VIRTUAL REALITY displays and popular in ACID HOUSE LIGHT SHOWS.

- *Hailed as the 'most psychedelic mind on the planet today', Terence McKenna, a Californian . . . tours the world spreading his message of 'Gaia, chaos, shamanism and plant hallucinogens'.*
  Independent, *13 January 1992*

CHARTER 88

A reformist pressure group formed in Britain in November 1988 in imitation of Charter 77, the Czech and Slovak human rights movement founded ten years earlier. The British initiative was taken by a small group of intellectuals and celebrities on the anniversary of the ambiguous 'Glorious Revolution' of 1688, which established the form the British constitution, or lack of it, took during subsequent regimes. The Charter was initially signed by 300 people and published in the *Independent*, the *Guardian* and the *New Statesman and Society*. By January 1989 5000 signatures had been collected and by the end of 1991 membership of Charter 88 stood at 29,000. The Charter demanded constitutional change and social reform in twelve specific areas, calling for: a bill of rights; guaranteed freedom of information; government accountability; judicial reform; reform of the electoral system; the restructuring of the House of Commons; the democratization of the Upper House in Parliament; the granting of national assemblies for Scotland and Wales; guarantees of redress for State abuses; the devolution of centralized State power; independence for local government; and a written constitution. The sole concerted postwar attempt at a non-doctrinaire critique of the British legal and political system, Charter 88 found itself up against the innate conservatism of British public opinion, the continuing domination of politics by the two main parties, and the accusation by some that it represented only the metropolitan minority of the so-called CHATTERING CLASSES and 'champagne socialists'.

- *Small wonder Messrs Kinnock and Hattersley saw it as essentially a movement of middle-class defeatists ('wankers' was Neil Kinnock's term) . . . Recently, however, events have begun to move Charter 88's way.*

  Robert Harris, Sunday Times, *August 1990*

CHATTERING CLASSES

A mock-serious social classification that became a media cliché of the early 1990s, the chattering classes were first identified by the journalist Frank Johnson in the 1980s. He was mocking the intellectual Left's tendency for earnestly debating and pontificating upon social issues in the media and at private functions. The phrase was subsequently adopted by other writers, including Alan Watkins, the *Observer*'s political commentator. Often applied to the promoters of CHARTER 88, it could be extended to refer to individuals of any political persuasion with easy access to media outlets for their opinions. Writers for the right-wing *Spectator*, the 'young Turks' of the *Modern Review* and frequenters of the Groucho Club (the Soho haunt

of London literary and media coteries) were also categorized thus at
different times.

CHELSEA BOOT

An elastic-sided ankle boot worn by men since the turn of the century,
the Chelsea boot became associated with upper-class Bohemians in
Britain during the late 1950s. Around 1961 it became one of the first,
discreet fashion statements of the emerging style-conscious MOD
movement. In that conservative and conformist period, footwear
was often the only available means for signalling a progressive
identity. Later, the original flat-heeled riding boot merged with the
Cuban-heeled flamenco boot to create the 'Beatle boot', which swept
Britain along with the MERSEY BOOM of 1963. During the PUNK era a
limited revival of Sixties fashions brought back the Chelsea boot, now
modified by confusion with the WINKLE-PICKER. Once reintroduced,
the style (reverting to its original appearance and no longer identified
with subcultures) has survived into the 1990s, worn by women as
well as by men.

- *Trilby Lane: 'How about shoes? The Chelsea boot has been played
  out, what's new?'*
  John Stephen: 'Shoes that are neat and a good shape are in.'
  Rave *magazine, February 1965*

- *To wear with your trousers – Chelsea boots are still the footwear,
  but now suede is taking over from leather.*
  Rave *magazine, February 1966*

- *Sexist, sadistic and currently superselling on the wrong end of Sunset
  Boulevard and the right end of Rodeo is the Chelsea Boot. This time
  around in black suede, not leather . . .*
  The Face, *January 1988*

CHILDREN OF GOD

A Utopian and apocalyptic religious cult begun in California in 1968
and led by David Berg, also known as Moses David and Chairman Mo.
The Children of God flourished in the USA, the UK and Australasia
particularly during the 1970s, and in the early Nineties there were

still an estimated 12,000 adherents in seventy countries. Members of the movement practised communal living and sexual pluralism. Police raids in 1992 removed children from the movement's communes in Melbourne. Like the daughter of EST's founder, Werner Erhard, Berg's daughter denounced the fugitive guru on network television.

● *Soon after the cult's inception it moved to Britain, where the practice of attracting new recruits by seduction earned its proselytizers the name 'Hookers for Jesus'.*

Sunday Times, *17 May 1992*

CHOPPERS

See BMX BIKES; HELL'S ANGELS.

CHROME-DOMES

See SKINHEADS.

CIDERPUNKS

See CRUSTIES.

CINÉMA VÉRITÉ

The term 'cinéma vérité' is the French translation of the Russian 'kino pravda', meaning 'cinema of truth', and was coined by the pioneering documentary film-maker Dziga Vertov (the nom de plume of Denis Kaufman) in the 1920s. As used by French critics, the term referred to a new tendency in documentaries in which disinterested observation, detached narrative, extensive editing and post-synchronized sound were replaced by the overt involvement in the events they were recording of the film-makers, who often confronted participants and commented on the film-making process. This more radical and dynamic technique, employed first by Jean Rouch in France in 1961, was made possible by advances in technology such as lightweight hand-held cameras and highly mobile sound-recording hardware. *Cinéma vérité* contributed elements to the *nouvelle vague* (see NEW wave) style, particularly in the work of Jean-Luc Godard, whilst in the USA Stephen Leacock and the Maysle brothers are also considered exponents of the genre, using a 'fly-on-the-wall' approach in their ROCK-music documentaries between 1967 and 1970. Early synonyms 'direct cinema' and 'catalyst cinema' having dropped out of use, *cinéma vérité* is now a generalized term for (apparently) unmanipulated reportage.

- Dragées au Poivre. *A group of French kids and their do-it-yourself* cinéma vérité *take the Mickey out of the* Nouvelle Vague, *among other things.*

Town *magazine, May 1964*

CLACKERS

A children's fad of 1971 in the UK, Clackers were a form of miniature bolas wound round the fingers and clicked together. There was an attempt by toy manufacturers to revive the craze in 1991 with an improved version attached to a stem, which was less likely to hurt the hand. Clackers are one of many fetish toys and accessories to have enjoyed a brief vogue with pre-teen schoolchildren since the 1960s; others include the SCOOBIDOO, SLAP-ITS and FRIENDSHIP BRACELETS.

CLASS WAR

A British anarchist sect with about 200 members in 1990 (but claiming a 60,000 readership for its broadsheet). Class War's activities overlap with the student, NEW AGE TRAVELLER, SQUATTING and CRUSTIE subcultures, and its members were at the forefront of the anti-poll tax riots of 1990. Its aim is the overthrow of late-capitalist consumer society by mobilizing the underclass against the rich.

CLOGS

Probably inspired by visits to Holland and Denmark by HIPPIES, clogs became part of the uniform of long-haired, denim-clad youth of both sexes during the early 1970s. Later in the decade attempts were made to popularize native Lancashire clogs as a left-wing fashion statement, with little success. In 1987 clogs were again declared to be back in style, but were lost in the many competing fads of a fragmented fashion scene. Yet another revival in 1992 culminated in the first Gucci clog.

- *Now available for the first time in Britain . . . Swedish fashion clogs for only 49/11 . . . They can be attractively worn with your maxi, midi, mini, trousers or bikini . . .*
    Advertisement in 19 *magazine, January 1971*

CLONE BANDS

See ROCK DOUBLES.

CLONES

By about 1972, effeminate or camp appearances and mannerisms had become outmoded in the gay male communities of New York and San Francisco and alternative visual stereotypes started to become more widespread. Among these were the parodic 'biker' look and the 'butch' construction worker or lumberjack/hiker look. As well as representing sexual icons, these images accorded with the new assertiveness of GAY LIBERATION and at the same time confused heterosexual critics. Once the GLAM ROCK bisexual flamboyance of the mid-1970s had passed its peak, the macho lumberjack/hiker style began to predominate, spreading to Europe in 1976 and supplanting all alternatives. The look consisted of plaid or denim work shirts, faded Levis and heavy boots, worn with cropped hair and a moustache. By the late 1970s those exhibiting this uniform appearance had been dubbed 'clones' (from the Greek *klon*, meaning twig, used in genetics to denote identical offspring) and their milieux 'clone-zones'.

- *The way the gays moved gave one a clue, from tentative camp to lumberjack clone, so that was what it had all been about all along (my body, your body, anybody).*
    Peter York, Style Wars, *1980*

CND

The Campaign for Nuclear Disarmament was founded in January 1958 to coordinate protest against the programme of nuclear weapons

testing embarked upon in the UK in 1952. A first public meeting
at Central Hall, Westminster, attracted 5000 people, and that Easter
9000 took part in the first CND march to Aldermaston, the site of the
Atomic Weapons Research Establishment. The annual Aldermaston
marches, together with other 'ban the bomb' demonstrations, provided
a focus for radical and libertarian activism in Britain throughout the
Fifties and Sixties. The CND symbol (designed by the artist Gerald
Holton) became the badge of EXISTENTIALISTS, Beatniks (see the
BEAT MOVEMENT), FOLK music aficionados, vegetarians and other free-
thinkers, and was later adopted as a general peace sign by HIPPIES
and still later, with its anti-nuclear connections largely forgotten, by
the ACID HOUSE movement.

CND was assisted by the support of celebrities such as the
philosopher Bertrand Russell, and by elements of the Church
and the left wing of the political establishment, and thus avoided
marginalization as an eccentric or extremist organization. It also
eschewed violent protest in favour of milder forms of direct action.
In 1962 CND revealed the location of secret nuclear bunkers – the
so-called RSGs (Regional Seats of Government) – but in the following
year the imprisonment of members of the coordinating Committee of
100 for infringement of the Official Secrets Act threw the movement
into disarray. The failure to react positively disillusioned many leftists
and progressives, pushing them towards militant Marxist or Trotskyite
groups or the beginnings of the libertarian COUNTERCULTURE. The
Committee of 100 was officially disbanded in 1968.

In the late 1970s CND campaigned against US military bases in
Britain, including Greenham Common, the site of the Women's Peace
Camp. The campaign's policy of unilateral disarmament was adopted
by the Labour Party in the early 1980s, but foundered due to hostility
among a majority of voters. This was compounded by the apparent
collapse of the nuclear threat from the Communist states, which was
seen by the Right as a vindication of its hard-line pro-nuclear stand.
Following the breakup of the Soviet Union and the end of the arms
race, CND lost a part of its *raison d'être*, but continued to campaign
against military expenditure, the arms trade and pollution by nuclear
waste. In the late 1980s its membership stood at a constant 60,000.

- *I think that CND and the Aldermaston marches were incredibly*
  important, because it was the first time that young people in this
  country had any reason to go anywhere else, and met people

completely out of their class and their ordinary background. And it was vaguely left wing and brown rice and lentils, handmade pottery mugs.
Sue Miles, quoted in Days in the Life, *Jonathon Green, 1988*

COCK ROCK

A term of the 1970s devised by the music press, but quickly adopted by FEMINISTS, to refer to aggressively macho HARD ROCK or HEAVY METAL music as pioneered by the group Led Zeppelin and perpetuated in more and more parodic forms through that decade. The phrase was inspired by such features as onstage pelvic thrusting, the wearing of codpieces, band names such as Whitesnake, and phallocentric lyrics.

COMBAT GAMES

Combat games became popular in the early 1980s among YUPPIES and those for whom they were a physically stretching outlet for aggressive and competitive instincts, as well as a test of strategic skills. The combat usually took the form of mock-military or guerrilla campaigns conducted in teams in woods or over rough terrain. Firearms were an important component, firing blanks or cartridges containing dye with which to mark a hit. This type of simulation was previously an established form of open-air training in the armed services; in the late 1970s the idea was picked up for management-training exercises in the USA, perhaps inspired by the attractions of SURVIVALISM. The modern version is typically a male fascination and is marketed under a range of names, including Paintball and Skirmish; it has obvious connections with the male-bonding countryside rituals of the masculinist (see the MEN'S MOVEMENT) and NEW MAN tendencies. A second variety of combat game that attracts more female participants is the role-playing fantasy re-enactment, based on such sources as the *Star War* films and the 'Dungeons and Dragons' board and VIDEO GAMES. These dramas are played out in costume, often using light-guns, as in Lasertag, for example.

COMIC BOOKS

See GRAPHIC NOVEL; HEAD COMICS.

COMPLEMENTARY MEDICINE
See HOLISTIC MEDICINE.

COMPUTER GAMES
See VIDEO GAMES.

CONCEPTUAL ARCHITECTURE

A notion appearing in the 1970s, Conceptual Architecture refers to
an exercise in which the concept and form of a potential structure
are of more significance than its actual construction. In other words,
the architecture consists of designing and planning on paper and
on computer buildings that are never built. An art form or aesthetic
gesture based on CONCEPTUAL ART, Conceptual Architecture allowed
architects to explore STRUCTURALISM and SEMIOLOGY without the
constraints of actualizing their projects in the real world. It also
permitted visionaries including the Danish painter and SITUATIONIST
Asger Jorn, the Italian designer Ettore Sottsass and the English
POST-MODERN architect Nigel Coates to create blueprints for imaginary
Utopias. In the 1980s the novel technologies of VIRTUAL REALITY
opened up new perspectives for imaginary or potential architecture.

CONCEPTUAL ART

A movement operating in the territory of fine art and sculpture in
which the idea is more important than the form through which
it is expressed. This approach, also known as Concept Art or
Conceptualism, subverts established aesthetics and questions theories
of art by using non-traditional materials, media and methods of
presentation. Conceptual Art was a vogue term of the late 1960s and
early 1970s still in currency in the early 1990s. Its first exponents
included the New Yorker Joseph Kosuth, who exhibited empty
frames and extracts from dictionaries and coined the slogan/title
'Art as Idea as Idea'; and the Californian Barry le Va, who combined
documentation and photography in his exhibits, as did his fellow
American Douglas Hueber, who also incorporated maps, letters and
sketches. These exemplifiers, using two-dimensional collages to
record ideas, communications, processes and journeys, now appear

unadventurous in comparison with some of the avant-garde users of gases, liquids, ready-made objects and bodily substances who succeeded them. By the end of the 1970s Conceptual Art had become a catch-all term for assemblages, installations and performances (see PERFORMANCE ART) that stressed concept rather than art object. Some practitioners, including Joseph Beuys and Richard Long, achieved international celebrity and mainstream acceptance in spite of the inherently controversial nature of their work. Non-figurative Conceptual Art was also dominant in British art schools at the beginning of the 1990s.

● ... *Nigel Greenwood has a kind of workshop show by two artists. One is far from conceptual ... but the other, a young American artist called Joel Fisher, can safely be given the new label; his pieces consist of scraps of 'paper' rendered down from clothing, and a stack of blocks of yellow soap made, believe it or not, out of best butter.*
Nigel Gosling, Observer, *June 1971*

CONCRETE POETRY

Following the direct inspiration of the French writer Apollinaire and the indirect effects of Dadaism and Futurism, poets in the late 1950s began to treat the poem as a visual as well as verbal art object, so that the arrangement of the letters on the page and the use of space and typography in revealing them became more significant than the meaning of the words. The effects of this approach were much derided by opponents of the MODERNIST avant-garde, but its influence continued to be important at least until the late 1970s. Elements of Concrete Poetry have been incorporated into CONCEPTUAL ART and mainstream graphics, and in the 1990s initiatives in the field seem to be coming from graphic designers and typographers more than from poets.

CONK

A 'process' hairstyle (one where the hair is straightened by the application of chemicals and/or heat) as worn by HIP young blacks in the United States from the 1920s until the late 1960s, when it was superseded by the racially affirmative AFRO style. Processed hair as worn by such celebrities as Michael Jackson and Prince continued to cause controversy in the 1980s, but the term 'conk' was no longer applied. It originated either as an alteration of Congolene, the trademark name of a hair-straightener preparation, or as a slang word for the head.

CONSUMERISM

By the mid-1970s it had become clear to Left and Right alike that it was consumption rather than production (as claimed by Marx) that formed the basis of social identity in the modern world. The term 'consumerism', which became a buzz word of the late 1970s, covers two concepts. The first is the idea, or ideology, which holds that maximum consumption of material goods and services is the ultimate goal of both the individual and society. The general acceptance of this tendency all over the developed world in the 1980s fostered the 'enterprise society', the introduction of 'market forces' into all areas of public activity and the conspicuous consumption and commodity fetishism that climaxed in the RECREATIONAL SHOPPING phenomenon of the middle of the decade.

Consumerism also describes the movement (first associated with Ralph Nader in the USA of the 1960s) to campaign for the rights of consumers. In Britain this has been carried on by mainstream watchdog organizations such as the Consumer Association and radical pressure groups such as CAMRA. Among social commentators, the SITUATIONISTS were the first to highlight the sinister power and intricacy of consumer society. Later, in the Seventies, marketing analysts posited three stages of consumerism: the first stage involves consumption of goods, the second sevices, and the third – a mark of advanced 'post-industrial' economies – is dedicated to the consumption of experience (for example, travel, fitness programmes, NEW AGE therapies, and VIRTUAL REALITY). More recently the POST-MODERNIST cultural theorist Jean Baudrillard has analysed the HYPERREALITY of consumerism and advocated, perhaps mischievously, a willing and passive collaboration by individuals in the face of invitations to consume that recalls the late-Eighties phenomenon of the COUCH POTATO.

CONTEMPORARY STYLE

A term used to denote the self-consciously MODERNISTIC designs in
interior decoration, particularly furniture, of the late 1950s and early
1960s. The classless look in question incorporated the so-called
Airport Style and derived partly from FESTIVAL STYLE. In practice,
Contemporary meant modular units, rough brickwork, bare or
brightly painted wood surfaces and ceramic decorations.

- *Contemporary meant something more than mere style. It was a
  theory put into practice; a commitment to a wider range of design
  values that allowed maximum public participation. Well-designed
  consumer goods were no longer only available to the privileged few.*
  Catherine McDermott, Street Style, *1986*

CORNERBOYS

A pejorative term, now archaic, used by journalists and adult critics of
the 1950s TEDDY BOYS. At the time these youths were as notorious for
their delinquent gang image, congregating on inner-city street corners,
as for their dandified dress.

CORNISH PASTY

A shoe style that resolutely ignored fashion but became identified
with a particular social subgroup in Britain was the so-called Cornish
Pasty. The moulded wraparound sole of the shoe was attached
to the uppers by a row of heavy leather stitches, thus inviting
comparison with the savoury pastry. It was considered emblematic
of the deliberately unfashionable adult male in the late 1970s and
early 1980s, typically being worn (sometimes as part of an ensemble
including a safari suit or Norfolk jacket) by schoolteachers or college
and university lecturers.

COUCH POTATO

This expression from the late 1980s describes a person whose main
activity is to lie in front of a television eating and drinking. The
categorization is American ('couch' being the equivalent of sofa
or settee) and sought to define humorously a new form of passive

ultra-CONSUMERISM (its active counterpart would be RECREATIONAL SHOPPING). In the USA 10,000 people joined a couch potato movement launched by a Bob Armstrong from Sacramento, who claimed that television provided an ideal and otherwise unattainable life experience. The French POST-MODERNIST philosopher Jean Baudrillard actually defined the couch potato *avant la lettre* when he declared that 'hyperconformity' and a 'strategy of passivity' were the proper responses to the enveloping HYPERREALITY of late capitalism.

- *That new breed of American, the stay-at-home, VCR-watching couch potato, has been good news indeed for the US home video industry.*

    Guardian, *29 February 1988*

- *'Couch Potato', according to Lindsay Bareham, 'is American for a television addict': the potato, once again, is defamed as a symbol of dull lethargy.*
    Patrick Skene Catling, Daily Telegraph *Christmas Review, 1989*

COUNTERCULTURE

A synonym for the HIPPIE-era ALTERNATIVE SOCIETY and the UNDERGROUND, the term 'counterculture' was coined by the American publisher, editor and author Theodore Roszack in 1969. The *Making of a Counter-culture* was his blueprint for a future in which progressive and libertarian groups would provide a counterpart and eventual replacement for existing Western society. The suggestion of a unified culture and alternative institutions formed from the disparate elements of middle-class youth rebellion was most enthusiastically promoted in the United States, where the term 'counterculture' was commonly used. By 1973 the idea had subsided, as anti-Establishment movements continued to fragment rather than cohere.

COUNTRYBILLY

See ROCKABILLY.

CREW CUT

Between 1957 and 1962 the cropped hairstyle common among many male pre-teens and teenagers in the USA was a fashionable fad in Britain, worn by those emulating the 'progressive' aspects (rather than the more flamboyant ROCK 'N' ROLL look) of American pop culture. The style, which first evolved into a so-called semi-crew, then into a 'Roman' look, was out of fashion from about 1963 to 1967, when late MODS and proto-SKINHEADS revived it. The crew cut was revived by members of the TWO TONE movement from 1979, and a mutation of the crew cut, the FLAT-TOP, was a fad of the early Eighties. The name of the style probably derives from its popularity with American college rowing crews of the 1930s and 1940s.

CROP CIRCLES

By 1990 the UFO obsession of the 1950s and 1960s had waned as sophisticated tracking and recording techniques had failed to register a single unarguable sighting. Suddenly, however, a new phenomenon seized the imagination of the British public and aroused hysteria in the press. This was the appearance in summer corn fields of geometric patterns – typically circles joined by lines, but sometimes more intricate designs. Belief in the pictograms' extraterrestrial or supernatural origins became an article of faith amongst the NEW AGE mystical fraternity. Devotees of the NEW SCIENCE – including Rupert Sheldrake, who proposed 'morphic resonance' (see NEW SCIENCE), and Terence Meaden, who favoured 'vortices of ball lightning' – preferred to ascribe the formations to unexplained natural forces. Serious scientists investigated the happenings; similar patterns were reportedly discovered in the dust in the Tokyo underground system; a journal, the *Cerealogist*, was founded; and conferences and symposia were held. The music groups Led Zeppelin, Big Audio Dynamite and the KLF all used cut-crop logos to publicize themselves. Although farmers and others reported previous instances of corn circles going back for some twelve years, the press failed to establish how old the phenomenon really was. Speculation continued into 1991, when two hoaxers, Doug Bowers and Dave Chorley, revealed that they had been responsible for most of the first crop circles, creating twenty per year for fun. In spite of these and other confessions, and despite the results of a national competition in July 1992 which proved that 'authentic' circles could be quickly duplicated, the self-proclaimed experts refused to concede.

- *The wonderful thing about crop circles is how everybody behaves true to type. The believers are either be-kaftaned earth mothers or gently dishevelled and rather upper-class fogies with names like Montague, Wingfield, Michell and Martineau. The sceptics are sensible northerners with monosyllabic surnames.*
  Weekend Telegraph, *18 July 1992*

CROSS-DRESSING
See GENDER-BENDERS.

CRUISING
Cruising began in the 1950s in the towns and cities of the USA as one of the rituals of an affluent youth culture. It involved driving, often in convoy, along a main 'drag' or around a prescribed circuit in order to pose, show off one's car and attract members of the opposite sex. Cruising could also precede or follow impromptu HOT-ROD racing as a sort of *concours d'élégance*, and it came to be associated particularly with CUSTOMIZED automobiles. In the mid-1960s cruising was adopted by the PACHUCO (Chicano) street subculture of Los Angeles, when both cars and owners were known as LOW RIDERS. Around 1974 the spontaneous drive-pasts spread to London and Paris; in London the King's Road in Chelsea became the venue for a gathering of American car enthusiasts who, first on random Friday nights and later by agreement on the last Saturday of each month, paraded around a circuit linked by the Battersea and Albert bridges. Minor versions of the same tradition were staged at Canvey Island, Essex, Twickenham in London's southwest suburbs and in a few provincial towns. The Chelsea cruise, now also attracting sports-car drivers and exotic non-American vehicles, was still flourishing in 1992.

CRUSTIES
An amalgam of the values of HIPPIES, PUNKS, GREBOS and the TRAVELLERS of mid-1980s convoy fame, Crusty culture came to public attention in Britain in 1991 in the city of Bath. It was there that this

West Country-based movement achieved its highest profile through the activities of city-centre beggars. Crusties practise a militant self-degradation involving drink and drug abuse, personal filthiness and public obnoxiousness. Living rough or in communal houses or squats (see SQUATTING), the proponents of this lifestyle finance themselves by begging and social security payments, otherwise shunning bourgeois society as far as possible. Inspired by the cultivated encrustations on (generally military-surplus) clothing and hair, the name Crusty is only one of a variety of epithets applied to themselves by the members of this coalescing of subcultures; other terms include Smellies, SOAP-DODGERS, self-styled Cider Punks, SCROTES, FRAGGLES, NEW AGE Travellers and the rural vagrant Hedgers. The Crusty milieu intersects with the world of CLASS WAR anarchists and with the homeless of urban 'cardboard cities'. In historical terms, Crusty can be seen as an extremist gesture inspired by Punk, but fostered by both its geographical setting in the southwest of England and Wales, to which the remnants of the Hippie COUNTERCULTURE had retired in the 1970s, and by the spectacular and intransigent CONSUMERISM of the 1980s. Crusty ideology is a blend of nihilism, flaunted self-destructiveness and feigned vacuity, celebrated by its own post-Punk bands and echoed in the slogans 'Make Homebrew Not War!' and 'Disorder!'

- *The Crusties of Bath are, with their counterparts at the opposite end of the social scale, the smooth lawyers and medics, considerably more redolent of the city Jane Austen knew than anything else the tourist is likely to see.*
  Reader's letter, Independent, November 1991

CRYSTALS

A minor element of the HIPPIE repertoire, crystals came to the fore in the 1980s as part of NEW AGE healing techniques, also doubling as jewellery. The rather confused claims made to support the role of crystals refer to the identification of certain gems with birth signs and to the supposed power of crystal structures (see PYRAMIDS) to focus cosmic energy. Crystals were traditionally prized as amulets, talismans and love tokens. They were also sometimes crushed and mixed into potions. Their ability to transport or reflect beneficent vibrations is a more modern notion.

- *The more precious stones a person wears, the more strongly will they be charged with cosmic forces, which they will radiate out into their surroundings.*
  Mellie Uyldert, The Magic of Precious Stones, *1980*

CUISINE MINCEUR/CUISINE NOUVELLE

See NOUVELLE CUISINE.

CULT WITH NO NAME

A semi-facetious label given by the music and style press to the London club-based youth subculture that subsequently became known as the BLITZ KIDS, then as the NEW ROMANTICS.

CUSTOMIZING

Customizing began in earnest in the USA during the 1950s with the ornamentation of cars and motorbikes in order to individualize them; the practice may have been partly inspired by the decorating of planes and tanks by armed service personnel during the Second World War. Cars were also rebuilt, modified and glamorized for the purpose of HOT-RODDING or for displaying in CRUISING rituals (this techno-KITSCH hobby was celebrated by the UNDERGROUND film-maker Kenneth Anger in his *Kustom Kar Kommandos*). HELL'S ANGELS customized their Harley Davidson motorcycles into 'chopped hogs' or 'choppers', as well as their leather jackets. Among both HIPPIES and the fashion-conscious, the customizing of clothing spread in the late Sixties and early Seventies, particularly the embroidering and patching of denim and the decorating of boots and shoes with coloured dyes and appliqué. This trend towards consumer 'interference' and the reworking of consumer goods reached new heights in the 1980s when in addition to jeans, leather jackets, shoes and hats, amateur and professional designers began to remodel household appliances such as TVs, telephones and computers, especially hand-held VIDEO GAMES. Customizing thus formed part of the POST-MODERN tendency to break down barriers between art and technology and to move further towards 'interactive CONSUMERISM'. Many manufactured styles and artefacts, from SKATEBOARDS and MOUNTAIN BIKES to the UNISEX look, were actually reactions to earlier customizing by anonymous individuals.

CUT-UPS

A technique practised by the émigré poet Brion Gysin (a long-term American resident of Tangier and later of Paris) in collaboration with the BEAT novelist William Burroughs, the cut-up applies the techniques of collage to written fiction and poetry by literally cutting up and rearranging ready-made texts randomly. Similar subversions of orthodox writing had been done before – as party games in Victorian and Edwardian society, and as avant-garde juxtapositions by Dadaists, Futurists, Cubists and Surrealists – but it was Gysin who promoted the cut-up to postwar progressives, influencing poetry, ROCK music and graphics, particularly during the PUNK era.

- *The cut-up and fold-in technique he [William Burroughs] developed – the random stewing together of other men's writings – was an attempt to tune in to a numinous message delivered through the static of apparent nonsense.*

  Anthony Burgess, Independent, *March 1991*

CYBERPORN

A pretentious term coined in 1992 from 'cyberspace' and CYBERPUNK to describe high-technology sex stimulants such as pornographic computer programmes, VIDEO GAMES, laser discs, telephone chat lines, satellite broadcasts and, in particular, VIRTUAL REALITY. The fusion of (safe) sex and cybernetics, robotics and information technology had been anticipated by writers such as Philip K. Dick, by musicians such as Gary Numan in his 1979 ELECTRO-pop hit 'Are Friends Electric?', and by the 1991 film *Lawnmower Man*.

- *The sexual possibilities of Virtual Reality are already sending a thrill through Europe's fetish cliques . . . Those eerie rubber masks delete individuality and turn male and female alike into distorted and inhuman figures. The effect is like the hydrocephalic bulk of a VR helmet: both terrifying and poignant.*

  Time Out, *May 1992*

CYBERPUNK

A 1980s literary genre triggered by the publication in 1984 of William Gibson's novel *Neuromancer*. In the early 1990s the term was still in use, now generalized to denote a mood or tendency involving GRAPHIC NOVELS, comic-book art, film and video, computer games (see VIDEO GAMES) and TECHNO music, or narrowed down to describe, in the words of *Time Out* magazine, 'computer-users who loiter around on the communication networks like kids at a shopping mall – often disruptive'. The 'cyber' (from the Greek *kybernetes*, meaning pilot or governor) in Cyberpunk refers to the notion of a cybernetic reality, a computer-generated world (actualized in the later 1980s by VIRTUAL REALITY) in which the human brain is networked into electronic systems of information and control. The 'punk' conveys the iconoclastic nihilism that permeates the work of Gibson and other young science-fiction authors such as Bruce Sterling. None of the strains within Cyberpunk are original to these writers: their literary forerunners are Raymond Chandler, Philip K. Dick (whose character Palmer Eldritch introduced the man/machine merger and whose 1968 novel *Do Androids Dream of Electric Sheep?* was filmed as the influential *Blade Runner*), and the gay black American writer Samuel Delany. Other influences include the French science-fiction and fantasy comic books (*bandes dessinées*) of the 1970s.

- *The brash fusion of* Blade Runner *imagery,* What Computer? *technology and the spirit of Atari gave the critics the excuse to create a new ghetto: Cyberpunk.*

    The Face, *October 1987*

DA

Joe Cirello, a barber from Philadelphia, claimed to have invented
the DA (the initials stand for 'duck's ass' or 'duck's arse') in 1940.
In fact a similar hairstyle, sometimes called the ARGENTINE DUCKTAIL,
consisting of greased hair piled high on top and swept back at
the sides to form a ridge or seam at the back, was simultaneously
fashionable among the Mexican-American PACHUCOS of Los Angeles.
The DA was adopted as an emblematic coiffure by disaffected young
males all over the English-speaking world and beyond (particularly
in France and Sweden) during the 1950s. In Britain it was part of the
visual identity of TEDDY BOYS and ROCKERS, along with the QUIFF and
the ELEPHANT'S TRUNK.

DANCEFLOOR

In the early 1980s white post-PUNK ROCK-based music lost its
impetus and originality and, by dint of repetition of sounds and
gestures, ceased to be subversive. In contrast, DISCO-based music,
once derided as repetitive and conformist, began to take over the
vanguard role in youth culture, helped by its adoption in the gay (see
GAY LIBERATION) UNDERGROUND. The most innovative sounds and
the most dynamic dance and fashion trends were being generated in
the clubs of New York and Chicago, and in the street HIP HOP and
RAP environments of Brooklyn, the Bronx and South Los Angeles. In
Britain new sounds and styles were propagated by DJs and amateur
record producers working through a network of movable club events,
warehouse discothèques and semi-private parties. Advances in
technology allowed do-it-yourself mixing, SAMPLING, SCRATCHING,
recording and even illicit broadcasting on pirate radio (see PIRATE
BROADCASTING), whilst the entrepreneurial spirit of the mid-1980s
created a thriving subculture with its own graphics, clothing, record

distributors and voices in the music and fashion press. The whole classless and multi-ethnic movement was known as Dancefloor, and by the early 1990s encompassed the ACID HOUSE and RAVE scenes, mainstream HOUSE and TECHNO and HIP HOP, as well as all their subcategories (BALEARIC BEAT, GARAGE, Ragamuffin Rap, etc.), and even jazz. Except for INDIE POP (dismissed by many as insipid) and GRUNGE (a reworking of Punk and HEAVY METAL), Rock 'n' Roll and its derivatives were out of favour in HIP circles. Dancefloor can be seen as a synthesis of many strands of 1980s Anglo-American street culture, expressed, packaged and promoted by the tools of the enterprise society, but claiming an 'alternative' ethos of cosmopolitan hedonism – ignoring rather than threatening the existing orthodoxies.

- *Dancefloor culture reprised a romantic tenet of late seventies' punk: the conviction that any and everyone could find a part to play.*
  Cynthia Rose, Design After Dark: The Story of Dancefloor Style, *1991*

DANCEHALL (REGGAE)
See RAGGA.

DAVY CROCKETT

The American frontiersman and politician David Crockett (1786–1836), who died a hero at the siege of the Alamo, was the basis for a pre-teen craze of 1956. The actor Fess Parker played Crockett in an American television series and in two feature films, accompanied by the theme tune 'King of the Wild Frontier'. This triggered off a fashion for coonskin caps and, to a lesser extent, buckskin suits as an alternative to the then ubiquitous cowboy outfit. The Davy Crockett fad was one of postwar Britain's first experiences of concerted marketing and merchandising and for a brief period the early 19th-century pioneer and his forest-Indian opponents seemed set to replace the cowboy as the media's romantic Western stereotype. Davy Crockett caps (fur hats with attached tails) featured as minor fashion accessories in some HIPPIE circles and again during the early 1980s in the HIP HOP and SCRATCH subcultures.

DAYDREAMER

A NEW AGE toy serving as a sophisticated kaleidoscope and claiming
to induce a mind-expanding state in the user. When the device is
held to the eyes and blown into, a blade turns to create whirling
PSYCHEDELIC patterns. The gadget originated in the USA in 1991 and
recalls the cruder TRIP GOGGLES of the late 1960s.

DEATH METAL

A sub-genre of HEAVY METAL, THRASH and GRUNGE, Death Metal
– also known as Deathcore – was distinguished by its taste for
mutilation, cannibalism, gore and blasphemy in its lyrics and the
names of its bands. It took one strain of ROCK imagery (the taste for
the macabre, seen in an introvert form in the GOTH phenomenon) and
an adolescent fascination with the morbid and grotesque (coinciding
with the vogue for dramatizations of serial killings) and made these
the basis of a music craze. Like horror comics and SPLATTER MOVIES,
the style appealed particularly to relatively naive teenagers in the
USA (many bands emanated from Florida for some reason), the UK
and Northern Europe. Exponents included Napalm Death, Carcass
and Cancer, Morbid Angel, Cannibal Corpse and Decomposed. It
started to take on a distinct identity from about 1990, with groups
vying to produce the most repellent record covers and the most
ludicrously dense – and usually inaudible – shock lyrics. The British
Rock press promoted the fad as another harmless pseudo-extremist
pose, although more sober commentators were divided as to its real
potential for harm. In 1992 British customs authorities failed in their
prosecution of the Swedish band Dismember for obscenity.

- *Death Metal music, the ugly stepson of Thrash, with its grisly
  graveyard lyrics and that disgusting deep-throat roar, sounds like
  the audio equivalent of the video nasty – just one more symptom
  of decline in a sickening world. But in Britain, its fans are mostly
  just benign little teenies with silver skull rings on a naughty night
  out . . .*
  Independent on Sunday, *6 September 1992*

DECONSTRUCTION

A concept and technique developed by the French philosopher and
critic Jacques Derrida, Deconstruction was first and foremost a close
analysis of literary texts that disregards their socio-historical setting
or their attempts to evoke 'meaning' and instead sees them as an
interplay of surface assumptions and signs. This approach, in which
the critic looks beyond the author's intentions and is able to follow a
variety of subversive relationships and speculations, pushed literary
theory – and subsequently progressive thought in general – beyond
STRUCTURALISM, on which it was based, into POST-STRUCTURALISM and
POST-MODERNISM. Derrida, a contemporary of Barthes (the proponent
of SEMIOLOGY), Foucault, Lyotard and Baudrillard, expounded
his theories in the late 1960s using abstractions, subjective claims
and plays on words, notably between *différence* – differing – the
notion that it is only the oppositions between ideas or words that
give them significance, and *différance* – deferring – the notion that
the resolution of the meaning of a text is endlessly put off by the
interpreter while processing its many facets.

Those influenced by Deconstruction turned it into a literary
orthodoxy (in the case of the American Yale School led by Paul de
Man) and a tool for the radical assessment of other aspects of culture.
By the 1980s it had become a vogue term in all areas of progressive
thought, often meaning no more than an attack on conventional
representations. Its positive effect could be said to be its unmasking
of the hidden strategies and bogus theories behind both bourgeois
and leftist communication systems; its negative effect the belittling
of creativity and feeling and its exaltation of the quasi-objective
commentator. FEMINISTS, anti-racists and other radicals have
extrapolated Deconstruction's notions of the power assumptions
behind the choice of words into the Political Correctness (see PC)
campaign to purify language.

Derrida himself was the focus for controversy when he defended
the reputation of Paul de Man, revealed after his death to have been
a wartime anti-Semite and collaborator. In February 1992, he also
attracted media attention when he addressed the Oxford University
Union and drew a crowd of 900 against the actor Warren Beatty's
400. In March of the same year he was proposed for an honorary
doctorate from Cambridge University, provoking an acrimonious
split between academics who accused him of 'intellectual nihilism'

and 'bogus philosophy', and those who defended him as the most important representative of the heirs of Saussure and Lévi-Strauss. After a debate that was also carried on in the media a vote was taken and the degree was awarded.

- *Deconstruction was conceived as a difficult and very specific set of practices or operations within written texts. But it is a shadowy presence in the pop of the '80s.*
    Paul Oldfield, After Subversion: Pop Culture and Power, *1989*

- *Popping up in poems and conversations, spicing up book reviews and sports reports, deconstruction is used with the cheerfully airy abandon that once marked existentialism. Part of the charm is that few people, in or out of academe, have a very firm grip on what deconstruction means.*
    David Lehman, Independent on Sunday, *8 September 1991*

DEELYBOBBERS

A set of imitation antennae worn on the head by children. This novelty item enjoyed a brief vogue in the USA in 1975. The name is an arbitrary coinage, although inspired by the fact that the ball-ends of the antennae do indeed bob on their flexible or sprung stems. The contraption is a combination of extraterrestrial and insect antennae as seen in children's stories and TV programmes.

DEEP HOUSE

See HOUSE.

DIANETICS

See SCIENTOLOGY.

DIGGERS

The first Diggers were a radical 17th-century Puritan sect led by Gerard Winstanley. They attempted to set up egalitarian alternative communities by cultivating the common lands of England, their manifesto being to 'lay the foundation of making the Earth a Common Treasury for All . . . not Lording over another, but all looking upon each other as equals'. In 1966 Emmet Grogan led an offshoot of the Haight-Ashbury HIPPIE subculture, which took the same name and organized free food programmes and 'crash pads', a free store and newsletter, as well as setting up rural communes elsewhere in California. In Britain a small group set itself up in 1967 as the Hyde Park Diggers, expanding the following year into a loose confederation of small farming communes. As a coherent movement the Diggers were short-lived, but their communal model persisted into the mid-1970s and was taken up by the TRAVELLERS.

● *When we've got the communes on the groove, we'll support and expand the whole of Hipville by giving away some of our surplus produce free to hippies and diggers in need of them, and by selling the rest in hippie shops, preferably at prices which will appreciably undercut those of the profiteering hucksters of Squareville.*
  London Diggers' Love Commune declaration, February 1968

DIRTY REALISM

A literary genre celebrated in 1983 by the British paperback magazine *Granta*, Dirty Realism is an American 'school' that includes Jayne Anne Phillips, Raymond Carver and Richard Ford. Taking its inspiration partly from the mood of 1970s cinema and the blue-collar ROCK songs of Bruce Springsteen, it concentrates on the experience of the rootless and disaffected, using a laconic or hardbitten, unaffected prose style.

● *It was a fiction – spare, unillusioned, but compassionate – of the belly-side of American life: trailer parks, roadside cafés and small mid-western towns.'*
  Granta *magazine, 1986*

DISCO

Disco music appeared at the beginning of the 1970s as a fusion of Tamla Motown, SOUL and black pop ballads, creating a synthesized, messageless dance music that owed as much, if not more to producers as to performers. Recordings featuring lush orchestrations over handclaps and FUNK rhythms began to take on an anonymity and uniformity that suited the repetitive discothèque format. This music was anathema to most progressives, who only started to take

notice when in the mid-1970s German producers and arrangers
such as Giorgio Moroder started to blend in harder electronic pop
MINIMALISM to create an international genre called 'Disco'. Disco
dancing evolved from its black American model into a simplified
parody practised by a multiracial, multinational mass audience for
whom the disco, with its increasingly sophisticated lighting and
sound systems, had replaced the dance hall, nightclub and bar-room.
The music industry began to be led from the dancefloor as dancers
and DJs created hits.

Throughout the late 1970s Disco existed in parallel to ROCK, which
entertained its devotees in live concerts in traditional venues. Rock's
culmination in PUNK in 1976 was the antithesis of conformist,
apolitical, anti-intellectual Disco. Significantly, the Sex Pistols'
singer, Johnny Rotten, wore a badge inscribed 'Death to Disco'
in 1977; two years later his group PIL produced 'Death Disco', a
distorted homage to the genre which marked the beginnings of a
crossover that would dominate 1980s youth culture. Black street
rhythms and dance styles reappeared in the discos and clubs in the
late 1970s as post-Punk white music began to assimilate the 120
beats-per-minute tempo. During the 1980s the word 'disco', always
a potential pejorative, gave way to DANCEFLOOR – a catch-all category
encompassing new mutations such as HOUSE, GARAGE and TECHNO.
In a 1991 retrospective, *Sky Magazine* nominated the following as
the five seminal Disco records of the 1970s: 'Spacer' by Sheila B.
Devotion; 'The Glow of Love' by Change; 'Try Me, I Know We Can
Make It' by Donna Summer; 'Shame' by Evelyn 'Champagne' King;
and 'I Specialize in Love' by Sharon Brown.

- *Sound that could be spiced and shaped and served up in any flavour
  of the month you wish – like soya beans. Thus there was classical
  disco, Latinized disco, which became popular when New York's
  gay groups decided that Spic chic was it in 1975, party disco,
  nostalgic disco.*

  Peter York, Style Wars, *1980*

- *Disco took most of its musical cues and lyrical manifesto from the
  James Brown song 'Get Up, I Feel Like Being a Sex Machine', and
  has stuck to those guns ever since.*

  Robert Sandall, Sunday Times, *July 1991*

DISCO-BALL
See LOLOBAL.

DISTRESSING

The various forms of distressing all involve treating or damaging surfaces in order to create an artificial appearance of age. A long-standing practice in the antiques business, it became a hallmark of 1980s interior design and decoration. In popular culture, distressing began with the bleaching and stressing of blue jeans in the late 1960s, followed closely by the taste for 'antique finish' leather, which during the 1970s re-created the patina of the second-hand for a more fastidious consumer market. When applied to environments rather than clothing, distressing came into its own in the mid-1980s with the new desire for instant 'heritage'. This was in some senses a parody of the new conservatism of the early 1980s that in the UK had been manifested in such vogues as the SLOANE RANGER look and the taste for country pine furniture. The more adventurous design trends of the YUPPIE, NEW GEORGIAN and YOUNG FOGEY era included a POST-MODERN liking for pastiches of classical forms and finishes. In practice this often meant dragging, stippling and chemically peeling walls and ceilings. Art objects, furniture and accessories were also distressed, sometimes under the influence of the JUNK ART fad. By the early 1990s the distressed look had become a cliché of Western European and North American design and was no longer in favour in avant-garde milieux.

DIVINE LIGHT MISSION

The Divine Light Mission was one of many enlightenment movements of the 1970s led by a living guru. This particular sect followed the teenage Guru Maharaj Ji, who held open-air meetings in the parks of London and New York and appealed particularly to the young. Rumours of the boy's opulent lifestyle (devotees were expected to renounce wealth) aroused both the interest of the press and widespread criticism, as did accusations of diamond-smuggling. At the end of the decade the guru was ousted by members of his family and disappeared into obscurity.

- *At midsummer in 1971 the free festival movement held its most successful event, the Glastonbury Fayre . . . The Guru Maharaj Ji addressed 10,000 from a specially constructed pyramid aligned to attract the beneficent forces of the region.*

  Robert Hewison, Too Much, 1986

DMs

One of the most lasting fashion accessories of the last two decades, DMs – 'Doc Martens' – are boots and shoes manufactured under the Doctor Martens label and featuring the Doctor's 'AirWair' patent moulded waterproof, acidproof, lightweight rubber soles. The cherry-red, high-lacing boots were adopted as part of the SKINHEAD uniform when army (BOVVER) boots were abandoned at the end of 1969; in the mid-1970s pre-PUNK progressives, art students and members of leftist groups began to wear the shoe versions. Doc Martens persisted as a classless, genderless non-fashion fashion into the 1980s, when they became part of a standard post-Punk black ensemble and American and European fans began importing them or producing imitations. The company reacted to increased popularity in the early 1980s by introducing loafer, jodhpur, CHELSEA BOOT, brogue and shaped-toe models to supplement the traditional plain versions. Readers of the *New Musical Express* voted DMs – as they came to be called – fashion item of the year in 1990.

- *[A boutique called] Boy's PR poster shows a working-class affray, photographed in black-and-white. A boy lies unconscious, face bleeding, on the pavement, framed by two pairs of legs in shortish trousers and rubber-soled Doc Martens. Skinhead.*

  Peter York, Harpers & Queen, July 1977

- *MA-1 flying jacket, 501s, matt Doc Martens. In the mid-Eighties hip young creatives wore this the way the Fifties company man wore his grey flannel.*

  Arena, November 1991

DRAG RACING

Drag racing involves racing two or more cars in a straight line from a standing start. The practice began on public roads and streets ('drag' being a slang term for (main) street dating from the turn of the century) among HOT-RODDERS in North America. As the amateur sport developed along with its own terminology and surrounding subculture, celebrated in Jan and Dean's 1963 hit, 'Drag City', the modified production cars mutated into specially designed dragsters with radically slimmed and elongated bodies riding on giant rear and small front wheels. Airstrips were borrowed for off-road races, later replaced by purpose-built dragstrips. Originally restricted to the affluent American youth culture of the 1950s and 1960s, drag racing became a minority hobby in Western Europe in the early 1970s. In Britain Blackbushe, a wartime aerodrome, was redesignated 'Santa Pod' and used for drag racing.

- *Santa Pod, our next stop, was very different. A concrete slab in the middle of vast potato plains, it is the centre of drag racing, that weird sport where competitors spend literally hours priming their scorpion-like machines for a brief, ecstatic lift-off down the quarter-mile stretch.*

  Nova *magazine, January 1975*

DREADLOCKS

The most visible symbol of the RASTAFARIAN movement, dreadlocks – long, tightly plaited or knotted strands of hair worn to the shoulders – were first adopted in Jamaica before the Second World War as an affirmation of identity. They originated as an imitation of hairstyles worn in Ethiopia under Haile Selassie (Ras Tafari), also recalling the lion's mane evoked in his title 'Lion of Judah'. Dreadlocks carry a religious significance, both in their name ('dread' is a key word in Rastafarian culture, encompassing such concepts as awe of God and the awe inspired in His enemies by the righteous) and in the fact that they must not be cut, in accordance with an Old Testament injunction in the Book of Numbers. Originally worn only by a small number of true believers, dreadlocks spread through the black community, first in Jamaica and soon after in Britain, with the increase of black consciousness and the popularity of REGGAE music. By the mid-1970s, locks (as they were usually known by wearers) were a familiar sight in London, also being worn by some young whites of both sexes. Short locks were fashionable in the mid-Eighties among devotees of revived FUNK, SOUL and HIP HOP culture in the UK and the USA. Later in the decade tangled ringlets, often hennaed, were one of the badges of the CRUSTIES.

- *Somewhere between Trenchtown and Ladbroke Grove, the cult of Rastafari had become a 'style': an expressive combination of 'locks', of khaki camouflage and weed which proclaimed unequivocally the alienation felt by many young black Britons.*
  Dick Hebdige, Subculture – the Meaning of Style, 1979

DUB

An evolved form of the REGGAE of the early 1970s, Dub originally referred to the rhythm tracks created by producers and arrangers of Reggae records. The throbbing, echoing, murky instrumental sound of Dub was based on reverberation, multitracking, overlays and delays, over which an optional vocalist (often performing a TALKOVER live, rather than on the record itself) could perform. The shuddering Dub sound was particularly tuned to the realities of playing through the giant home-made sound systems used in parties and clubs in Jamaica, in black communities in London, and later in New York; its effect was to slow down and deepen the Reggae sound into something MINIMALIST and hypnotic. In many ways Dub, appearing in the UK in 1974 and existing as a recognizable genre until about 1980, was the foreunner to the SAMPLING, REMIXING and RAPPING DANCEFLOOR underground of the 1980s. Although it was admired by the PUNK subculture and incorporated into a few avant-garde white musicians' repertoires, Dub remained identified with the street culture of black youth and RASTAFARIANS, and was ignored by the mainstream music industry.

- *Nothing could have prepared you for the sheer audacity and texture of early Dub records like Skin, Flesh and Bones' 'Everlasting Dub' (High Note, 1975); they still sound terrific.*
  Jon Savage, England's Dreaming, 1991

DWARF-THROWING

A sport in which competitors vie to throw compliant (and usually helmeted) dwarfs as far as possible. The novelty practice was imported to Britain from Australia in the mid-1980s; it has also been popular in Germany and in France, where it was officially banned in 1991 after catching on on the Côte d'Azur.

- *Manuel Wackenheim, a French dwarf known as 'Mr Skyman' . . . is suing over an interior ministry order in November to halt 'an intolerable attack on human dignity'. His lawyer said his client is an entertainer who does not consider his profession either dangerous or degrading.*

Independent, 18 January 1992

DWEMs

See PC.

See ECSTASY.

EARTH ART

See LAND ART.

EARTH SHOES

With its spade-shaped toe and moulded, heel-less sole – raising the front of the foot, rather than the back – the earth shoe was a negation of fashion rather than a fashion statement. The new form of footwear was introduced in 1970 to counteract the poor posture and aggressive/erotic style connotations associated with contemporary boots and shoes. Accordingly, it became identified throughout the 1970s with the environmentally aware, vegetarians and anti-materialist liberals, as well as with a generation of young American tourists. The earth shoe design probably influenced that of the CORNISH PASTY, a much-ridiculed adult style of the late 1970s.

ECOLOGISTS

See GREEN MOVEMENT.

ECSTASY

The nickname for the drug MDMA (3, 4 methylene dioxymethamphetamine) derives from the fact that users experience a sense of physical and emotional well-being, and an affectionate warmth towards others. The preparation was synthesized and patented in 1914 and rediscovered in the USA in the late 1960s for recreational use (related chemically to 'speed', it resembles a mild form of LSD in its effects), but it remained a minority taste until the early 1980s. Used by Californian therapists among others, it was legal until 1985. MDMA became a fashion in sophisticated media and nightclub circles in the USA and Britain around 1984, appealing to club and DISCO aficionados in particular because its amphetamine base bestows increased energy and wakefulness. Use of Ecstasy, also known in Britain as 'Adam', 'E', 'X' and 'Epsom Salts', coincided with the growth of DANCEFLOOR culture, and the drug was adopted as a mainstay of the ACID HOUSE and RAVE cult. Just as the nature of LSD fundamentally affected the mood and ethos of the late 1960s and early 1970s, Ecstasy helped define the later 1980s and early 1990s, both contributing to and reflecting the hedonistic, non-cerebral tendencies of progressive youth culture. Its adoption by, among others, working-class former CASUALS and football supporters helped to neutralize the violent strain in those milieux. Several deaths were reported from prolonged use of the substance and law enforcers chose to treat it as a serious danger; nevertheless its illicit sale flourished all over the British Isles in the early 1990s, devotees enhancing its effects by anointing themselves with VAPORUB.

- *Every generation finds the drug it needs . . . the cold, selfish children of 1985 think that ecstasy will make them loved and loving.*
  P. J. O'Rourke, Republican Party Reptile, *1987*

ELECTRO

The terms Electro Pop and Electro ROCK were first used in Britain at the very end of the 1970s to refer to white, progressive, Rock-based music created exclusively with synthesizers and drum machines and partly inspired by the earlier experimental electronic music of German (KRAUT ROCK) groups such as Kraftwerk. Exponents of this particular strain of post-PUNK music included the Human League, the Flying Lizards, Dépêche Mode, the Normal and, later, Erasure.

By 1982 the black American street-based subculture that included RAP and BREAK DANCING had moved towards creating 'space-age' electronic sounds, inspired both by European pop and the sounds of VIDEO GAMES. The record 'Planet Rock' by Afrika Bambaataa is acknowledged as the first example of this genre, which was dubbed

Electro and which mutated by 1984 into HIP HOP and by 1986 into
HOUSE. Electro was also a direct ancestor of TECHNO, the frenetic
synthetic fad of the early 1990s.

- *How to recognise it [Electro] . . . Fairly pathetic, tame lyrics about
  shooting little bug-eyed monsters or how fresh the MCs were, or
  jive-talk nonsense. Tinkling, ant-size drum sound on weeny drum
  machines. Very little funkiness amidst the electronics . . .*
  NME, *December 1991*

ELEPHANT'S TRUNK

A spectacular male hairstyle of the TEDDY BOY era, the elephant's
trunk consisted of a tubular QUIFF projecting over the forehead.
The arrangement was an elaboration of the earlier DA. Worn by the
proto-GLAM star Bryan Ferry of Roxy Music in 1971, it was revived by
some adherents of the ROCKABILLY look in the early 1980s, including a
small number of females.

EMIN

A British-based enlightenment cult of the early 1980s led by
Stephen Armin, the Emin movement was attacked consistently by
the satirical (see SATIRE) magazine *Private Eye* in its 'Cult Corner'
column.

ENCOUNTER GROUPS

Originally a form of radical THERAPY, by the end of the 1960s
the encounter group had become a widespread practice in such
diverse fields as psychiatry, social work, professional training,
education and theatre. The encounter group, rather than providing
one-to-one analysis or prescriptive advice, uses the dynamics
of group activities and confrontation – including touching,
feeling, screaming, and reacting to music – to release frustrations
and inhibitions and improve interpersonal relations and skills.
After attracting attention and notoriety when first introduced,
the technique has become an accepted part of the repertoire
of respected therapists as well as a mainstay of GESTALT and
PRIMAL techniques and more controversial self-improvement cults.

ENVIRONMENTALISTS

See GREEN MOVEMENT.

ESSEX BOY

Essex Boys were the SPIV wing of the YUPPIE subculture of the City
of London in the mid-1980s. Variously characterized as 'Waynes',
'Kevins' or 'Darrens', they were the young men of working-class
origin who typically commuted into the City from the overspill
suburbs of south Essex to take advantage of the opportunities for
enrichment that existed in the financial boom before and after the
BIG BANG. A decade before, they might have worked as messengers on
the floor of the Stock Exchange; in the Eighties they were more likely
to be brokers, marketmakers or dealers. In City circles, Essex Boy
came to denote a flashy style and an uncultured assertiveness; the
nickname did not cross over into the media, unlike ESSEX GIRL and
the slightly different ESSEX MAN of the 1990s.

- *An 'Essex Boy', one of the new breed of half-commission men,*
  Darren's making a lot of money considering he's not 30 yet. His
  Mum and Dad still both work on the assembly line at an electrical
  component factory in Romford, and they can't understand how it is
  their boy's doing so well.

  Peter Pugh, The City Slicker's Handbook, *1988*

ESSEX GIRL

A joke figure featuring in popular folklore and the mass media
in Britain in 1991 and 1992, Essex Girl personified vulgarity,
promiscuity and dim intellect. The figure of the heavily made-up
working-class young woman wearing white stiletto shoes and
dancing round her handbag at discos had been lampooned since
the 1970s, often designated as a 'Sharon' or 'Tracy' (the female
counterpart to a 'Kevin' or 'Wayne'; see ESSEX BOY). Viz magazine's
northern 'fat slags', the TV comedy *Birds of a Feather* and the realist
dramas of Mike Leigh all contained incarnations of her. Around 1990
she was tied to a specific location – the area of south Essex supposed
to epitomize the upwardly mobile working class. Essex Boy already
existed as a stock figure in the jargon of the City of London; Essex
Girl began to appear in the comic riddles flashed on to terminal

screens and networked round the financial centres, becoming the new focus for a number of old blue jokes and the source of many new ones. In 1992 the Sun newspaper began to print the jokes, prompting protests from some Essex citizens, investigation by TV documentarists, and the coining of SURREY GIRL and KNIGHTSBRIDGE GIRL as middle-class alternatives. The Essex Girl jokes, by no means confined to a male audience, formed part of a world of Rottweilers (see FIGHTING DOGS), satellite TV and tabloid newspapers; a consistent tradition of unashamed, self-aware and assertive popular culture celebrating philistinism and materialism and, like ESSEX MAN, nurtured by THATCHERISM and John Major's 'classless society'.

- *Q: How does an Essex Girl turn off the light after sex?*
  A: She slams the door of the Cortina.
                          The Official Essex Girl Joke Book, *1991*

- *Young white working-class girls are now the only social group that may be mocked with total impunity. Imagine a book of Brixton Girl jokes or a newspaper column featuring the young black men, Delroy and Delbert.*
           Julie Burchill, Sunday Times *Book Review, 15 March 1992*

ESSEX MAN

Unlike the spivvish (see SPIVS) ESSEX BOY and the cheerful tart, ESSEX GIRL, Essex Man was an invention of political commentators during the Thatcher (see THATCHERISM) administration. The phrase was first used to define the typical male member of the lower-middle or upper working classes who would vote Conservative in spite of sharing none of the pre-Thatcher Tory characteristics. Essex Man (coined in imitation of a prehistoric hominoid category, as in 'Selsdon Man') could be poor or *nouveau riche*, but would inevitably be uncultured, aggressively right wing and unashamedly materialist. The choice of Essex as the location of this archetype was based partly on the character of Norman Tebbit, Member of Parliament for Chingford, and partly on the demographic reality of the county, where East Londoners had been relocated in postwar years. A number of press articles attempted to delineate Essex Man, the more charitable seeing him as a well-meaning blue- or white-collar supporter of John Major's 'classless society', though the *Sunday Telegraph* described him in 1990 as 'young, industrious, mildly brutish and culturally barren . . . drinking with his mates, watching sport on Sky television, playing with his car and thinking about (and occasionally attempting) sexual intercourse'. In May 1992 the *Sunday Times* proposed WESSEX MAN as a NEW AGE counterpart.

EST

The initials EST stand for Erhard Seminar Training, a California-based self-improvement process of the 1970s founded by an ex-car salesman, John Paul Rosenberg (Rosenberg changed his name to Werner Erhard after being inspired by Ludwig Erhard, the West German chancellor and one of the architects of the postwar 'economic miracle'). The EST technique included elements adapted from radical psychotherapy, including the deliberate disorientation of subjects through isolation, public humiliation and verbal abuse by trainers. The resultant purging of negative and obstructive characteristics would enable a new clarity of purpose and focus on personal achievement. Although claiming affinities with Oriental philosophies (it was dubbed 'the ZEN of free-market capitalism') and spiritual enlightenment programmes, EST projected an aggressively materialist, ego-reinforcing message that appealed to a wide range of self-improvers. Even critics generally conceded the seminars' short-term effectiveness, but by the 1990s Erhard's activities (his organization had thirty-five centres in the USA and operated in seventeen countries) were hampered by lawsuits brought against him by former course participants, accusations of abuse from one of his children, and the confiscation of his assets by the US Internal Revenue. A new series of programmes under the 'Forum' title were nonetheless promoted internationally during the early 1990s.

ETHNIC MUSIC

See WORLD MUSIC.

EUROSTYLE

A term used by fashion magazines and social commentators to refer to the trends in casual clothing and sportswear that originated from Continental Europe, particularly Italy, France and Spain, during the 1980s. This international look, comprising primary colours and featured labels, was a palatable high-street version of the parodies of American Fifties and Sixties styles produced by Fiorucci at the end of the 1970s. The conformist, cosmopolitan and well-finished Eurostyle products ousted both the remnants of the PUNK look and the relatively tawdry sweatshop clothing previously sold in Britain for the mass youth market. Reinforced by business links with the EC and low-cost foreign holidays, Continental recycling and repackaging of traditional Western modes (first imported by MODS and more recently by CASUALS) dominated the consumer boom of the mid-1980s. Eurostyle also brought to the British consumer a new label-consciousness and the flaunting of labels on the exterior of clothing, as well as a previously un-British concern with accessories (bags, belts, jewellery, pens, etc.) and cosmetics for both sexes.

EUROTECHNO

See BALEARIC BEAT; TECHNO.

EXECUTIVE TOYS

See NEWTON'S CRADLE; PET ROCKS; TRAMPOLINING.

EXEGESIS

A controversial self-improvement programme which involves subjecting students to stress and abuse, Exegesis (the word means critical interpretation or exposition) was founded by a former actor, Robert Fuller, who took the surname D'Aubigny. Based in Britain with subsidiaries in France and Ireland, Exegesis also encompassed professional training, public relations and computer software, as well as controlling a complex financial empire. In the 1980s the organization, like the similar EST in the USA, faced criticism over its use of psychological programming and questions over its tax affairs.

EXISTENTIALISM

From the 1940s to the end of the 1960s, Existentialism was undoubtedly the most influential, if not the only, philosophy directly to influence popular culture and the intellectual life of the West. The Existentialism that permeated the Bohemian café society of Paris in the late 1940s, and from there spread to the USA and Britain to influence the BEAT Generation in particular, was largely derived from the writings of Jean-Paul Sartre and Albert Camus. Sartre, and to a lesser extent Camus, had been influenced by the strain of philosophical thought initiated by the Danish theologian Søren Kierkegaard in the 19th century and propounded in the first half of the 20th by the German philosopher Martin Heidegger. The implications of this mode of thinking are that the human individual is isolated in a potentially absurd universe in which only fellow humans possess consciousness, conscience and will. The individual must create his or her own identity and morality by an act of will and involvement taken in a void.

The Second World War created the environment in which this radically disillusioned and by now atheist creed could take hold, and in the postwar years it fused with absurdism (see THEATRE OF THE ABSURD) and Marxism to create a potent movement that encouraged dramatic self-expression and poetic despair. In Paris, the Left Bank provided a setting for the transformation of Existentialism into a fashionable pose for authentic and would-be intellectuals. In the Anglo-American context, Existentialist influences can be seen in the cult of adolescent angst that pervaded the Beat Movement, the ANGRY YOUNG MEN and the rise of the teenager. By the end of the 1960s communal and collectivist political and social theories were in the ascendant and the Existentialist focus on the individual seemed out of place. In Paris it was supplanted by the theories of the generation of 1968, STRUCTURALISM and SEMIOLOGY in particular.

● *But existentialism is no longer a very powerful influence in philosophy; in fact, it is almost dead. Which leaves the British philosophers the run of the field.*
    Colin Wilson, Daily Telegraph *magazine, November 1968*

FACES

See MODS.

FANZINES

Collectors of comic books, devotees of film, ROCK 'N' ROLL and
Country music, and the fan clubs of particular stars were already
circulating mimeographed newsletters in the mid-1970s when the
new availability of cheap photocopying was seized upon by the
PUNK movement, triggering an explosion of home-made magazines.
The first American fanzines of this period were often phototypeset
or printed by offset lithography, but the typical British fanzine
was made up of stapled A4 sheets containing typewritten text
with handwritten captions and crude photomontage in black
and white. The magazines were distributed at music events and
through independent record shops and bookshops, providing
an information network and forum for polemic in keeping with
Punk's do-it-yourself philosophy and proselytizing. One of the
first significant examples was *Punk*, published in the USA
in January 1976; this was quickly followed by *Sniffin' Glue* in
London and *Ripped and Torn* in Edinburgh. By 1977 dozens of
fanzines were in existence. The deliberately primitive visual style
they introduced was co-opted by the mainstream music press,
commercial graphic design and the fashion industry, while their
radical pamphleteering approach was taken up by FEMINISTS and
other political activists, and in the early 1980s by, among others,
football fans (the first alternative football paper, *Foul*, had been
started in 1972), GRAFFITI enthusiasts and SKATEBOARDERS. In Britain
these fanzines were the training ground for a generation of style and
music journalists, including Danny Baker, Ian Penman and Paul
Morley.

- *Practically all writing on the new indie pop takes after the style of the fanzines that service the scene – excessively focused on the writer's own excitement, full of surface agitation, low on insight.*
  Simon Reynolds, Against Health and Efficiency: Independent Music in the 1980s, *1986*

FEMINISM

The so-called 'second wave' of feminism (the first being the Edwardian suffrage movement) began in the USA in the early 1960s when Betty Friedan published *The Feminine Mystique* and Gloria Steinem began to publish magazine articles redefining women's role and identity. A new focus on women's issues gathered momentum alongside the civil rights and racial equality movements and in 1966 the American National Organization of Women was set up.

The effects of the American initiatives began to appear in Britain after 1968. At first part of the general mobilization of the Left and the COUNTERCULTURE, the Women's Liberation Movement grew as the first flush of student unrest and HIPPIE ideology waned (the ALTERNATIVE SOCIETY, at least in manifestations such as the UNDERGROUND music scene, was generally phallocentric). The *Shrew* newspaper was published in Britain in 1969, and Germaine Greer's *The Female Eunuch* appeared the following year. The underground press devoted special issues to women's liberation, and in 1971 two of its writers founded the magazine *Spare Rib*, which survived and prospered, as did the feminist publishing house Virago, founded in 1975.

Feminism quickly attracted the attention of the media, whose commentaries generally focused on the sensational surface – the burning of bras in public demonstrations (the Living Bra was demonized by US feminists but the burning was actually limited to two or three occasions) and the disruption of beauty contests. This did, however, ensure that women's issues penetrated the mass consciousness, albeit slowly, and the passing of the Sex Discrimination Act in Britain in the mid-1970s marked a real advance. Deeper structural and attitudinal changes were more difficult to achieve, and in the United States and Europe the women's movement was always to some extent fragmented. In Britain, the USA and Australia there was a three-way division between the radical separatists, the leftists and more liberal gradualists. In France and Italy the tendency was less overtly political and more concerned with philosophical and psychological theories (the works of French writers such as Simone de Beauvoir and Anaïs Nin had helped to trigger the Anglo-Saxon movement).

During the late Seventies militant rhetoric and lesbian politics aroused the hostility of the media and alienated some women who preferred to work through orthodox channels for betterment. In the early 1980s explicit feminism as a movement could be said to have faltered, but in many significant areas the changes in awareness it had achieved remained and continued to evolve. Real changes in women's status in the home and workplace began to register in statistical surveys in the 1980s and in the latter part of the decade specific issues such as sexual harassment, violence by men, and child-care provision were debated seriously for the first time, as were the concepts of the NEW MAN, political correctness (see PC) and the risk of a masculinist (see the MEN'S MOVEMENT) backlash.

- *I myself have never been able to find out precisely what feminism is: I only know that people call me a feminist whenever I express sentiments that differentiate me from a doormat.*
  Rebecca West, 1913

- *A woman who cannot organise her sex life in her own best interest is hardly likely to transform society.*
  Germaine Greer, Oz magazine, February 1970

- *Contemporary feminism cut itself off from history and bankrupted itself when it spun its puerile, paranoid fantasy of male oppressors and female sex-object victims.*
  Camille Paglia, quoted in GQ magazine, January 1991

FESTIVAL STYLE

Sometimes also known as CONTEMPORARY STYLE or Airport Style, Festival Style was the title given to the trend in design and decoration that became fashionable in the UK in the wake of the Festival of Britain in 1951. It consisted of vivid colours, futuristic or abstract motifs and bold, often geometric shapes; popular materials included nylon, plastic, Formica and glass. Expressed in murals, carpets and curtains, as well as in lamps, coffee tables and other furniture, the look was a MODERNIST reaction to the drabness of

the Forties. As the style percolated from the fashion-conscious
élite to the mainstream, it was transformed by an admixture of
pseudo-Mediterranean influences into a KITSCH cliché by the end of
the decade. Elements of Festival Style reappeared in the free-for-all
eclecticism of 1980s POST-MODERNISM, and original items of
Fifties furniture and ornament became valuable collectables at the
same time.

FIBRE-OPTIC LAMP
See LAVA LAMP.

FIGHTING DOGS
The vogue for 'hard dogs' trained to attack humans or other animals
arose in the USA during the mid-1970s in conjunction with the
post-Vietnam SURVIVALIST movement, and was maintained by, among
others, drug dealers defending their territory. Private ownership of
attack dogs became a working-class and underclass status symbol
in Britain in the late 1980s, contributing to the long-established
UNDERGROUND practice of staging dog fights for 'sport' and profit. By
1991 the number of attacks on members of the public by these dogs
forced the Conservative Government into hasty legislation to restrict
ownership and to register and muzzle certain breeds. Widespread
police raids were still being carried out the following year in an
attempt to enforce these laws. Doberman pinschers and alsatians
were the first breeds to become popular in these milieux, followed
by rottweilers (a press sensation of 1989), American pit bull terriers
(bred especially to kill), and the Japanese tosa.

FILM NOIR
The term 'film noir' was coined by French film critics to categorize
low-budget black-and-white suspense thrillers of the 1940s and
1950s, particularly those suffused with pessimism and employing an
expressionistic visual style. Films belonging to this genre include
Marcel Carné's Le Jour se lève (actually made in 1939), John
Huston's The Maltese Falcon and Samuel Fuller's Underworld USA.
Their unredeemed 'blackness' (hence noir; reinforced by La Série

Noire, the title under which pulp detective novels were published
in France) was imitated in the 1980s in such releases as the remake
of James M. Cain's *The Postman Always Rings Twice*, and the Coen
brothers' *Blood Simple*. By the 1980s the phrase had become familiar
enough for it to be shortened to '*noir*' (adjective or noun), or the
un-French '*noiresque*', in the HIP Anglo-Saxon media.

FILOFAX

Expensively bound combinations of pocket diary, wallet, notebook
and address book had been fashionable in France, Italy and Spain
for three decades before being picked up in English-speaking
countries as the emblematic fashion accessory of the YUPPIE era.
By 1984 the Filofax (the personal organizer manufactured by Filofax
Limited, formerly Norman & Hill) was *de rigueur* for all real or
would-be young professionals. The pack's main purpose was as an
appointment book, but the ring binder and large format allowed for
the insertion of extra components such as maps, checklists and even
condoms and miniaturized novels (so-called 'Filo-fiction'). More and
more exotic presentations were introduced, although the iguana and
crocodile finishes were simulated in calfskin. Filofaxes had been on
sale in Britain since 1921 (they were particularly popular from the
1930s to the 1970s among the clergy and with officers in the armed
forces because they fitted ecclesiastical and military pockets), but
they proved to be uniquely suited to the needs of those working
in finance and the media in the 1980s, providing a portable filing
system that doubled as a brand-name fashion accessory. Imitators
such as Lefax and Microfile and the Psion electronic organizer
failed to supplant the Filofax, which became a standard corporate
gift, although abandoned by fashion leaders. By 1990 the company
was anxious to avoid the exclusive ABC1 Yuppie identification and
targeted students and housewives, among others.

- *Celia Lyttleton's fat Filofax of Sloane daubers has made her the
  Peggy Guggenheim of W11.*
                                                    Tatler, *April 1988*

FLAT-TOP

The flat-top hairstyle originated as a modification of the American army-issue CREW CUT (the 'GI crop') following the Second World War. The short all-over military crop was lengthened and levelled off geometrically on the top, while the sides were brushed back. (In a more radical version known as the 'Mac Curtis' after a ROCKABILLY star, a kiss curl and duck tail were included.) In the USA, the flat-top became the emblematic hairstyle of adolescent males – particularly working-class youths and Rockabilly devotees – around 1956. When the neo-Rockabilly movement replaced PUNK for some British fashion followers in 1979, the flat-top took the place of the spiky crop to provide a vogue style comparable to the similar black 'Philly-crop' (prominent in HIP HOP culture) and the avant-garde geometric successors of the WEDGE (taken to extremes by the black model and singer Grace Jones in 1981). Between 1980 and 1986 the flat-top thrived among the representatives of the 'clean-cut' wing of male fashion, having shed its specific Rockabilly overtones.

FLOP

Also known as the Eton flop and the floppie, this male hairstyle consists of a short back and sides with a long hank of hair swept across the top of the head to fall over the eyes. Inspired by the appearance of pre-Second World War aesthetes, the flop is actually common to many British public schools, where it allows languid gestures – the tossing of the head, the flicking of the wrist – without offending against rules prohibiting long hair, which usually stipulate that the collar must not be obscured. The flop flourished through the 1980s and was still in evidence in the early 1990s, when it was not confined to schoolboys but was also worn by college and university students of differing class backgrounds and by some INDIE POP, SHAMBLING and SHOE-GAZING musicians.

FLOWER POWER

Later a mildly derogatory media term for the HIPPIE COUNTERCULTURE, 'flower power' was first employed positively, if briefly, as a rallying cry during the 'Summers of Love' (1966 in San Francisco; 1967 in London and elsewhere). The first Hippies carried flowers as offerings to passers-by or as symbols of a gentler consciousness, influenced by such diverse precedents as Hindu ceremony, Pre-Raphaelite decoration and romantic nature-worship. Flower power was the notion that an alternative to military and economic power was a real possibility; in the USA flowers were used literally to spike the guns of the Establishment during anti-war demonstrations. The terms 'flower children' and 'flower power' were abandoned by their exponents as the mass media appropriated them, usually in order to condescend or ridicule, around the beginning of 1968.

- *We turned to the burning question of the hour – Flower Power . . . 'The Grateful Dead are just the Pretty Things in drag. The groups all get record sleeves that look as though they were designed by Aubrey Beardsley when he was stoned.'*
  Interview with Paul Jones, Melody Maker, 19 August 1967

- *Flowers don't have power.*
  Herbert Marcuse, speaking at the Dialectics of Liberation Congress, London, 1967

FLUXUS

The Latin word for flow and change was adopted as the name of a would-be subversive American/West German artistic movement that began in the 1960s and which influenced many of the subsequent avant-garde tendencies in international art, including HAPPENINGS and PERFORMANCE ART. Fluxus was begun by the Lithuanian-American publisher George Maciunas in 1962 and was associated with artists and performers such as the musician John Cage, Wolf Vostell, Allan Kaprow and, most notably, the German teacher, sculptor and Performance artist Joseph Beuys. Fluxus, inspired to some extent by Dada, was more significant as a clearing-house and disseminator of ideas than as a source of art objects or coherent philosophies. It pioneered the breaking-down of barriers between different artistic disciplines and attacked the distinction between artistic and political involvement and the exalted status of the gallery artist. By the time of Maciunas's death in 1978 the movement, which had never been the subject of media attention, was virtually defunct.

FLYGIRLS

The female counterparts of B-BOYS, Flygirls, also known as B-girls, were teenage devotees of HIP HOP and RAP culture. Originally used by black urban youth in New York, the name spread to other English-speaking areas by the late 1980s. 'Fly' is a key word in street slang, meaning both sharp-witted and attractive.

FOLK

During the 1950s, Folk music in the UK was principally the province of antiquarians such as Cecil Sharp and others who recorded and anthologized traditional memorized ballads. Performers tended to be purists, often conforming to a masculine stereotype of beard, knitted pullover and beer, singing, often unaccompanied, in a quasi-rustic nasal whine. 'Folkies' tended to belong to the puritanical Left and/or disarmament milieux; they operated through a network of clubs and coffee bars in which they overlapped with the Beatnik (see the BEAT MOVEMENT) tendency of the late Fifties and early Sixties. Irish Folk music was mainly restricted to the Irish émigré community until the Dubliners broke through into mainstream popularity in the 1960s. In the USA, Pete Seeger and Woody Guthrie kept alive the strain of poor white rural folksong until it was picked up by civil rights, student and Bohemian circles at the end of the Fifties.

The various strands of this then generally earnest and clean-cut genre were brought together by the Newport Folk Festival: Joan Baez appeared there for the first time in 1959; in 1966 Bob Dylan, originally inspired by Guthrie and Dave van Ronk, shocked the old guard and launched Folk ROCK when he played an electrified set there. It was probably the image of the Beatnik troubadour as cultivated by Dylan (and paralleled by singer-songwriters such as Leonard Cohen, Tim Buckley and Simon and Garfunkel) that did most to push Folk into a more hard-edged and fashionable role where, along with the PROTEST SONG sub-genre, it became central to the burgeoning progressive youth culture of the mid-1960s.

From 1965 to 1969 there was also a middle-of-the road craze for melodic Folk songs, as sung in the USA by the New Christie Minstrels, the Kingston Trio and Peter, Paul and Mary, and the Seekers and the Spinners, for example, in the UK. In Britain Dylan was idolized in 1965; he was also imitated, notably by Donovan

(Leitch), who evolved into a gifted musician and who for a short period straddled the fields of Celtic music, Folk, Rock and early PSYCHEDELIA. Folk Rock, comprising groups such as The Byrds, the Loving Spoonful, Jefferson Airplane, Crosby, Stills, Nash and Young in the USA and Fairport Convention in Britain, was in vogue until about 1970, but the bedrock of Folk clubs (and the Keele and Cambridge festivals) and performers continued to operate in Britain from the early 1960s to the mid-1970s independently of fashions. Singers such as John Renbourn, Bert Jansch and Davy Graham moved around this circuit playing Folk blues, while John Martyn, Al Stewart, the Strawbs, Rab Noakes, Finbar and Eddie Furey, the Corries and many others represented an eclectic mixture of regional, traditional and pop-influenced styles.

Among electric Folk groups in Britain there was a move back to traditional and Celtic influences led by Fairport Convention and Steeleye Span, followed by Fotheringay and the Albion Country Band. A more experimental mixture of Folk, mysticism and exotic influences was pioneered by the Incredible String Band and the Third Ear Band among others. During the eras of GLAM ROCK, HEAVY METAL, PUNK and TWO TONE, Folk music in Britain and the USA thrived discreetly in small venues. In the early Eighties new strains of Folk-based music appeared: the Pogues combined traditional Irish music with Punk to become a cult success throughout the decade; Clannad and others combined Irish and NEW AGE music. The WOMAD festivals, supported initially by the Rock star Peter Gabriel, incorporated Anglo-Celtic Folk into WORLD MUSIC.

- *It's fashionable among college students to like folk, and it's generally folksy acts who have success playing college dates . . .*
  Rave *magazine, February 1965*

- *Ewan MacColl, one of the leaders of the folk revival, says . . . that singers like Donovan and Dylan, who have never experienced the things they sing about, are just obtaining a reflex action out of the nihilistic feelings of despair in the air at the moment.*
  London Life, *14 October 1965*

FOODIES

The Foodie was a phenomenon of the 1980s; the gourmet manifestation of the YUPPIE-era cult of discerning, if conspicuous, consumption. The patronizing of fashionable restaurants and home-made *haute cuisine* were both mainstays of the upwardly mobile lifestyle of the twenty- and thirty-something generation riding on the mid-Eighties economic boom in the USA and the UK. Helping to spread the new interest in diet and cosmopolitan delicacies were NOUVELLE CUISINE and, particularly in the USA, the vogue for SUSHI. Once coined, the term was extended to refer to pre-existing wholefood enthusiasts, vegetarians and devotees of MACROBIOTICS. In marketing terms it denoted consumers who based their high spending on novelty and innovation in food products, whether of the junk or gourmet variety.

- *A couple of weeks ago I went to a party at the Dorchester Hotel, the launch of the* Official Foodie Handbook, *a celebration of gluttony masked in mockery . . . This comedy of bad manners was crowned with a tragedy, the book coming out in exactly the same week as the Ethiopian story finally broke, a blight of bad publicity that the most vivacious of PR girls could not wave away easily.*

  Julie Burchill, Sunday Times, *November 1984*

FOREST THERAPY

See TREE-SNIFFING.

FRACTALS

See CHAOS THEORY; LIGHT SHOWS; PSYCHEDELIA.

FRAGGLES

A subdivision of the CRUSTY phenomenon. Fraggle (from the American TV puppet show *Fraggle Rock*) is a British slang term for a deranged and/or dishevelled youth.

FREE JAZZ

A genre that flourished around 1960, and which reflected the MODERNIST tendency to abstraction and improvisation, as seen in ABSTRACT EXPRESSIONIST painting and modern dance, for instance. The self-consciously avant-garde approach of free jazz appealed

mainly to white intellectuals who saw TRAD as regressive and
Bebop as superficial. The style, which dispensed with regular
rhythm or predetermined melody, was said to be inspired by
Charlie Mingus, although he rejected it. Practitioners included John
Coltrane, Ornette Coleman, Eric Dolphy and Cecil Taylor. While it
remained a significant movement through the 1960s and avoided
the commercialization to which nearly every other progressive
form of music succumbed, free jazz alienated many, particularly in
Britain. These people increasingly turned to the blues as an authentic
musical expression of emotion, or to ROCK for excitement. While
improvisation and experimentation remain within the repertoire
of modern jazz musicians, the 'excesses' of free jazz are now out of
favour.

FRIENDSHIP BRACELETS

A recurrent pre-teen schoolgirl fad of the early 1990s recalling
the SCOOBIDOO of the Sixties, friendship bracelets are woven from
coloured or multicoloured wool and tied round the wrist. They
are exchanged as tokens, as well as functioning as fetish toys like
CLACKERS and SLAP-ITS.

FRINGE THEATRE

The concept of fringe theatre appeared at the beginning of the 1960s,
inspired by the independent, often avant-garde productions mounted
on the fringes of the Edinburgh Festival. These performances were
in the European tradition of cabaret and café theatre and challenged
the political orthodoxy and immovably bourgeois values of most
of London's West End productions. The Traverse Theatre Club in
Edinburgh gave this form of theatre a permanent home from 1962. In
London the Institute for Contemporary Arts coexisted with various
clubs and workshops until the influence of radical politics and the
COUNTERCULTURE gave experimental theatre a new impetus in the later
Sixties, helped by the removal in 1968 of censorship by the Lord
Chamberlain's office.

The new spirit of cooperatives and mobile groups such as the
People Show and the Welfare State, who staged HAPPENINGS
and PERFORMANCE ART via a network of ARTS LABS and arts
centres, firmly established a genre in which barriers between

audience and performers and between political agitation and entertainment/spectacle were broken down. By 1975 there were around 100 fringe groups active in the UK, operating in literally hundreds of venues, including a first wave of pubs (the Gate in Notting Hill, the Bush in Shepherd's Bush and the King's Head in Islington were the best known in London). This was followed by a second wave, opened up by the PUB ROCK and ALTERNATIVE COMEDY booms. The fringe was always more cohesive and more articulate than the counterculture or the music business, for example organizing itself to negotiate with local authorities, the Arts Council and the acting union, Equity, for funding and better conditions. By the end of the 1970s it had merged with the mainstream theatre world to the extent that there was no longer any clear-cut distinction between audiences, venues, formats or ideologies.

FRISBEE

Improvised games of catch using the lids of tin cans had been played for decades before the inventor Walter Frederick Morrison, inspired by the first post-Second World War UFO reports, began hawking a plastic 'flying saucer' at California fairgrounds. The object became popular locally as a beach toy and was picked up by the co-founders of the Wham-O company, Rich Knerr and Spud Melin (also responsible for the HULA-HOOP and LIMBO BAR), who began manufacturing the saucers in January 1957. Knerr heard the term 'Frisbie-ing' on a marketing trip to Ivy League colleges, where flat tins used by the Frisbie Pie Company had been tossed around for many years. Wham-O appropriated the term phonetically and in 1959 registered Frisbee as a trademark.

Playing with the plastic discs first flourished as part of the SURFING subculture of the early 1960s, then as part of the HIPPIE repertoire of hedonism. Relaxed and essentially non-competitive, Frisbee play meshed perfectly with the soft drug-inspired 'play-power' of the late 1960s and early 1970s. The banking, swooping, rising and falling and complex trajectories of flight inspired a mystical zeal in many players, summed up in the enthusiasts' dictum: 'When the ball dreams, it dreams it is a Frisbee'. A Frisbee association was formed in Britain and during the 1970s several national conventions were held in which dogs as well as humans occasionally performed, but the craze was never as popular as in the USA, where there has been an annual championship since the 1950s and a lobby to have Frisbee accepted as an Olympic sport. Several team games have been developed, and individuals compete in accuracy and power of throws, but the true spirit of Frisbee is represented in freestyle events, where cooperating pairs or trios compete in terms of balletic grace, style, ingenuity and swagger. Each team's efforts are marked not by judges but by their fellow competitors.

- *Frisbee play joins man's greatest tool, his hand, with his greatest dream, to fly.*

  Dr Stancil Johnson

FUDS

Juggling balls known as Fuds were a NEW AGE toy and a minor fad among neo-HIPPIES and RAVERS during the early 1990s.

FUJI

A form of rhythmic dance music from Nigeria that has been absorbed into the WORLD MUSIC catalogue. Fuji competed with JUJU in the dancehalls of Lagos in the 1980s and early 1990s as successors to the earlier HIGH LIFE.

FUNK

A slang word meaning earthy or raw, but originally used in the 17th century to mean fetid or stinky, and ultimately derived from the Latin *fumigare*, to smoke, the term 'funky' has been used since the 1950s to refer to urban black American music using heavy rhythms and bass and simple melodies. The back-formation noun Funk has denoted a kind of histrionic SOUL music that blends African, jazz and ROCK influences and uses brass instrumentation. Funk as a genre emerged at the end of the 1960s and flourished in the early 1970s; its impetus came largely from James Brown – the 'Godfather of Soul' – and was perpetuated by such artists as George Clinton and Parliament, the Ohio Players, Funkadelic, Kool and the Gang and the Fatback Band. Funk employed a visual style of outrageous showbiz KITSCH (PLATFORM SOLES, satin, lamé, lace and heavy jewellery were the staples of a black version of the GLITTER look) and flamboyant stage performances. Its musical riffs were later SAMPLED and imitated by RAP artists, and its costumes influenced the HIP HOP uniforms of the 1980s and the spectacles staged by Prince and Michael Jackson.

Although seen by its detractors as tasteless and overblown, the extrovert Funk tendency had a social significance over and above the musical excitement it generated: it promoted black pride and moved black consciousness away from the ghetto and the street. Jazz Funk was a related hybrid of the same era that added jazz virtuosity to the rhythms of Funk. Played by Grover Washington Jr., George Benson, Bobbi Humphrey and Donald Byrd among others, it remained a minority taste into the 1980s. In the early 1980s a cooler form of Funk became fashionable in white clubland, and in the late Eighties and early Nineties Funk was incorporated into the musical lexicon that made up the DANCEFLOOR culture.

GAIA HYPOTHESIS

James Lovelock's theory that the Earth is an organic entity was named, on the advice of the author William Golding, after the personification of the earth as a goddess in Greek myth (also spelt Gaea and deriving from 'ge', earth). The British chemist and ecologist proposed a view of the Earth and its life-forms as a self-regulating system, implying a sort of planetary consciousness, or at least a self-correcting mechanism, that transcends humankind. His hypothesis, although dismissed by some as pseudo-science and by others as a metaphorical restatement of the obvious, has provided an immensely influential philosophical rationale for the GREEN MOVEMENT.

- *. . . in an arc stretching from Somerset to Cornwall . . . Wessex Man is bemusedly searching for salvation for the planet, closeness to Gaia, and the Spirit Horse perfection of his outdoor drumming skills . . .*

    Sunday Times, *3 May 1992*

GARAGE MUSIC

The term 'garage band' was first applied to amateurish American ROCK groups of the late 1960s who attracted small cult followings but who failed to make a commercial impact. The name referred to their custom of practising – and sometimes recording – in the garages of suburban homes. (Among many others these included the Barbarians, the Magic Mushrooms, the Seeds, the Standells and the Hollywood Argylls.) The appellation was revived in the mid-1970s to refer to young groups such as the Ramones who played simple, usually three-chord pop. These groups (their British contemporaries were involved in PUB ROCK) were the originators of the PUNK sound.

In the late 1980s a quite different musical tendency was dubbed

'Garage Music', after Paradise Garage, the name of a New York gay DISCO flourishing in 1986. Music journalists adopted the phrase to categorize one of the many strands of post-HOUSE dance music, this one featuring elements of SOUL, gospel and R & B.

GARDEN GNOMES
See KITSCH.

GAY LIBERATION
In the relatively libertarian climate of the late 1960s, bars and nightclubs catering for a male homosexual clientele began to operate more openly in the USA, Australia, Holland, Denmark and, to a lesser extent, the UK. In June 1969 disturbances broke out in New York City following police harassment of the patrons of one such bar, the Stonewall. The Stonewall riots triggered off a tide of gay solidarity across North America, which coalesced into the Gay Liberation Front (GLF), a loose association that promoted 'gay pride', helped repressed gays to 'come out' (of the 'closet'), and fought for gay rights for men and women. The movement spread to other countries in 1970 and by 1972 had succeeded, despite strong opposition, in promoting its cause and achieving some relaxation of anti-gay legislation. Newspapers and magazines were established, including *Gay News* in London; telephone help lines were also set up, as were 'respectable' pressure groups such as the Campaign for Homosexual Equality. By 1973 – at the time of GLAM ROCK – it had actually become fashionable in hip media and entertainment circles to acknowledge bisexuality and an androgynous aesthetic.

In the late 1970s the militant gay movement subsided and the male gay UNDERGROUND devoted itself increasingly to hedonism. The beginnings of the macho-parody CLONE look were accompanied by a cult of sado-masochism and promiscuity that, combined with the discovery of Aids, seriously damaged the status of gays in society in the 1980s. After 1982 much of the energy of the gay community was expended on caring for Aids victims and promoting safe sex, although militancy reappeared in Britain in the fight against discriminatory legislation (Clause 28 of the 1988 Local Government Bill and Clause 25 of the 1991 Criminal Justice Act) and in the US in the fad for 'outing' (publicly naming covertly homosexual activities).

New pressure groups for the 1990s were ActUp (the Aids Coalition to Unleash Power) in the USA and in the UK, the Stonewall Group of reformist lobbyists and OutRage!, a direct-action movement.

The word 'gay', which had formerly had the sense of showy as well as happy, was originally used in British slang of the 18th and 19th centuries to mean sexually immoral or available and was invariably applied to women. The English-speaking homosexual community adopted it as a secret code word in the 20th century; it was widely used in the theatrical milieu by the mid-1960s, and with the advent of gay liberation entered the vocabulary of standard English. In practice, gay often referred to males, the word lesbian specifying gay women. Ironically, in the early 1990s some radicals were reverting to the old pejorative 'queer' to distance themselves from what they saw as an acquiescent gay community.

- *In 1970 two LSE students, Bob Mellers and Aubrey Waters, came back from the States and started Gay Liberation Front meetings . . . The counterculture was there, drag queens were there, a minority of lesbians, heavy-duty political people.*
  Andrew Lumsden, quoted in Days in the Life, *Jonathon Green, 1988*

GENDER-BENDERS

A vogue journalistic term of the early 1980s referring to the adoption by HIP youth culture of transvestism or cross-dressing. Formerly an aberrant minority practice, the new androgyny was endorsed by the mass media and quickly entered British KITSCH folklore. The main proponents of gender-bending were the singers Boy George (George O'Dowd) and (the male) Marilyn. Annie Lennox of the Eurythmics duo provided a female counterpart by posing and performing in male guise. Androgyny had been fashionable in earlier pop culture – notably in the era of GLAM and GLITTER – and David Bowie and the Rolling Stones had flirted with transvestism on occasion in the late Sixties, but it was the bisexual underground club culture which provided a haven for the BLITZ KIDS and the NEW ROMANTICS that gave rise to the gender-bender fad. It was probably the innocent flamboyance of the New Romantics, recalling pantomime dames and bedroom farce, rather than deviance and subversion, that struck a chord with the British and then North American and Continental public. Boy George's cross-dressing and use of make-up was in any case more ambivalent than the stereotype feminine outfits of earlier drag acts. Gender-bending influenced a number of WANNABES, and persisted among a few young bedsitter eccentrics after its 1984 peak.

GENERATION X

A term that has appeared three times in references to popular culture in the last three decades, Generation X was first employed as the title of a collection of interviews with young people compiled by Charles Hamblett and Jane Deverson at the time of the MOD and ROCKER disturbances of 1963 and 1964. The book, whose sensationalist title evoked science fiction and prefigured the Who's anthem, 'My Generation', was the first serious attempt in Britain to treat youth culture in objective close-up. In 1977 the book's title was adopted as a name by a PUNK group comprising Billy Idol, later a pop star in the USA, and Tony James, later of the grotesque 1980s parody group Sigue Sigue Sputnik. Then, in 1992, the thirty-year-old Canadian author Douglas Coupland wrote the lightweight fictional *Generation X: Tales for an Accelerated Culture*. In his book, Coupland identified a disillusioned post-YUPPIE generation rebelling against materialism and conspicuous consumption in favour of travel, irresponsibility and/or apathy. The same age group had been focused on a year before by journalists who had referred to them as the 'twenty-somethings' or the new BLANK GENERATION; in France their equivalents have been called '*la génération nulle*', and in California, 'the Slackers'.

- *. . . the narrator of the book is the archetypal X-er. He lives in a rented bungalow (X-ers don't have mortgages), works as a bartender (X-ers have low-pay, low-prestige, ersatz 'McJobs') and suffers from paralysing millenarial gloom.*
  Sunday Times, *26 April 1992*

GEODESIC DOMES

The best-known and most enduring legacy of Richard Buckminster Fuller (1895–1983), geodesic domes are prefabricated structures made up of a grid of polygons formed from short, straight metal or plastic bars with sheets of plastic or glass. The practical advantage of the dome, which was first constructed in 1959, was that, whatever its size, it used the minimum materials to cover the maximum space. Fuller was a visionary masquerading as a functionalist; he combined a mystical aesthetic with a social conscience and a profound faith in high technology and energy-saving, which made him a cult figure among HIPPIES and other progressives, particularly in the late 1960s and early 1970s, when hundreds of his domes were constructed. A geodesic dome (the word geodesic, or geodetic, is from the Greek and refers to the shortest line between two points on a curved surface) was the centrepiece of Expo '67 in Montreal; in 1968 Fuller proposed enclosing Manhattan within a giant geodesic dome as a method of pollution control. Exponents of the American COUNTERCULTURE and their British counterparts made geodesic domes in the countryside or erected them on urban rooftops, and Fuller's ideas went on to influence both HIGH TECH design and POST-MODERNIST architecture in the West and Japan, as well as the philosophies of the NEW AGE movement.

GESTALT

Gestalt is a German word meaning shape, form or structure; it has come to signify a bundle of phenomena or concepts that operate as a unified whole not reducible to its parts. Gestalt psychology, influential from about 1910 until the early 1960s, argued against analysis from the observation of details, parts or constituents, and in favour of looking at configurations. In American psychotherapy of the later 1960s, Gestalt referred to the idea of confronting actual states of mind or emotions by examining the collection of experiences that worked together to create them. In practice this approach, pioneered by Fritz and Laura Perls at the Esalen Institute in California, used radical awareness techniques including ENCOUNTER GROUPS, breathing exercises, touching and feeling. Fritz Perls' image was that of the archetypal Western COUNTERCULTURE guru, encouraging followers to liberate and improve themselves. As such, he promoted the self-indulgence and hedonism of the HIPPIE era as well as prefiguring the 'Me Generation' of the Seventies and Eighties. By the mid-Seventies, however, the philosophical underpinning of Gestalt was being seen as simplistic and the practices associated with it merged into the general repertoire of alternative THERAPY. The term 'gestalt' continues to be used as a buzz word whenever a field, matrix or functioning arrangement is emphasized instead of its components, but HOLISTIC, both as a vogue term and as a concept in treatment, has tended to supplant it.

GHETTO-BLASTER

The cumbersome but portable stereo cassette player and radio which became emblematic of the nascent New York HIP HOP culture of the late 1970s. Carried on the shoulder or placed on the pavement, the ghetto-blaster – also known as the boogie box, beat box and boom box, and in Britain as the Rasta box, wog box and Brixton briefcase – provided a powerful miniature version of the Jamaican and South Bronx sound systems and was used for impromptu parties, to accompany public displays of BREAK DANCING, or just for personal entertainment. Even after the advent of the personal stereo, or Walkman, devotees of RAP and REGGAE continued to favour the ghetto-blaster for symbolic as well as economic or acoustic reasons.

- *Boyle and his buddy, music PR Olly Daniaud, threw a slamming, beer-fuelled party in Hyde Park last week . . . Tom Conran was there, as was Harriet Guinness. Groovy video producer James Lebon was loitering by a ghetto-blaster.*
  Sunday Times *magazine, 30 August 1992*

GLAM ROCK

In 1971 T-Rex and Roxy Music (vehicles for Marc Bolan and Bryan Ferry, respectively) fused Sixties finery with Fifties vulgarity and pushed post-HIPPIE ROCK and pop music further towards a decadent, androgynous, narcissistic stance in which the only ideology was glamour. By 1972, via his 'Ziggy Stardust' persona, David Bowie had taken this tendency into an area of bisexual fantasy and science-fiction imagery that became known as Glam Rock; other exponents included Sweet, Alice Cooper, Mott the Hoople, and the slightly less flamboyant Slade and Mud. After initial flirtations by progressives, who were interested in the sophisticated axis of Ferry, Bowie and Lou Reed, Glam Rock became the domain of white teenyboppers who had been excluded from PSYCHEDELIA and HARD ROCK. The influence of Glam Rock, the associated GLITTER tendency and their attendant fashions (which were, in fact, evolved versions of 1960s styles and included such artefacts as PLATFORM boots) continued until 1976, when they were brutally supplanted by PUNK. Black musical fashion ignored Glam Rock in favour of SOUL and REGGAE, but adopted its sartorial vulgarity, especially in the case of FUNK bands.

- *Glam was a rite of passage for Pop/Rock – retaining the tackiness of hippy garb . . . [it] salved the pain of transition in a kind of Panto ineptitude; and it cheered up the seventies.*
  Ian Penman, 'The Shattered Glass: Notes on Bryan Ferry', 1989

GLASGOW PUPS

A group of figurative painters based on the Glasgow School of Art in the late 1980s, the so-called Glasgow Pups (the categorization was made by Waldemar Januszczak, art critic of the *Guardian* and later head of arts programming at Channel 4) helped to raise the profile of the city, which was nominated European City of Culture in 1990. The artists concerned included Ken Currie, Peter Howson, Steven Campbell and Adrian Wisniewski. The name, though not the style, probably recalled the 'Glasgow School' of the 1890s.

- *The central focus of the exhibition is of course the voluble group of painters – with the ersatz title of the 'Glasgow Pups' – who have had a tumult of critical and popular acclaim over the past few years.*
  The Face, *October 1987*

GLITTER

Contemporary, and virtually synonymous, with GLAM ROCK, Glitter was a word and a concept applied first to pop musicians such as Marc Bolan of T-Rex (who pioneered the wearing of actual glitter-dust as make-up on stage), and later to parodists of the glamour scene such as Gary Glitter himself (born Paul Gadd). Musically, Glitter implied a crude, thumping drum beat (in the case of the Glitter Band provided by two drummers) overlayed by simplistic guitar riffs and chorus singing. The effect was anthemic and bombastic, but in the manner of a football chant rather than the operatic pretensions of some HARD ROCK. Glitter was a white phenomenon, marking the return of showbiz vulgarity to mainstream pop, but in a camp and self-mocking form. It began in 1972, peaked in 1973, and survived until late 1975, although its main exponent, Gary Glitter, continued to stage successful comebacks into the 1990s.

● *I've never seen such a strange gathering of people . . . For a
start there were many people who resembled Christmas trees on
legs. There was much glitter, and several men dressed as ladies.
As somebody quite rightly said, 'The 60s are over, well and
truly over.'*

Report on David Bowie's first New York performance,
Melody Maker, 7 October 1972

GLOBAL VILLAGE

A term coined by Marshall McLuhan (see MCLUHANISM) to describe
the world in the age of information networks (in the pre-computer
late 1960s McLuhan was stressing telephones, film and broadcast
media), a world in which individuals have access to virtually
instantaneous communication, rendering previous notions of
space and time obsolete. The word village implies the intimacy
of a unified and shared culture. McLuhan's phrase became a
cliché of the HIPPIE era, appealing both to a desire for a common
consciousness and to the wish for a convergence of primitivism and
technology.

GLOTTAL STOP

See MOCKNEY.

GOBBING

Gobbing (from the slang word 'gob' for mouth, ultimately of Celtic
origin) was the ritualized spitting at performers on stage indulged
in by British PUNKS. Spitting is an established adolescent gesture of
bravado, and perfectly fitted the Punks' self-conscious pose of anger
and defiance. Most Punk musicians disapproved of the practice (Joe
Strummer of the Clash claimed to have been infected with hepatitis
from a fan's saliva), but gobbing persisted until the movement itself
subsided.

GOBOTS

Gobots were fit-together multifaceted toy robots on the same
lines as TRANSFORMERS. Both these so-called 'promotional toys'

(i.e. manufactured fads) were a hit with pre-teen boys during the mid-Eighties.

GO-GO

A sub-genre of acoustic, percussion-based and originally live dance music, based on FUNK and forming part of the HIP HOP tendency. The style, which deviated from other electronically synthetic HOUSE and DANCEFLOOR music, seems to have originated in Washington, DC, in 1983. It was picked up in fashionable British nightclubs and DISCOS shortly after, but the leading exponents continued to be American. The term 'go-go' reflects the high-energy pumping dance moves previously displayed by 'go-go girls', and is a convergence of 'Go! Go!' and *à gogo*, French for 'galore'.

GONK

A troll-like doll that became a craze among pre-teen children and a fetish object among younger teenagers (particularly girls) in 1968 and 1969. The Gonk was part of a tradition of cuddly grotesques that included TROLLS, WOMBLES, MUPPETS, SMURFS, CABBAGE PATCH DOLLS and MY LITTLE PONY. Like Muppet and Smurf, the word Gonk, originally an arbitrary trademark name, lived on as a schoolchildren's term of abuse, applied to dull-witted or otherwise unfortunate fellow pupils.

GONZO JOURNALISM

A journalistic tendency allied to the so-called 'New Journalism' and pioneered by Hunter S. Thompson in *Rolling Stone* magazine in the early 1970s, gonzo involved the writers of reportage in the (typically hedonistic and excessive) action and events they describe. As a literary style, it presupposes unrestrained and slangy language, with a great deal of hyperbole. Thompson inspired imitators on *Rolling Stone* and elsewhere and the gonzo label was still in use in the 1980s, applied, for instance, to the right-wing humourist P. J. O'Rourke. The word itself is an adjective meaning crazy and extremist and derives either from a HIPSTER expression made up of 'gone' (as in ecstatic, uncontrolled) and an '-o' suffix (with the 'z' for ease of pronunciation), or directly from the Italian *gonzo*, meaning a buffoon or simpleton.

- *. . . the style of modern journalism known as 'gonzo': the free-wheeling and often self-indulgent method which has been copied by countless writers.*

  i-D, *November 1987*

GOTHS

One strand of PUNK imagery – exemplified by the groups Siouxsie and the Banshees and the Damned – consisted of doom-laden or anthemic guitar-based ROCK music accompanied by black clothing, bleached hair, powdered faces and the wearing of occult or mock-medieval paraphernalia. This horror-film iconography preceded Punk; it had been used by a variety of performers (including Bobby 'Boris' Pickett and the Crypt-kickers, Screaming Lord Sutch, the Undertakers, Hawkwind, Black Sabbath, Alice Cooper and *The Rocky Horror Show*) since the 1950s, as well as by comic books and the camp Sixties TV comedies *The Addams Family* and *The Munsters*. In the post-Punk era the humorous aspects of the style were picked up by such neo-PSYCHEDELIC bands as Gaye Bikers on Acid and Zodiac Mindwarp, as well as by the enduring Damned. The introverted and serious vein evolved via groups such as Bauhaus, the Cure, Southern Death Cult, Nick Cave and the Bad Seeds and the Sisters of Mercy to become Goth.

The term itself (based on 'Gothic Rock', a music journalist categorization) began to be used in 1984 of a youth cult that had during the previous year been focused on the Batcave, a Soho music club. This had been touted as a revival of Punk values but although its label, 'Positive Punk', and its leading exponents, Brigandage, did not last long, the Goth pose of pallor, black leather, crucifixes and a sort of morbid passivity caught on among adolescents. Goth proved to be the most enduring direct legacy of Punk, but without Punk's energy, anger or subversion. At its edges it blurred into GREBO or CRUSTY culture, but its mainstream presented a remarkably unified appearance and attitude; an impressively forbidding fantasy mask for youth angst and sensitivity.

- *Plumage is all-important to the Goth, it represents an extension of the darkest parts of the soul, it is asexual, it upsets grannies and it*

*can't be 'put away' during the day when you go to work, proving
all-importantly that you don't go to work.*
Andrew Collins, NME, November 1991

GRAFFITI

Subversive graffiti in public places was a feature of SITUATIONIST
tactics, popularized by PROVOS and KABOUTERS in Amsterdam, and
by the May 1968 student activists in Paris and elsewhere; later
exponents included FEMINISTS, who, with environmentalists and
anarchists such as the Australian Bugerup group, often amended
the texts and graphics of advertising hoardings. American street
gangs had been using graffiti symbols, pseudonyms and slogans
as territorial markers and badges of identity for many years when,
around 1974 in New York City, prompted by the availability of
cheap car-paint aerosols, the practice grew into a large-scale fashion.
As well as walls, teenage graffiti-writers spray-painted the sides
of subway trains (adding an extra risk element to the hobby) and
elaborated their autograph initials into more complex symbols
and pictograms. Although discouraged by civic authorities, graffiti
flourished and was quickly picked up by social commentators and
then the art Establishment, first for collection in coffee-table books
and then for transferral to galleries, where it was promoted as the
successor to POP ART. Other enthusiasts celebrated graffiti as the new
folk art, some going further to describe it as a recolonizing of the city
space by the black and Hispanic dispossessed. Some graffiti artists
were subsequently hired by community projects in the USA and
Britain to create murals.

The craze also produced its own slang lexicon: the autograph
became a 'tag', a work of art a 'piece', spray-painting a public place
'bombing', and stealing someone's tag 'biting', for example. The 'art'
itself remained very limited in its conventions, concentrating on Day-
Glo typography or the very simplest images. At the end of the 1970s
graffiti was incorporated into HIP HOP subculture, along with BREAK
DANCING and RAP. At the end of the 1980s it was still thriving on the
streets, and the gay New York artist Keith Haring, among others, had
helped its crossover into mainstream graphic design.

- *Graffiti painting is an immediate realisation of self, through no
  other mediation than one's name.*
  Atlanta and Alexander, ZG magazine, 1981

GRAPHIC NOVEL

A logical mode for an image-conscious age, the graphic novel
has been slow to emerge into popular culture in English-speaking
countries, and has yet to win any significant following. Whilst in
France the *bande dessinée* (strip cartoon or comic book) has been
used as a medium for extended and semi-serious fiction since about
1970, in the USA its use has remained confined to lightweight
science fiction, horror and comedy, and in Britain the genre has been
very much a minority taste. In the USA, *Maus*, the 1987 graphic
novel by Art Speigelman portraying victims of the Holocaust as mice,
sold well, whilst *Watchmen* by Alan Moore and Dave Gibbons and
Dark Knight Returns (a Batman update) by Frank Miller had some
cult success, as did the more painterly graphics of Bill Sienkiewicz
and Dave McKean. An annual convention in Angoulême, France,
consolidated the graphic novel's status in the Latin countries, but its
Anglo-American appeal has remained restricted mainly to a mid- and
late-adolescent readership. Graphic Novels nevertheless continued to
take themselves seriously – the 1992 titles *Signal to Noise* and *Skin*,
for instance, dealt with communications theory and the politics of
Thalidomide respectively.

- *The comic book still suffers from the perception that, because kids'
  books are illustrated, anyone who reads comics must be retarded;
  but I try to make my work as sophisticated and multi-layered as a
  novel or short story.*
                                    Neil Gaiman, graphic-novel author, 1987

GREASERS
See ROCKERS.

GREBOS
Grebos (also spelt Greebos or Greboes), a British phenomenon of
the mid- to late-1980s, were scruffy young ROCK music enthusiasts,
typically long-haired, intentionally unkempt and unhygienic, and
leather-jacketed. Nearly all Grebos were white and working- or
lower-middle-class, many coming from country towns and villages

rather than cities. The name itself seems to have been coined in the Midlands around 1985, based on 'Greaser' (see ROCKERS). The music press seized on the self-deprecating term to categorize an existing subculture of earnest, gauche, HARD ROCK devotees who blended the scruffier characteristics of PUNKS, Rockers, HIPPIES and GOTHS, and were reminiscent of the PSYCHEDELIC biker (see HELL'S ANGELS) image promoted in the early Seventies by the group Hawkwind and their entourage. The Grebos' self-conscious embracing of dirtiness and uncouth attitudes and their liking for cheap alcohol and certain drugs (cannabis, magic mushrooms and LSD, rather than cocaine or heroin) was later taken to extremes by the CRUSTIES.

- *Greboes drink stout and snakebite, smoke Players Number 6 (packets of 10), wear Y-fronts and dirty torn jeans, drive big bikes and go out with girls who don't shave their armpits.*

  i-D, *November 1987*

- *Brummie 'grebo' boors Pop Will Eat Itself sound frightful on paper and even worse (in the best possible sense, you understand) in the flesh.*

  Independent, *11 May 1989*

GREEN MOVEMENT

In 1962 the American naturalist Rachel Carson's book *Silent Spring*, which dealt with the effects of chemicals on the countryside, focused attention for the first time on environmental pollution. During the late 1960s, the search for alternative lifestyles and the notion of the GLOBAL VILLAGE gave rise to a movement that swelled during the following two decades. Initially known as ecologists, or derisively as 'eco-freaks', activists concentrated first on deforestation, river and sea pollution and the threat to animal species. The energy crises of the 1970s focused attention on the danger of nuclear fuel and the need to investigate renewable power sources; the first UN Conference on the Human Environment was held in Stockholm in 1972, the year in which a worldwide upsurge in awareness was accompanied by predictions of imminent catastrophe, many of which proved to be premature. In the 1980s concern over ozone-layer depletion and global warming was added to these issues.

At first a minority activity, Green consciousness (the 'Green' label predominated from around 1982, replacing the term 'environmentalist') provided a cause that could transcend earlier political affiliations and corral the considerable energies of leftists, liberals, post-HIPPIE NEW AGE enthusiasts and anarchists alike. In the USA, local environmental initiatives achieved some notable successes, and in Germany the Green Party won a number of seats in the 1987 elections. The British Ecology Party changed its name to the Green Party in 1985, but failed to make a strong impact on voting preferences. In spite of the mainstream parties' attempts in the mid-1980s to annex the Green platform, most environmentalist activity in Britain was channelled through groups such as Friends of the Earth and the more radical Greenpeace. The Green Movement in its various forms did succeed in two areas in the period leading up to 1990; it made it necessary for both industry and the education system at least to pay lip-service to its ethos, and it provided the only sustained critique of the values of the so-called 'enterprise culture'.

- *If current trends are allowed to persist, the breakdown of society and the irreversible disruption of the life-support systems on this planet, possibly by the end of the century, certainly within the lifetimes of our children, are inevitable.*
  'Blueprint for Survival', Ecologist *magazine, 1972*

- *A new 'green' Cabinet committee which was one of the key initiatives in last year's Government White Paper on the environment has yet to meet, 10 months after Chris Patten, the former Secretary of State for the Environment, announced its existence.*
  Independent, *8 June 1991*

GREY POWER

By partly facetious analogy with the BLACK POWER movement of the 1960s, the term Grey Power appeared in the 1980s to describe the growing influence of that part of the population aged over fifty. (In fact, an article entitled 'The Greying of America' by Jean Gimpel had appeared in the *National Review* in 1976.) As the decline in the birth rate in Western Europe, the USA and particularly Japan coincided with increased longevity, it became clear that, although on the one hand there would be more and more pressure on health care and social services, on the other hand affluent older consumers and savers would be demanding the attention of the commercial sector and the media. An EC survey published in 1991 estimated that by the year 2020 more than one in four Europeans would be aged sixty or over, whilst fewer than one in five would be aged twenty or under. Hitherto ignored in favour of the youth market, these 'grumpies' ('grown-up mature professionals') were being catered for in 1992 by their own magazines (including *The Oldie*, launched in London by Richard Ingrams, former editor of *Private Eye*), holiday schemes and consumer products. Meanwhile, in Japan a pair of 100-year-old female twins became cult pop stars.

- *US companies have also stepped up their courtship of the 78 million Americans of the baby boom who are now reaching middle age. Products include wide-seated jeans, frilly girdles and expensive pairs of bi-focal spectacles . . .*

  British Airways *Business Life, November 1991*

GRUNGE

Grunge (a colloquialism for dirt or squalor) was adopted by ROCK music journalists in the mid-1980s to refer to the deliberately offensive posturing of GREBO and HEAVY METAL musicians. In 1992 a Grunge Rock movement, consisting of American bands such as Hole, Babes in Toyland, Helmet, Nirvana and Bastard, as well as the British Membranes and the Australian Cosmic Psychos, was being touted as an aggressive alternative to the insipid SHOE-GAZING tendency. The groups categorized as Grunge in fact recycled familiar shock tactics and musical influences from PUNK and HARD CORE, adding a more explicit obsession with pain, bodily fluids, disfigurement and dirt.

- *Bands like Unsane make music which is designed not to soothe Pop's slightly fevered brow but to crush its skull.*

  Steven Wells, NME, *4 January 1992*

GURNING

The competitive sport of pulling faces. It was a well-established novelty folk custom which caught the public imagination in the UK after television publicity in the 1960s. During the Seventies, championships widened their scope to take on an international dimension. The verb 'to gurn' is a northwestern British dialect version of the word grin, which in Middle English could also signify grimace or snarl.

HACKERS

The penetrating of computer systems by outsiders, either for industrial espionage, sabotage or simply for fun, has been hailed by fans of the CYBERPUNK movement as a new form of guerrilla heroism. Known in data-processing jargon as 'hacking' (from the image of cutting one's way into a tangled network), the activity attracted worldwide attention in the mid-1980s when computer viruses were planted, and has been exalted by some CONCEPTUAL ARTISTS and journalists. *i-D* magazine queried whether hackers were 'cybernetic wrecking crews . . . or freedom fighters of the information age.'

Hacking originated at the end of the 1960s with the vogue for 'Phreaking' whereby adolescent experts tapped into the US telephone service with the aid of home-made electronic equipment. While some Phreakers went on to careers in high technology (including Steve Jobs and Steve Wozniak who founded Apple Computers), others evolved into hackers, forming a loosely linked underground of data criminals who are estimated to cause £2 billion-worth of damage per year in the Anglo-Saxon countries. Experts also estimate that 85 per cent of computer crime is undetected or unreported and that 17 per cent of the world's computers will be infected by viruses in the 1990s. The virus – a hidden self-replicating program designed to subvert or sabotage existing systems – is spread by the transfer of infected software. As well as carrying out remote-control destruction, hackers can steal information, transfer funds and perpetrate blackmail and extortion, although the majority are more innocently motivated by a sense of mischief and adventure. Hacking seems to be a male-dominated activity and flourishes particularly in the USA, the UK, Germany and the former socialist countries of Eastern Europe, where large numbers of highly trained programmers were left un- or under-employed. The language and ethos of the hackers overlaps with that of CYBERPUNK, GRAPHIC NOVELS and VIDEO GAMES; *noms de guerre* are *de rigueur* and include Doctor Diode, Captain Crunch, Captain Zap, the Masters of Destruction, the Legion of Doom and the Galactic Hackers Party.

HAPPENINGS

Artistic events or performances named after the work *18 Happenings in 6 Parts*, presented by Allan Kaprow in the Reuben Gallery, New York, in the autumn of 1959, Happenings were a high-profile feature of the avant-garde scene of the early 1960s. (The word had added resonance due to its HIP TALK slang sense of exciting or up to the minute.) Whether staged or impromptu, the one-off Happening aimed to draw upon the interaction of performer, audience and environment in a logical extension of multimedia art beyond assemblages and kinetics into spontaneous involvement. Artists associated with the trend (although they rejected both the term and any suggestion of a movement) were Al Hansen, Claes Oldenburg, Jim Dine, Red Grooms, Robert Rauschenberg and the FLUXUS Group, all based in New York. Elsewhere, Yves Klein, Wolf Vostell and Joseph Beuys presented similar works.

Far from being an isolated phenomenon, the Happening was a successor to the events and juxtapositions of the Dadaists and Surrealists before the Second World War, and to the experiments of the composer John Cage in the 1950s. It brought PERFORMANCE ART to the public attention through press fascination with the seemingly wilful, arbitrary and unpredictable content of the pieces. Its gestural power quickly faded, however; its 'meaning' was ephemeral, if apparent at all, and after 1966 the distinctiveness of the Happening disappeared, although audience involvement, environments and spontaneity continued to feature in theatre, dance, poetry and music, if not in gallery art. One of the first British events to parallel the Happening outside the art gallery milieu was organized by the Liverpool poet Adrian Henri as part of the Merseyside Arts festival of 1962.

- *Jim Dine . . . drank from jars of paint while painting 'I love what I'm . . .' on a large canvas, before pouring the remaining paint over his head and leaping through the canvas. The evening ended with Dick Higgins counting in German until everybody left.*
  RoseLee Goldberg, Performance Art, *1979*

HARDCORE

The term 'hardcore', first applied in the 1960s to explicit and
uncompromising pornography (probably originally as a pun on hard
core – compacted rubble used as a road-building foundation), was
later generalized to describe relentless depravity or squalor, as in the
film title *The Hardcore Life*. It was taken up by the music business
as a categorization in the early 1980s and was first applied to a North
American genre of post-PUNK ROCK music on the border between
Punk and HEAVY METAL. Similar strains were known as THRASH METAL
or, if even more frenetic, as Speed core. In the early 1990s the same
term was employed to denote a speeded-up version of TECHNO music,
as practised particularly on the RAVE scene in Britain, Belgium and
Holland.

HARD EDGE

The term Hard Edge was first applied to a school of American
painters and sculptors of the late 1950s and early 1960s. The style
consisted of cool, uncompromising abstract geometric forms made
up of uniform surfaces with sharply defined limits, hence the
description, which was probably coined by the American critic
Jules Langsner. Hard Edge works were typically untitled, or bore
minimal, uninformative titles, provoking the amusement of some
non-aficionados. Some of the best-known exponents of Hard Edge
painting include Lewis Stein, Leon Polk Smith, Frank Stella and
Kenneth Noland. In Britain the critic Lawrence Alloway – also
claimed as the originator of the phrase – applied this label to the
work of Richard Smith, Harold and Bernard Cohen, Robyn Denny
and William Turnbull. The categorization overlaps the tendency
known as POST-PAINTERLY ABSTRACTION; both were a contrast to the
messy spontaneity of ABSTRACT EXPRESSIONISM. In more recent years
the term has come to be used to describe anything uncompromisingly
and starkly delineated.

HARD ROCK

A music-business designation first appearing in the United States
in the late 1960s, Hard Rock was probably originally a play on
the words used by miners to refer to difficult drilling conditions

(as opposed to soft-rock mining). The term refers rather vaguely to any electric ROCK music played with a strong driving rhythm and minimal elaboration, and as such may sometimes be synonymous with HEAVY METAL, although it implies less pomposity or anthemic overtones. Soft Rock, by contrast, is slower and gentler Rock-based music, often influenced by FOLK or Country styles.

HARE KRISHNA

'Hare Krsna' ('O Lord Krishna') is a Sanskrit prayer or invocation to the Hindu god that forms the opening of a psalm chanted by devotees. The chant has been one of the most noticeable aspects of the public devotions carried out in urban streets and other open spaces by members of the International Society for Krishna Consciousness. This missionary cult began to attract Western adherents in California during the late 1960s and quickly spread to Britain, where it was helped by the patronage of George Harrison of the Beatles. Dressed in saffron robes with heads shaved, members of both sexes renounce personal wealth and seek converts, particularly among the young and dispossessed. Unlike other religious movements of the 1960s and 1970s, they have not promoted the personality cult of a particular guru, although Krishna Consciousness does owe its existence to one individual, the late Swami Prabhupada.

- *Unlike in Britain, where Krishna devotees are generally viewed as lunatics who dance down Oxford Street wearing very little, but making a helluva lot of noise, in India they are highly respected.*
  Independent, *1 August 1992*

HEAD-BANGING

At ROCK music concerts where audiences were confined to seats or packed tightly by the stage, excitement could best be expressed by frenzied shaking and even literal banging of the head in time to the music. The practice substituted for IDIOT DANCING among the early devotees of HARD ROCK and HEAVY METAL music, had become a standard part of the repertoire of the Heavy Metal subculture by the late 1970s, along with the playing of imaginary guitars (see AIR GUITAR) and, later, MOSHING. Head-banging, both in public and in private, continued into the 1990s in spite of a number of fatalities and injuries. Apart from its literal use, the term became generalized in colloquial language to describe any relentless, uncontrolled or self-destructive behaviour.

HEAD COMICS

A genre of comic strips and comic books spawned in the HIPPIE culture of San Francisco during the late 1960s, their name deriving from the slang use of 'head' to mean a drug-user or 'turned-on' individual. They were parodies of the *Marvel* comic format of the 1950s and featured uncensored humorous or subversive cartoons by such artists as Robert Crumb and S. Clay Wilson. These Hippie graphics were published under various banners, including the influential Zap Comix, and provided a potent vehicle for UNDERGROUND ideas in the era before affordable technology allowed home-made FANZINES to develop.

HEAVY METAL

A music-business categorization first appearing in 1969 and still in use in the early 1990s. The term denotes heavily amplified ROCK music stripped of all overt black influences and based on simplified, repetitive, but essentially melodic riffs. (The phrase 'Heavy Metal [Kids]' was coined by William Burroughs and was first used in a musical context by the group Steppenwolf in 1968). The music is played loudly, usually by a traditional four-piece guitar-dominated male group, and is typically accompanied by stylized, aggressive poses. Heavy Metal also describes the subculture that coalesces around this music, whose predominantly male adherents favour leather, denim and long hair, wear cabalistic paraphernalia and indulge in IDIOT DANCING and HEAD-BANGING. Early focuses of the musical style were Deep Purple in the late 1960s and Led Zeppelin and Black Sabbath in the early 1970s; more recent figureheads include the Scorpions. Heavy Metal succeeded in fossilizing the essential sounds and gestures of the 'progressive' Rock music of the late 1960s, using them to inspire succeeding generations of adolescents. In the 1980s Heavy Metal influenced sub-genres such as HARD CORE, THRASH METAL, GREBO and GRUNGE.

- *Heavy Metal has fans among the student population, but it also*

*has a large working-class following. It seems to represent a curious
blend of hippy aesthetics and football-terrace machismo.*
        Dick Hebdige, Subculture: The Meaning of Style, *1979*

- *When you think of Heavy Metal you think of sexist innuendos and
  pseudo-Satanism. A lot of metal kids are just plain dumb.*
        Dave Grohl of Nirvana, NME, *January 1992*

HEDGERS

See CRUSTIES.

HELL'S ANGELS

Just as SURVIVALISTS attempted to re-create the combat lifestyle of
Vietnam veterans in the American countryside during the 1970s
and 1980s, so the earlier Hell's Angels had tried to continue on the
roads of America the camaraderie and mobility of Second World
War flyers by substituting for fighter planes CUSTOMIZED Harley
Davidson motorcycles, known as 'chopped hogs' and later 'choppers'
('chopping' being the slang term for lengthening front forks and
raising handlebars). The nickname Hell's Angels was one of many
chosen by flight crews in wartime; in peacetime California it was
adopted by the first biker gangs. Calling themselves 'one-percenters',
after the American Motor-cyclist Association declared that 99 per
cent of motorcyclists were law-abiding citizens, these groups of
motorcycle enthusiasts gradually evolved a self-styled 'outlaw',
hedonist, macho existence, living communally, wearing insignia
known as 'colours', which were won in initiation rituals, and
gathering on 'runs' (mobile debauches).

The Angels, usually in their thirties and accompanied by
subservient 'Mommas' or 'Old Ladies', shocked the straight society
they had rejected by wearing swastikas and death's-heads and by
practising a self-conscious cult of personal filth, violence and excess.
The American media discovered the existence of these marauding
bands in 1964; at the same time the future GONZO journalist Hunter
Thompson joined a chapter of Angels and recorded their lifestyle,
before being 'stomped' and ejected. The nascent COUNTERCULTURE
and the Hell's Angels came together for the first time in August 1965,
when Ken Kesey and the MERRY PRANKSTERS met a group of them in

La Honda, California, for a prolonged drug party. In 1968 American Hell's Angels visited London, receiving local admirers at the Chelsea Bridge meeting-place for ROCKERS and Greasers. Soon afterwards a London chapter of Angels was authorized by Oakland, California, and around the country a number of other unauthorized groups appeared, including the Road Rats, the Hangmen, the Outlaws and the Aces.

The HIPPIE UNDERGROUND, fascinated by the Hell's Angels, enlisted them to police concerts, festivals and SQUATTING activities, but in spite of having an anti-Establishment stance, sexual libertarianism and drug use in common, the contradictions between the love generation and the Angels' aggression soon surfaced. One of the most graphic examples of this was the experience of the 'bad-boy' Rolling Stones – used to the relatively placid British bikers – when Californian Angels hired to keep order at the Altamont Festival terrorized the band and audience and killed one onlooker. Hell's Angel groupings existed throughout the 1970s in the UK, living outside society and attracting media attention only when feuds between rival gangs ended in deaths, as happened several times. A sanitized version of the American non-gang biker, inspired in part by the cult film *Easy Rider*, also became a fashion stereotype from the early Seventies. Harley Davidsons were ridden by a small élite, and by the end of the decade Japanese manufacturers and producers of children's bicycles were imitating the chopper.

- *When you're around them and they're feeling good towards you, man it furnishes you with something that is unmistakable. Like you walk down the street surrounded by great big Angels through any district in the world and you feel good about it.*
  Ken Kesey, interviewed in Oz magazine, April 1969

- *Meanwhile a small group of Angels, led by Wild Child, a perpendicular, gesticulative figure in a gruesomely ornate leather dress, adorned with a Nazi helmet – the Auntie Mame of the pack – knotted their way through the swelling pressmen, ruthlessly inspecting blue and red cards.*
  IT, August 1969

HIGH LIFE

Also spelt Hi-Life, this electric, percussion-based dance music of Nigeria and elsewhere in West Africa was popularized by Fela

(Ransome) Anikulapo Kuti. More recent rival musical styles are JUJU and FUJI.

HIGH TECH

A style in design and architecture that celebrates modernity and functionality, generally using lightweight, flexible or tensile materials such as steel, rubber, glass and plastic. High Tech (also spelt Hi Tech) is a radical, unsentimental successor to MODERNISM rather than a form of POST-MODERNISM, its architectural contemporary and rival in the early 1980s. Typical High Tech buildings flaunt their industrial and mechanical aspects and often display their workings – air-conditioning and heating systems, lighting, lifts and doors – as decoration. In Britain such buildings were still rare in the early 1990s and the style had more effect on consumers in the context of interior decoration (epitomized by the work of the Czech émigré Eva Jirična) and design objects, furniture and electronics. The international architects Richard Rogers, Norman Foster and I. M. Pei are among those to whom the High Tech label has been applied. *See* LOW TECH.

HIP HOP

Hip Hop is the name given to the black American subculture that grew up around RAP music, GRAFFITI and BREAK DANCING at the end of the 1970s, and which went on to establish itself as a source of international adolescent fashions, styles and attitudes. Hip Hop began in 1974 in New York's South Bronx housing project when DJs plugged sound systems into the street lights to provide music for mass block parties. While the disc jockeys and MCs, influenced by Jamaican models, chanted over a variety of mixed and SCRATCHED dance records, creating Rap, the black and Hispanic partygoers evolved the acrobatic styles of dancing known as BODY POPPING and BREAK DANCING. Local gangs began to signpost their identities and their 'turf' with a newly flamboyant strain of graffiti. The summer open-air gatherings moved into community centres in the winter and rival groups with allegiances to particular DJs formed 'crews' or 'posses', paralleling the network of street gangs that already existed. Leading black DJs such as Afrika Bambaataa used their influence to promote black pride and African identity, as well as encouraging young people to use Rap and dance rather than violence to compete in the neighbourhood. In November 1979 the Sugarhill Gang's 'Rapper's Delight' reached number five in the record charts and the phenomenon started to emerge from the ghetto underground. In 1982 Run DMC pioneered the B-BOY and FLYGIRL tendencies, reducing the showbiz element in Hip Hop and elevating teenage street style.

By the mid-1980s, graffiti artists were exhibiting in fashionable midtown Manhattan galleries and Rappers and break dancers were entertaining at white trendsetters' parties. Rap music was featured on MTV for the first time in 1983. Meanwhile, the performers' original environment had thrown up a visual uniform of sportswear, including TRAINERS, gold chains and baseball caps, as well as an attitude to accompany the musical style. From the mid-Eighties this became known as Hip Hop, after the dancers' slogan 'Hip Hop (Be Bop) Don't Stop!', the title of a recording by Man Parrish. Both inside and outside the USA this was seen as a colourful novelty until about 1986, when white teenagers started to buy black music in huge volumes and to imitate the dance and clothing styles that went with it. At the same time, white musicians (Aerosmith, Bob Dylan, John Lydon and the Beach Boys among them) queued up to record 'crossover' songs with Rappers and Hip Hop FUNK musicians such as Run DMC, Afrika Bambaataa, Kurtis Blow and the Fat Boys, or imitated the music themselves (as in the case of the Beastie Boys). Hip Hop became the third force in modern pop music, competing in the DANCEFLOOR scene with HOUSE, and rivalling the white successors to ROCK, HEAVY METAL and INDIE POP.

In terms of its influence on young people worldwide, Hip Hop was more important than any of its predecessors; its street-based sports clothes and musical blend of DISCO, SOUL, Funk and Rap made it readily exportable to Third World as well as to developed countries. What was more problematical was its increasing identification in the USA with racism, sexism, crime and drug culture. While some Hip Hop artists continued to promote Afro-American ethnic awareness and others, from 1988, invoked the benign neo-HIPPIE 'Daisy Age', from 1985 onwards another strain adopted gangster poses, glorifying violence and belittling women. This exposed one of the contradictions in the whole black urban culture, where the ethos of the 'homeboys' and 'gangbangers' of New York, Chicago and particularly Los Angeles, fighting each other to control the 'hood', clashed with the pleasure principle of the dancers, the commercial ambitions of the entrepreneurs and the political agitators reviving

the BLACK POWER of the late Sixties. Hip Hop at the end of the 1980s
was marked by the involvement of Hispanics, whites and Asians, and
by more and more overlap with other musical styles such as REGGAE,
TECHNO and Rock.

- *While all the rap boys are putting their guns in some muthafucker's
  face, Toi Jackson, 22 years old from Queen's, New York City, and
  Joyce Spencer, 19 years old from the Bronx, have put together the
  best hip hop groove of the year.*

  The Face, *May 1987*

- *. . . hiphop has functioned as the main bulletin board for the
  black underclass. Furiously cross-referential, bluntly committed to
  the word as its elemental motor force, it has grown increasingly
  ambitious in its drive to map this landscape of violently simple
  struggle between good and evil . . .*

  Mark Sinker, New Statesman and Society, *February 1990*

HIP HOP REGGAE

See RAGGA.

HIP HOUSE

See HOUSE.

HIPPIE CONVOY

See TRAVELLERS.

HIPPIES

The proponents and members of the ALTERNATIVE SOCIETY or
COUNTERCULTURE movement that opposed bourgeois values and
Western orthodoxies in the late 1960s. The Hippie movement was
a much wider-based successor to the Bohemian Beatnik (see BEAT
MOVEMENT) and HIPSTER tendencies that had existed in the United
States since the 1950s. The merging of libertarian activists from the
civil rights campaign with experimenters with Utopian lifestyles
(themselves influenced by Asian and Oriental philosophies and
the use of LSD) first happened in California in 1965 and 1966,
galvanized by opposition to the Vietnam War and to the aggressive

materialism of the society that was promoting it. In the summer of 1966, reports reached Europe of mass gatherings of young people preaching pacifism and hedonism on America's West Coast. The following year's 'Summer of Love' was also celebrated in Britain, where the Hippie philosophy blended with a local vogue for exotic and nostalgic fashions, decadent poses and provocation of the older generation. True Hippies never referred to themselves as such, but rather as 'freaks' or 'heads', the term Hippie (from HIP or 'Hipster') originally being a condescending nickname bestowed on a younger generation by older musicians and Bohemians. It was quickly adopted by the press, however, following the lead of the San Francisco columnist Herb Caen.

The worldwide Hippie movement had lost its main impetus by about 1974. In 1977 PUNKS singled out Hippies as objects of contempt, accusing them of vacuity and passivity and blaming them for the commercialization of youth culture. Remnants of the subculture such as the TRAVELLERS continued to promote its philosophies through the Seventies, however, and during the Eighties these resurfaced in different incarnations in NEW AGE and WORLD MUSIC, and in the ACID HOUSE and CRUSTY phenomena.

- *'You are our leader, George [Harrison]', a hippie told the Beatle. 'No,' said George. 'Wrong.' 'Oh yes, man,' the hippie insisted, running to keep up with the line of a thousand or more, surging eight abreast along Haight Street.*

  Melody Maker, *19 August 1967*

- *Cathy Schwarzenberg is an eighteen-year-old hippie who believes that paintings should come under the National Health, that money should never have been invented and that any form of work makes for dull people.*

  Rave *magazine, June 1969*

HIPSTERS

The Hipster was an American phenomenon of the 1950s that began in the black bebop jazz milieu of the 1940s and helped to evolve the SATIRE boom and the COUNTERCULTURE of the 1960s. Hipsters were white (usually male) Bohemian aficionados of black and Hispanic street culture, especially as it manifested itself in jazz music and the 'jive' or HIP TALK that accompanied it. Hipsters were usually lower-middle-class would-be intellectuals, whereas the Beatniks (see the BEAT MOVEMENT), whose subculture overlapped with theirs, were college-educated and middle class. The two parallel UNDERGROUND cultures were also distinguished by the way they dressed, hipsters imitating the ZOOT SUITS and, later, mohair or shiny cotton suits of jazz musicians and pimps, Beatniks the self-consciously dramatic dishevelment of artists, EXISTENTIALISTS and mystics. The slang word 'hip', originally an all-purpose term of approval probably deriving from a shout of exhortation or encouragement, and also rendered as 'hep', was a key term in the lexicon of black musicians of the 1940s onwards, when it came to signify aware, in touch and 'cool'. Those who had these qualities were 'hep cats', 'Hepsters' or 'Hipsters'; a derisive version of the latter word, applied by an older generation to younger upstarts, was the name HIPPIE.

The typical Hipsters of the 1950s (unlike Beatniks they did generally acknowledge their nickname) were habitués of Greenwich Village or San Francisco nightclubs, subversive in their identification with black values and their taste for marijuana, but often displaying what in retrospect looks like crass machismo in their attitudes to women and their admiration of sporting heroes. The two best-known products of the Hipster scene were the novelist Norman Mailer – who defined the Hipster as 'a white negro' – and the comedian Lenny Bruce, who, with Mort Sahl, launched the satire craze in the US and Britain. By the early 1960s the separate urban Hipster and footloose Beatnik strands making up the American avant-garde had merged; by about 1966 the word itself was outmoded, overtaken, like its milieu, by the wider-based Hippie phenomenon.

HIP TALK

The argot favoured by jazz (see FREE JAZZ; TRAD) musicians, HIPSTERS, Beatniks (see BEAT MOVEMENT) and other Bohemians in the USA during the 1950s. It is a version of jive talk, which derived from a blending of West African terms, Caribbean Creole and black slave codes with the dialect of Southern 'white trash' and native North American underworld slang and neologisms. In the Harlem music venues of the 1920s and 1930s, jive talk developed into a jargon that helped to define the subculture of jazz musicians, as well as bar and nightclub habitués and their admirers and hangers-on. This exclusive and fashionable patois crossed over into mainstream slang in stages over a very long period. JITTERBUGGERS and BOBBYSOXERS employed some words, as did the ZOOT-SUITERS of the late 1940s. Much of the vocabulary of ROCK 'N' ROLL and JIVE, including the terms themselves, come from hip talk, but it was the Beatniks of the later 1950s who assiduously cultivated the hip vocabulary and spread terms like 'hep', 'pad', 'cool', 'man', 'cat', 'chick' and 'scene' and phrases like 'it sends me' across the English-speaking community. The greatest influx of hip talk came during the HIPPIE era, when expressions such as 'groovy', 'far out', 'too much' and 'heavy' became commonplace in the speech of a generation of young people almost all unaware of the prewar origins of these terms. By the mid-1970s everything associated with the preceding COUNTERCULTURE – its jargon in particular – was considered extremely *passé*, except in those milieux where the slang had originated. Hip talk continued to be used unselfconsciously by black musicians, gamblers and sports enthusiasts, but it was not referred to as such. The black slang disseminated through the HIP HOP and RAP movements was a new and evolved variety.

HOLISTIC MEDICINE

A holistic (from the Greek *holos*, meaning whole) approach to medicine involves combining current conventional treatment with alternative medicine and unorthodox therapies to treat whole systems, rather than focusing on parts in isolation. The application of holistic methods avoids the supremacy of the doctor or healer and the passive acquiescence of the patient, instead promoting an interaction between them that takes account of the total experience and circumstances of the patient.

HOMEOPATHY

One of the most respectable forms of alternative (see HOLISTIC) medicine, homeopathy has been endorsed by the British royal family, amongst others. Within the orthodox medical professions attitudes towards homeopathy vary. Homeopathic treatment is available under the British National Health Service, but conventional research has failed to prove its basic assumptions. These are that taking a highly diluted form of a particular substance will stimulate the body to heal and protect the sufferer against the symptoms caused by that substance in higher doses. Developed by the 19th-century German physician C. F. S. Hahnemann, the treatment takes its name from the Greek *homeo-*, meaning same or like, and *-patheia*, meaning suffering. Its obvious attractions are the folk notion of sympathetic magic it seems to support, its use of natural remedies and the fact that it is quite free of the dangers of conventional treatment by chemical drugs. Homeopathy seems to be more effective in the treatment of minor disorders and nervous or allergic conditions than in the curing of diseases, which may lend some weight to arguments for a psychosomatic or placebo explanation.

HOT PANTS

Hot pants (the nickname is a slang term meaning sexual arousal) were a worldwide female fashion craze of 1971. They seem to have evolved through a merging of the home-made shorts worn by HIPPIES and black Americans, made by cutting down blue jeans, with the matching shorts worn under microskirts (see MINISKIRT) as visible underwear. Hot pants provided women with a sexy, abbreviated garment without the vulnerability associated with short skirts. Often attached to a tunic top, the short shorts were typically made of velvet or satin. The fad lasted about two years and attempts to revive it as part of Eighties nostalgia had limited success.

- *The sexy, bottom-hugging street shorts are not original . . . shorts have been talked about and worn by a handful of trendies for months.*
  Sunday Times *magazine, 21 February 1971*

- *Hot pants (worn with a skin-hugging, sleeveless top, thigh boots and lots of ice) were floated as the female equivalent of the Pimp look, but didn't take off like they had in the States.*
  Jon Savage, The Face, *February 1988*

HOT-RODDING

The American hot-rodding cult, which, like the associated DRAG RACING cult, began in the 1940s and flourished in the 1950s, involved CUSTOMIZING and modifying standard production cars to give dramatically better speed and acceleration. The practice of building, racing and CRUISING these cars, which had its own jargon and mystique, remained a feature of North American youth affluence until the early 1970s, when hot-rodders appeared in Australia, Britain, Germany and Scandinavia. In those countries it remained very much a minority hobby for participants, although hot-rodding magazines sold to a wider public. The nickname was originally a play on words, combining mechanics' jargon, where hot rod has the literal meaning of a heated-up piston or connecting rod, with the slang sense of hot as (made more) potent, and rod as device, machine or gun.

HOTTING

An illegal craze surfacing in England in 1991, hotting is an elaborate form of joyriding – itself a cult in Belfast since the 1970s and in Dublin since the early 1980s – in which teenagers and children sometimes as young as eleven steal cars and then stage high-speed performances in front of onlookers before crashing or abandoning the vehicles. Often a high-powered car is stolen to order by a thief who then turns it over to a 'star' driver. The thefts and displays are usually meticulously planned by a number of individuals using radio scanners and lock-up hiding-places; spectators will then sometimes pay to watch the usually male drivers speed along side streets or central roads on council estates at up to 100 mph, crashing gears and carrying out handbrake turns.

Hotting (the term itself plays on the two slang senses of 'hot': stolen and powerful) is a phenomenon produced by a subculture based on large council estates, for example the Blackbird Leys in Oxford, in which socially deprived and/or unemployed males enjoy local celebrity by bravado driving and are encouraged, tolerated or protected by parts of the community. The thieves and drivers, who are known in slang as 'twockers' after the initials of the offence, 'taking without owner's consent', sometimes seek to defend their activities by maintaining that theft is the only way for them to enjoy the fruits of the 'enterprise culture', adding that insurance companies, rather than individuals, suffer as a result. Hotting, along with the associated RAM-RAIDING, caused an outcry in the national press after a sharp increase in hit-and-run deaths involving stolen cars, and at the end of 1991 the British Government rushed through legislation creating a new offence of joyriding. In the USA a similar offence, often involving the taking of cars at gunpoint from owners caught in traffic, is known as 'car-jacking'.

- *The hotters . . . range in age from 14 to 24 and have so far foiled police attempts to apprehend them. They say they are more skilful than police drivers and, driving stolen cars, have less to lose. 'A beast [police officer] who crashes a car ends up back on the beat,' one said.*

  Independent, *3 September 1991*

DANCE HOUSE

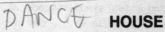

House music, named after the Wharehouse (sic) club in Chicago, where the DJ, Frankie Knuckles, claimed to have invented the style, was a radical fusion of 1970s DISCO sounds and minimalist gospel-style vocals that used REMIXING, synthesizers, multilayered computerized tracks, clattering percussion and the distinctive bass sound of the 808 drum machine. The repetitive, hypnotic dance music flourished in the intensely competitive semi-underground Chicago club scene of 1985 and was quickly adopted in the UK, particularly in the North of England, whence House hits were exported back to the US. In 1987 SAMPLING became an integral feature of the House sound, moving it even further away from musician-based music towards a totally synthetic concoction created by DJ or producer. The underlying rhythm and structure of House was in fact not dissimilar to the heavy Disco – tempered by DUB and SCRATCH – of the early 1980s, retaining that subculture's camp and S & M overtones. As it evolved, sub-genres appeared such as TECHNO, so-called Deep House, Hip House, which incorporated HIP HOP and RAP, and the ECSTASY-fuelled ACID HOUSE, which became the most significant British musical cult of the late 1980s.

- *House has given British dance music a credibility it's never had before . . . There are none of the problems with it that you get with Hip Hop because you don't have to wear a flying jacket and shout 'Yo!' to dance to it or to make it.*

  Club DJ Mike Pickering, The Face, *February 1988*

- *Despite reggae and ska, punk was always a white boys' fad. House is the first subculture that's been open to everyone.*

  Sarah Champion, Blitz, *May 1991*

HULA-HOOP

Often cited as the quintessential short-lived craze, the Hula-Hoop
was a trademark name for a light plastic hoop spun around the waist
by swivelling the hips. Cane hoops had been used in schools for
group exercises during the early 1950s as part of physical education,
but in 1957 the mass-produced coloured hoop, manufactured in the
USA by Wham-O (founded in 1947 by 'gadgeteers' and toymakers
Rich Knerr and Spud Melin, who also launched the LIMBO BAR and
the FRISBEE), swept the world. The fad reached Britain in September
1958 and was the subject of press hysteria during the last quarter
of the year. In November the *Daily Express* reported a marathon
performance under the headline, 'Four-hour Hula Girl'; the Hoop
was featured in a Giles' cartoon; the *Evening Standard* reported that
shops in Windsor and Eton were out of stock after public-school
boys went on a buying spree; and the *Sunday Times* reported the
death from a cerebral haemorrhage of a seventeen-year-old Japanese
Hula fan. In the same month American commentators announced
the demise of the craze, and in December British newspapers agreed,
marvelling at the nine-week wonder. In fact it was far from over.
Children in particular continued to buy the Hula-Hoop, and in 1961
six- and seven-year-olds wrote to the *Observer* newspaper vying to
set Hula records (total revolutions claimed were between 3000 and
9000). Resurgences of the Hula-Hoop's popularity were forecast in
1978 and 1988, but failed to materialize, although sports and toy
shops continued to stock it.

A manufactured gimmick in keeping with the period's growing
taste for novelty, the Hoop emerged from mid-Fifties America's
fascination with Hawaii, which was an accessible but exotic holiday
destination (it became the fiftieth US state in 1959). The energetic
swivelling of the hips needed to keep the Hoop spinning served four
purposes: it provided aerobic exercise and aided slimming; it allowed
otherwise taboo erotic movements in public, and it formed the basis
for a competitive family endurance sport. The movements and
the name were from the Hawaiian Hula culture, part of an ancient
Pacific tradition also including Samoan and Maori war dances. In
this tradition, mass dances retell heroic or romantic legends, as well
as serving as mental and physical discipline. Stamping, squatting,
undulating and pelvic-thrusting are strictly prescribed moves in a
complex ritual full of symbolism. It was versions of these competitive

dances, performed since the arrival of Christian missionaries by women as well as men, that were presented as tourist entertainment for fascinated North Americans and which featured in bastardized forms in films, TV programmes and the Hoop craze. Hula-Hooping anticipated the TWIST in its blend of veiled eroticism and innocent exertion, and presaged AEROBICS as a keep-fit fad marketed to a mass audience.

HUNT SABOTEURS

See SABBING.

HYPERREALISM

A genre of painting deriving from the highly coloured figurative acrylics of POP ART. Hyperrealism originated in the USA at the end of the 1960s and consisted of usually large-scale paintings of figures, street scenes and consumer hardware, for instance, that were almost indistinguishable from colour photographs. Artists sometimes imitated the side effects of photography by perversely focusing on details, cropping images arbitrarily and giving all the components of the picture an equal gloss. The style is also known as photorealism. Exponents of the genre included Howard Kanovitz, Richard Estes and Malcolm Morley, the Swiss artist Franz Gertsch, and the makers of polystyrene and polyester human replicas, Duane Hanson and John de Andrea.

HYPERREALITY

A term and concept used by the French sociologist and POST-MODERNIST philosopher Jean Baudrillard, hyperreality is supposed to describe the all-enveloping power of the consumer society of the late 20th century. In this new state of being, an ever-changing display of empty electronic images referring only to themselves has replaced the old notions of time, space and social relations. The superstructure created by the news and entertainment media and by multinational corporations is a self-perpetuating spectacle whose only purpose is to encourage consumption; there is no longer a deeper logic, or a more authentic 'reality' existing behind this capitalist carnival. In the mid-1980s, Baudrillard, a former Marxist, SEMIOLOGIST and POST-STRUCTURALIST, provocatively suggested that the only way to confront this updated version of McLuhan's GLOBAL VILLAGE (confirming the MCLUHANIST claim that 'the medium is the message') was by a kind of knowing collaboration. He called this celebrating and using of the new reality for one's own ends 'hyperconforming', a strategy put into practice in the 1980s by the COUCH POTATO and the RECREATIONAL SHOPPER.

Baudrillard's ideas are obviously both a product of and a comment on the cosmopolitan 'enterprise culture' of the 1980s. He himself hyperconformed by embracing celebrity and materialism, becoming a cult figure among fashion-conscious intellectuals in the USA and UK, as well as in France. Hyperreality ('hyper-' was a vogue prefix of the early Eighties) established itself as a cultural buzz word by about 1990; in the following year the Italian writer Umberto Eco published a work with the title *Travels in Hyperreality*.

- *Culture has become a vast hyper-reality. Our new life of perpetual shopping constitutes a fundamental mutation in the ecology of the human species.*

  Jean Baudrillard, 1989

- *Baudrillard is obviously projecting himself as the Globe-trotting Bad Boy of Postmodern Philosophy. However, his recent fixations (Alfa Romeo cars, mattresses, mistresses, Stevie Wonder, Rio, his paunch, mud-wrestling and porn) reveal just another ageing, square-eyed slob.*

  Weekend Guardian, *September 1990*

ICEBALL

A novelty sport launched in 1986, iceball was a calculatedly
aggressive and spectacular combination of ice hockey and basketball.
It was part of the vogue for fast-moving updates of established team
games that was triggered by the ROLLER DISCO craze of the late 1970s,
and which later included ROLLERBLADING, STREET HOCKEY and the
amateur game BROOMBALL, beloved of YUPPIES and also played
on ice.

I-CHING

The I-Ching (pronounced 'yi jing' meaning Book of Changes) is a
prehistoric Chinese method of divination. It involves the casting of
coins or dried yarrow stalks (the plant is a kind of daisy) to form
a configuration that gives one of sixty-four hexagrams, or six-line
hieroglyphs. The hexagram is then checked against an 'oracle'
book of predictions. Although it is based on no orthodox scientific
principles, the I-Ching, like TAROT and astrology, offers a sophisticated
and poetic world-view. The Chinese system was one of the five
prized books of wisdom that formed the basis of Confucianist
and, to some extent, Taoist thought. During the 1960s, it moved
from being an obscure curiosity of interest only to occultists and
antiquarians to become a major component in the HIPPIES' mystical
compendium. Earlier, the avant-garde composer John Cage had based
some compositions on the results of throwing the I-Ching and some
enthusiasts went as far as to depend upon its advice for their daily
actions and decisions. It was an article of faith to believe that MAOIST
tacticians in China and other mysterious forces also used the book.
By the 1980s it had been subsumed into the multiplicity of NEW AGE
practices and fads, alongside RUNES, tarot cards and palmistry.

IDIOT DANCING

Idiot dancing was the name given by the music press and musicians, as well as by the dancers themselves, to a frenzied style of dancing practised from 1968 by fans of ACID ROCK, PSYCHEDELIC music and boogie. This frenetic and clumsy dancing on the spot – invariably consisting of writhing hand and arm movements and head-shaking – was influenced by a notion of Indian and oriental religious ecstatic dancing, and was the result not only of imitating (in some cases experiencing) the effects of hallucinogenic drugs but also, more prosaically, of the limited space for any more expressive movement allowed by the packed concert halls and festival sites that were the natural habitat of the idiot dancer. By the mid-1970s, idiot dancing had mutated into the less picturesque HEAD-BANGING.

INDIE POP

The 'Indie' abbreviation started to be used by the music press and music industry in the 1970s to describe an independent record label (i.e. one not affiliated to any of the big business conglomerates, known as the 'majors'), having previously referred to American films made without the support of the Hollywood studio system. It was the advent of PUNK, with its do-it-yourself ethic, that boosted small-scale record companies and threatened the near-monopolies of the majors in the UK. At the beginning of the 1980s the independents were releasing records in a variety of genres, from INDUSTRIAL MUSIC through ELECTRO pop to FUNK and DISCO, but by the middle of the decade a different category of music had evolved that was so closely associated with the small labels that it was known as 'Indie' or 'Indie Pop'.

This white pop music was inspired by mid-1960s ballads, the folksy (see FOLK) end of the PSYCHEDELIA spectrum and the more melodic and nostalgic elements of Punk. The music was accompanied by a studied pose involving a feigned innocence, introversion and distractedness. The clothing style that went with this pose was based on children's non-fashion clothes of the Fifties and Sixties, with a special significance for the anorak (taken by students and others for use as a synonym for 'wimp') and the duffel coat. Indie bands, among them Orange Juice, the Soup Dragons, the Mighty Lemon Drops, the Woodentops and Lilac Time, affected dreamy, fey vocals over jangling guitars and simple insistent drumming. The epitome of Indie in terms of popularity were the Smiths, whose anguished, sexually ambivalent singer Morrissey was probably the most important cult white singing star of the decade. Towards the end of the 1980s longer hair (sometimes the FLOP), leather jackets and more overt drug influences were added to the Indie repertoire. The new style was part of a matrix incorporating the SHAMBLING and SHOE-GAZING tendencies and overlapping with the BAGGY and RAVE scenes, as well as with GRUNGE. The 'Indie' (but not the 'Pop') appellation was then also applied to DANCEFLOOR records.

- *What's most British today is the aspiration to be like the Americans: what's marginal, dissident, practically unpatriotic is the Indie scene's defensive Englishness – a patriotism located in the past, a nostalgia for a never-never Britain, compounded from Sixties 'social realist' films and the golden age of British pop.*
  Simon Reynolds, Against Health and Efficiency: Independent Music in the 1980s, *1986*

INDI-POP

A genre of pop music dating from the early 1980s, Indi-Pop (also known as Asian pop) mixes Anglo-American ROCK-based sounds with Indian 'rags'. Its best-known exemplifiers were the group Monsoon, fronted by Sheila Chandra, and the eccentric Sons of Arqa. It should not be confused with INDIE POP.

INDUSTRIAL MUSIC

Industrial Music was a kind of avant-garde post-PUNK ROCK-based electronic music that intersected with PERFORMANCE ART. Its first exponents were the occultist provocateurs Psychic TV, led by Genesis P-Orridge and Cosey Fanni Tutti, who introduced the phrase in 1978 to describe a relentless, almost atonal wall of sound. In the early Eighties two groups, the German Einsturzende Neubaten ('Collapsing New Buildings') and the British Test Department, celebrated urban decay and post-industrial angst by playing their versions of Industrial Music, using conventional instruments and heavy tools and machinery, sometimes partially demolishing stages and sets in the process. The style (which may have had an unacknowledged inspiration in Captain Beefheart's soundtrack for Paul Schrader's film *Bluecollar* and Public Image Limited's *Metal Box* album) was fashionable until about 1984, although Test Department continued to promote it thereafter.

- *Mechanistic music with shouting over the top is such a cliché in 1987 that it makes nonsense of [Test Department's] manifesto . . . Life is mediocre they say. Liberation will blossom out of noise, power, spectacle, physical intensity, short hair, decrepit machinery, American GI chic, chiaroscuro lighting, rain and rust.*
  The Face, *November 1987*

IRIDOLOGY

This alternative diagnostic technique claims that medical problems can be identified by close examination of the patient's eye. Markings on the irises are said to correspond to conditions present in other parts of the body. Practitioners consult maps of the eyes that resemble the meridian maps used by ACUPUNCTURISTS.

JACKING

Referring specifically to the jerky style of dancing accompanying
HIP HOP and HOUSE music, jacking carried wider connotations in the
black American subcultures of the late 1980s and early 1990s, where
it also meant living a 'streetwise' life, being part of the DANCEFLOOR
scene, and sometimes also being an active member of the gangster
underground. The latter sense was embodied in *New Jack City*, a 1991
film by Melvin van Peebles.

JANOV

See PRIMAL SCREAM.

JAPS

The initials JAP (pronounced like the first syllable of Japanese)
signify Jewish American Princess, a social group first identified and
then extensively commented upon in the late 1970s. (The mildly
derogatory term was not exclusively racist but was also used by
many Jews, in keeping with a tradition of self-deprecating humour.)
The JAP is a young Jewish girl, especially a wealthy or spoilt one,
who supposedly conforms to a number of clear-cut stereotypes.
These include behaving in a comically self-indulgent, acquisitive
way and single-mindedly cultivating eligible marriage partners.
The JAP is also mocked (JAP jokes were still circulating in 1988) for
her dim intellect and her vulgarity. In 1983 the phenomenon was
established by the publication in the USA of the *JAP Handbook*, an
exhaustive guide to the tastes and attitudes of the Jewish American
Princess on the lines of the earlier *Preppie Handbook* (see PREPPIE).
In 1992 JAP jokes reappeared in the UK, now ascribed to the local
KNIGHTSBRIDGE GIRL.

- *Q. What does a JAP make for dinner?*
  A. Reservations.

Evening Standard, *9 May 1988*

JAZZ

See FREE JAZZ; TRAD.

JELLIES

The nickname given to cheap sandals manufactured in brightly coloured transparent plastic, as worn in Britain by SOUL BOYS at the end of the 1970s and by art students, amongst others, in the early 1980s. At the end of that decade they were revived by the designer Paul Smith under the name 'Jellybeans'.

JELLO SHOTS

A transient novelty in the search for innovative ways to package alcohol, Jello Shots were chunks of solid fruit jelly containing vodka. They appeared in 1991 in the USA and were being marketed in the UK the following year. Originating among YUPPIES but continued by the NEW AGE and RAVE subcultures, the craze for exotic high-tech stimulants was also reflected in ROCKET COCKTAILS and so-called 'psychoactive' cocktails containing SMART DRUGS.

JESUS BOOTS

The nickname given to sandals, particularly thong-type, ankle-high sandals as worn by Beatniks (see BEAT MOVEMENT) of the late 1950s and early 1960s. The jocular term was used by British students, MODS and other teenagers at the time – specifically between 1962 and 1966 – when CHELSEA BOOTS were in fashion.

JESUS FREAKS

A disparaging term applied to Christians, particularly those 'born-again' or belonging to evangelical or mystical cults of the HIPPIE era. It was also used by British students in the late 1960s and early 1970s to refer to members of university Christian unions, amongst others.

JIGABOOS

A term applied to young, politically aware blacks in the USA. The word was particularly associated in the 1980s with high-school and college factions seeking to promote black awareness and opposing collaboration with the white Establishment. It was originally a racist epithet (of unknown derivation) used by whites from the early years of the 20th century. Like 'nigger', it was adopted by blacks in defiance of their oppressors. In Spike Lee's 1988 film *School Daze*, a fictional all-black Deep South campus is riven between 'Jigaboos' who want the authorities to renounce links with South Africa, and the lighter-skinned WANNABES who are apolitical and emulate white student pastimes and rituals.

JIT

A variety of Zimbabwean dance music, blending electric ROCK and SOUL with traditional rhythms and melodies. Jit, whose best-known exponent is John Chibadura, spread from its country of origin in the 1980s to become a component of WORLD MUSIC.

JITTERBUGGING

A dance of the 1930s and 1940s based on a speeded-up two-step similar to the LINDY HOP, the jitterbug was performed by couples to the accompaniment of swing music. It consisted of fast acrobatic movements and spectacular solo improvisations, some of which were carried over into JIVE and ROCK 'N' ROLL dancing in the 1950s. In their day the young jitterbuggers were considered by many of their elders to be scandalous and subversive: the dance was associated with ethnic minorities, the poor and the infamous ZOOT SUITERS. By the later 1940s 'Hot Rhythm' music and jitterbugging had been introduced to Britain and Australia.

JIVE

A style of fast dancing to swing or ROCK 'N' ROLL music. Jiving (the word is of unknown origin, but first surfaced in the black community of the USA) initially appeared in the dance halls of Britain during the early 1950s and came to be associated with the nascent culture of the teenager. With a change in musical style from swing jazz to Rock 'n' Roll around 1955, the jive mutated to incorporate hip-swivelling and rhythmic shuffling in addition to the sweeping moves, twirling and over-the-shoulder flourishes inherited from JITTERBUGGING and LINDY-HOPPING. Jive became a key word in TEDDY BOY circles and a symbol of depravity and abandon to many adults. In the late 1950s the semi-comical hand jive (performed with semaphoric arm movements while sitting or standing) was introduced. The jive was the last of the postwar dance crazes to be based on partner contact; many subsequent styles used some of its moves, but were semi-improvised or performed solo. Jiving became an integral part of the repertoire of respectable modern dancing as well as of periodic Fifties revivals, and as such survived into the 1990s.

JOYRIDING
See HOTTING.

JUDO
See KUNG FU.

JUJU
A variety of Nigerian dance music popularized in Europe and the USA during the early 1980s by its best-known exponent, King Sunny Ade. The heavy rhythmic, multitextured music played on a combination of traditional and electronic instruments has been influenced by ROCK and REGGAE. Its rival genre in Nigeria is FUJI; both are the successors of the HIGH LIFE music of the 1960s.

JUNK ART
Drawing on a long tradition that included the letter-based collages of Kurt Schwitters and Marcel Duchamp's found objects, as well as the graphics of PUNK, Junk Art, which appeared in the early 1980s, had the added attraction of ecological awareness in that it recycled industrial or domestic refuse. It also fitted with the prevalent POST-MODERN notions of mixing high and low culture and removing the remaining distinctions between art objects, design accessories

and consumer artefacts. Semi-figurative sculptures and assemblages constructed from discarded metal and sold in short-lived galleries around London's Portobello Road recalled the primitivist and minimalist works of Max Ernst, Picasso and even Epstein's 1913 *Rock Drill*. Salvage – the obsession of the PERFORMANCE sculptors of the Mutoid Waste Company – also became a mainstay of avant-garde jewellery (notably in the work of the male designer Judy Blame), clothing (the British designer Anne Delaney fabricated a skirt from phonecards), furniture-making and graphic design. Junk Art thus fused with recycled fashion, itself inspired by the toys, sculptures and decorations produced in developing countries using scavenged materials.

- *Using bits of wire, tins, old flip-flops, half rubbed-out india rubbers, pieces of plastic, they make sophisticated bicycles, motorbikes and ice cream carts. In most of these countries there's now a price tag on these toys-cum-objets d'art, and they are even ending up in rarefied art galleries.*

  The Face, *September 1992*

K

KABOUTERS

Named after mischievous and benevolent elves of Dutch folklore,
the Kabouters were a group of UNDERGROUND activists operating
in Amsterdam during the late 1960s. They organized squats (see
SQUATTING), 'sleep-in' dormitories for travellers and the homeless,
and the famous White Bicycle scheme whereby bikes were left in
public places for the use of anyone in need. They also declared the
creation of an 'Orange Free State', a microcosm ALTERNATIVE SOCIETY.
The Kabouters' libertarian ideas and alternative welfare schemes were
given a boost when twelve members (habitually dressed in elf hoods
and boots) were elected to Amsterdam's city council. Their following
overlapped with that of the more radical PROVO movement founded
in 1965. Organized COUNTERCULTURES were probably more successful
in Amsterdam and Copenhagen than anywhere else, and provided a
model for squatters in Britain and France. By the late 1970s, however,
the occupied quarters of both cities were involved in drug wars
and permanent confrontation with the authorities, the pacifist and
humorous tactics of the Kabouters having been largely abandoned.

- *Since February [the Kabouters'] imaginative anarchistic
  demonstrations have removed them from the rest of most
  subcultural activities which consist of ego projections or spectacular
  consumptions.*
  Time Out, August 1970

- *At first the Kabouters adopted the familiar Provo smokescreen,
  playing small public jokes like stealing the Mayor's chair from the
  City Council chamber and holding it to ransom . . . but the election
  success suddenly brought back a pre-1965 political idea, that of
  overturning the system from within.*
  Bamn, edited by Peter Stansill and David Zane Mairowitz, 1971

KAFTAN

Although it was only truly fashionable for a brief period around
the end of 1966, the kaftan has entered 20th-century folklore as
the emblem of the HIPPIE era. The traditional kaftan (the name is
a Russian version of an earlier Turkish word, itself deriving from
Persian) was a loose, ankle-length tunic worn, usually under a coat,
by Middle Eastern men since the 16th century. Adopted by a few
exquisites and sophisticates in Europe since the 18th century, the
kaftan inspired Parisian *haute couture* designers, who adapted it for
evening wear for women. In the late 1950s Pierre Cardin's Eastern
look for men hinted at the coming Orientalism, which was unleashed
fully in the late 1960s. Kaftans, now usually thigh- or calf-length,
provided a light, relatively cheap and exotic UNISEX garment that
liberated the wearer not only from restricting collars, cuffs and belts
but also from a bourgeois image. Kaftans were a key component –
along with beads, bells and flowers – of the FLOWER POWER ensemble
identified by the media in 1966 and 1967. They were imported in bulk
from India to the USA and Europe until the mid-1970s, but quickly
relapsed into a marginal role as housecoats or nightdresses for most
wearers. In the Eighties and Nineties kaftans were *de rigueur* for those
involved in neo-PSYCHEDELIC revivals and THEME DISCOS.

KARAOKE

The importing of karaoke (Japanese for 'empty orchestra') into Britain
in the early 1980s illustrated two significant trends of the period.
The first was the new willingness to look beyond the United States as
a source of popular culture, in particular to Japan, where 'Western'
fashions and technology were now being created rather than recycled;
the second was the move by ordinary members of the public rather
than representatives of progressive subcultures to take control of the
entertainment media.

Karaoke originated in Japan as a bar-room distraction for off-duty
businessmen who would sing current hits or traditional songs through
a microphone over an amplified backing track, often supported by
scrolled lyrics on a video screen, entertaining their colleagues and
often poking fun at their bosses. This ritualized form of release from
corporate life was and is an almost exclusively masculine indulgence
in Japan. In the USA and Britain, karaoke first appeared at a small

number of bars catering for Japanese visitors, then in a few exclusive wine and cocktail bars as a novelty. However, it was not until it was picked up by working-class pubs as a high-technology update of traditional sing-alongs, with the added *frisson* of public fame or humiliation, that the craze took hold, flourishing from around 1987 to the early 1990s. Whereas video- and computer-based entertainment is largely a private activity, the public performance element of karaoke seemed to strike a chord in the British. Karaoke (in Britain generally pronounced 'carry-oakie') sessions were televised in 1989, national competitions were organized the following year, and equipment consisting of twin-tape decks, eight-track backing tapes, amplification and optional video unit could be hired for private functions.

- *In its place of origin, Karaoke is so firmly established that after staggering out of a Karaoke bar the dedicated punter can hire a specially equipped Karaoke taxi and carry on singing all the way home . . .*

  Geoff Deane, The Face, January 1988

- *A mother of a nine-month-old baby and a housewife, Jackie turns into Whitney Houston at night. Her growling and falsetto version of 'I Wanna Dance With Somebody' was undoubtedly the most professional performance of the night, and the most in keeping with the karaoke ethic of bringing something of yourself to the performance.*

  Sean Macaulay, ES Magazine, September 1991

KARATE

See KUNG FU.

KINESIOLOGY

A NEW AGE THERAPY technique involving muscle-testing and 'energy-balancing', applied in the treatment of allergies and to promote general health. Kinesiology uses touching rather than massage in order to transmit mystical healing forces, or to awaken and release those forces in the patient. Like many New Age approaches, it is influenced by the ancient Chinese principles (the body's meridians and energy flow) behind ACUPUNCTURE.

KINETIC ART

From the Greek *kinetikos*, meaning moving, Kinetic Art encompasses any painting, sculpture, assemblage or installation that comprises a mobile element. The best-known examples are the suspended abstract 'mobiles' of the American sculptor Alexander Calder, which in the early 1960s inspired a lasting popular fashion in home decoration, and the electric motor-driven constructions of the Swiss-French Jean Tinguely. In the 1960s, as gallery art moved beyond the traditional modes of presentation into mixed media, many artists experimented with moving parts, liquids, gases, and works in which the viewer could manipulate the art object. In its widest sense, Kinetic may also refer to the static canvases of OP ART, in which geometric patterns create the illusion of movement by their effect on the retina.

KINKY BOOTS

Women's knee- or thigh-high leather boots as worn in Britain from 1962 to 1965. This kind of footwear, inspired by fetishistic styles, was considered daring at the time and emblematic of the 'swinging Sixties'. The leather repertoire, of which kinky boots were a part, was one of the first examples of a deviant or underground mode being acknowledged by mainstream fashion (the vogue term 'kinky', originally part of the lexicon of pornographers and prostitutes, became diluted to denote merely fashionable or novel). Honor Blackman and Patrick MacNee, stars of the cult TV series *The Avengers* that brought the look to a mass audience, actually recorded a single entitled 'Kinky Boots' in 1965 (it was re-released and became a Chart hit in 1990).

KIPPER TIE

The extra-wide kipper tie was so called because of its supposed fish shape, and, it is claimed, as a play on the name of Michael Fish, whose Mr Fish boutique sold it. It appeared in Britain at the end of 1966 partly due to a brief interest in 1930s modes, replacing narrow leather or floral ties and remaining in fashion until 1968. The kipper is significant in that it marked the transition from colourful versions of traditional male clothing styles to the radically new shapes and colours of the HIPPIE era. Typically worn with a waisted, wide-lapelled jacket and bell-bottomed trousers (as caricatured in the

Beatles cartoon film, *Yellow Submarine*), the tie usually featured bold abstract OP ART or Paisley designs or figurative paintings, before giving way to the first consciously PSYCHEDELIC patterns and images. Shirts also mutated at the same time through pastel and primary colours to intricate patterns, whilst collars developed from pointed to rounded before the collar-and-tie convention was dispensed with altogether. The kipper tie has remained in the memory of style commentators as a quintessential phenomenon of 'swinging London' and the pioneering boutique culture that accompanied it. The same term was sometimes later applied to the wide and garish ties that were worn with wide lapels and flared trousers or Oxford bags as part of 1970s male fashion.

KIRLIAN PHOTOGRAPHY

A photographic technique used in NEW AGE treatments and THERAPIES whereby problems are diagnosed by studying photographs revealing the electromagnetic and thermal flow around and from the body. The procedure is a blend of the scientific and the paranormal and claims to detect problems before physical symptoms manifest themselves. Orthodox medical experts acknowledge the ability of the Kirlian high-frequency field machine to register changes such as the menstrual cycle, but doubt its validity in the case of more serious illnesses such as cancer for example. The process is named after its Russians inventors, Semyon and Valentina Kirlian, who developed it in the 1970s.

KITCHEN SINK DRAMA

A genre represented in the British theatre, cinema and on television since the late 1950s, 'kitchen sink drama' refers to a version of social realism that dwells on the squalor and tedium of working-class domestic life. The tendency followed on from the ANGRY YOUNG MEN, whose 'bedsitter alienation' put the lifestyles of the 'have-nots' centre-stage for the first time. Dramatists such as Arnold Wesker continued to do this with plays such as *Chips With Everything*. By the mid-1960s kitchen sink drama was in danger of becoming a cliché, if not a parody, as the semi-pejorative classification (first coined in 1954 by the critic David Sylvester to denote a school of painting typified by John Bratby) suggests. Far from celebrating working-class virtues or promoting social change, the effect of the approach on many commentators was merely to perpetuate stereotypes and reinforce pessimism. By the 1970s some of its conventions had been co-opted for comedy in such TV productions as *Till Death Us Do Part* and *Rising Damp*.

- ... *cinema-goers in Kansas City and Kuala Lumpur expose themselves patiently to the national inscrutablities of continental cinematic styles: the stark guilt-laden neuroses of Ingmar Bergman, the stylish ennui of Antonioni, the scruffy anti-heroism of Britain's sinking Kitchen Sink.*

  Town *magazine, May 1964*

KITSCH

An appreciation of kitsch (the word is German for gaudy trash, from the verb *kitschen*, meaning slap together or create carelessly) by the style-conscious was a characteristic of the 1960s, particularly in the UK. This appreciation took several forms; the sentimental collection of earlier mass-culture artefacts; the re-creation of garish and vulgar popular styles; and the knowing parody of 'bad taste'. POP ART had reintroduced consumer products and commercial images previously dismissed or denounced by MODERNISM in the early 1960s; by 1966 this had resulted in youth subcultures adopting BADGES, uniforms and medals, as well as a rag-bag of Victorian, Edwardian and 1930s clothing styles. Progressives in the fields of music (notably the Bonzo Dog Doodah Band and the Kinks) and design (art student tastes were crystallized in a 1967 manifesto in the Royal College of Art magazine, Ark) began to celebrate working- and lower-middle-class decorative icons: plaster-duck wall decorations and garden gnomes in particular were singled out. The seaside postcard illustrations typified by Donald McGill and the hitherto unfashionable 'metroland' look of 1930s suburbia were imitated, as was their high-culture equivalent, Art Deco, propagated by Barbara Hulanicki's Biba store. These 'retro' styles, which were nostalgia-based rather than innovative, ushered in the 1970s and then yielded to the increasing influence of the 1950s and mid-Sixties revivals that dominated the following two decades. The creation of authentic kitsch did not cease in the 1950s; artefacts such as the LAVA LAMP, the GONK and NEWTON'S CRADLE all attest to its survival through the Sixties and Seventies.

- *And when in the 1990s the mood of nostalgia is fulfilled by the recreation of the 60s, the cultist's prize possession will not be his Heal's chair or his Casa Pupo rug, but rather a beside lamp formed from a plaster negress's head with a glinting gilt stem and a shade in a delicate hue of peach lustre.*

  Ark *magazine, 1967*

- *The organising principle of the whole pop sensibility is, of course, kitsch, the self-conscious manipulation by those working within fine art or exposed to fine art values of those 'vulgar' themes and 'low' representational forms which are defined by traditionalists as being 'in poor taste' . . .*

  Dick Hebdige, Hiding in the Light, *1988*

KNIGHTSBRIDGE GIRL

A social stereotype invented in 1991 as a counterpart to ESSEX GIRL; the reference is to the London district between Chelsea and Kensington containing Harrods and many designer shops, as well as the homes of the very rich. Many of the jokes circulated mocking the Knightsbridge Girl's spoilt behaviour were in fact recycled Jewish American Princess (JAP) jokes originating in the USA. SURREY GIRL was Knightsbridge Girl's rural or suburban equivalent.

KODE

The complex system of language and signals used by the gay community in order to communicate covertly with one another, particularly about sexual proclivities. This included the wearing of key-rings, chains and specific colours of handkerchiefs in specific pockets. The linguistic element of this system is literally a code in that it takes terms from standard English, such as 'straight', 'CLONE' and 'boystown', and uses them ironically. The 'K' spelling is to give the English word overtones of Germanic or Slavonic exoticism and oppression, as in 'Amerika' or 'klan'. *See* also GAY LIBERATION.

KRAUT ROCK

A music-industry categorization of the early 1970s, Kraut Rock refers to the HEAVY METAL and avant-garde electronic ROCK music played by a number of West German groups, 'Kraut' being a slang term for German, taken from 'Sauerkraut', the national dish of pickled cabbage. Kraut Rock had three waves: the progressive Rock of Can, Neu, Faust and Amon Duul; the synthesizer-based semi-experimental music of Kraftwerk and Tangerine Dream; and the POMP ROCK of the Scorpions. Early 1980s INDUSTRIAL MUSIC exponents Einsturzende Neubaten were exempted from the category. Germany was the first non-Anglophone country to produce a significant body of Rock music, and the influences of some aspects of Kraut Rock – particularly that of Kraftwerk – fed back into later genres such as ELECTRO and TECHNO.

- *Krautrock had once been quite an intellectual fad but when the prevailing tone in 76 became anti-intellectual, Krautrock, notionally tarred with the same brush, was seen as a no go.*

  Peter York, Style Wars, 1980

KRISHNAMURTI

The Indian Krishnamurti (1895–1986) was chosen by the Theosophist Annie Besant and groomed from boyhood to be the 'world teacher', the future spiritual leader of her movement. In 1929, however, he rejected the messianic role arranged for him, saying 'Truth is a pathless land', and went on to criticize the notion of the divine guru who exerts spiritual authority over faithful devotees. Krishnamurti established centres in Ojai, California, the Rishi Valley and Benares in India and at Brockwell Park in England. He spent his life teaching a low-key doctrine of self-awareness and responsibility in everyday behaviour to a mainly 'respectable', rather than exclusively COUNTERCULTURE, following. Of the many gurus competing in the postwar era to offer ways to enlightenment, Krishnamurti was one of the few to escape public suspicion or criticism during his lifetime. In 1991 the publication of reminiscences by a confidante, Radha Rajagopal Sloss, raised questions about his asceticism and supposed celibacy. In the 1990s, Krishnamurti's movement continues his work.

KUNG FU

Chinese and Japanese martial arts have appealed particularly to the young and/or dispossessed of Western countries since the 1960s, when judo and, to a lesser extent, karate were popular youth-club hobbies (karate also enjoyed a brief vogue around 1970 among both SKINHEADS and members of the COUNTERCULTURE). In the early 1970s, however, attention shifted to kung fu. The name is from the Mandarin Chinese and denotes a balletic and acrobatic form of unarmed combat said to have been developed in the 6th century at Shaolin Temple in the Hunan Province of southern China. Kung fu movies exported from Hong Kong created a worldwide craze for the activity, particularly among ethnic minority communities, and made an international superstar of the actor and instructor Bruce Lee. From about 1972 there was a crossover: the Hong Kong films used black American SOUL and FUNK music in their soundtracks, while American film-makers created a new genre, the so-called 'blaxploitation' movies, which featured black heroes punishing enemies using martial-arts techniques as well as weapons. Both types of film were regularly shown on double bills to young audiences, and martial arts continued to form part of ghetto subculture until the 1990s, by which time the musical accompaniment was RAP and HIP HOP. A passing interest in kung fu among middle-class HIPPIES and self-improvers led to other disciplines such as Kendo, Tai Chi and Thai boxing being taken up.

- *'Superfly' and 'King Boxer' or 'Cleopatra Jones' paired with Bruce Lee . . . The aisles were perilously full of inspired youth practising its high kicks to the sound of a wah-wah pedal.*

  David Toop, The Face, *February 1988*

KWELA

The East African dance-music contemporary of the better-known Nigerian HIGH LIFE of the 1960s.

LAGER LOUT

A journalistic coinage of the later 1980s describing a drunken young male troublemaker. The term encompassed working-class CASUALS, football fans, ESSEX BOYS, YUPPIES and perpetrators of the outbreaks of anti-police rioting seen in many rural towns during that decade. Since the end of the Seventies, lager (both in its insipid domestic form and as a high-strength import) had largely replaced bitter as the preferred drink both of macho pub habitués and the more fashion-conscious frequenters of City bars. The loutishness in question was invariably mindless high spirits and drink-fuelled aggression rather than anything systematically subversive.

LAMBADA

A worldwide dance craze of 1989 and 1990, the lambada was launched in Paris as a hit record based on a Brazilian original (the ultimate authorship of the dance was the subject of litigation). Combining the fashion for WORLD MUSIC with the DISCO milieu's search for novelty (SALSA had been the most recent success), the lambada added an extra dimension of eroticism in that it involved couples engaged in vigorous hip-swivelling and lunging movements.

LAND ART

A categorization first used in the late 1960s and increasingly fashionable in progressive circles since then, Land Art covers a number of different artistic approaches, but the many techniques have in common the manipulating, celebrating and/or recording of the landscape. They include Earth Art (practised by the Americans Robert Smithson, Michael Heizer, Walter De Maria and Dennis Oppenheim, amongst others), in which artificial earthworks, trenches and holes are constructed; the placing of sculptures and assemblages in the countryside or the erection of stone circles and monuments (notably by the British sculptor Ian Hamilton Finlay); the wrapping or signposting of topographical features (made famous by the Bulgarian-American Christo, who wrapped one and a half miles of Australian coastline in 1969); and the arrangement of natural objects and the photographing and recording of journeys (as carried out by the British artist Richard Long). Beginning as a form of MINIMALISM or CONCEPTUAL ART, Land Art has blended with NEW AGE spiritual concepts of communion with nature and POST-MODERNIST ideas of merging interiors and exteriors, art and architecture. By the early 1990s the use of natural materials in outdoor settings had become almost commonplace, the prevailing approach involving the 'collaboration of nature' in a creative process. The British artist Wendy Lemley, for instance, hung forty-foot cloths from the banks of the Thames to be stained with tidal silt.

- *Andy Goldsworthy is an artist well known for his painstaking natural constructions; his recent work has ranged from vast wheels of ice, cut and built at the North Pole, to thousands of chestnut stalks latticed together into a curtain, a dozen leaves stuck with saliva, sailing down a river.*
  Independent, *4 September 1992*

LASERTAG
See COMBAT GAMES.

LAVA LAMP
First appearing as a futuristic decorative object in the late 1960s, the lava lamp became a symbol of the bad taste of the early 1970s. Consisting of an upright transparent cylinder filled with clear liquid on a usually brass or brass-coloured base, the lamp's unique selling proposition was the movement of globules of typically orange-coloured gel up and down, triggered by the heat from a bulb. The lamp became a standard item of KITSCH working-class decor, along with fluorescent man-made fabrics and plastic and Formica surfaces. It was quickly integrated into ironic parodies by design-conscious progressives in the early 1970s and again in the early 1990s. A slightly later rival in the same market was the fibre-optic lamp, a

domed plastic table lamp consisting of a mass of protuding fibres whose luminescent tips slowly changed colour. The noise of the contraption's motor detracted from the contemplative pleasure it was intended to afford.

LEATHER BOYS

See ROCKERS.

LETTRISTS

See SITUATIONISTS.

LIGHT SHOWS

The use of complex projected light displays originated in avant-garde theatre and KINETIC and PERFORMANCE ART, but it was as an accompaniment to the PSYCHEDELIC music of the late 1960s that light shows became a distinct category of spectacle. Throughout the early Sixties experiments had been conducted to examine the disorienting effects of flashing lights and the visual effects of projecting light through liquids of different viscosities. Combining both these techniques – stroboscopic emission and the heating of coloured oil and water on slides – produced the light show, a mobile and unpredictable pattern of shapes and colours enveloping performers, audience and surroundings to re-create the sensory confusion of an LSD trip or hashish or opium reverie.

In Britain the technique was pioneered in 1963 by Mark Boyle, but it was the Soft Machine and Pink Floyd groups in mid-1966 who introduced club audiences to the light show. In the autumn of the same year the Who pop group tentatively used the first psychedelic light sequence on television in a special edition of the cult programme *Ready Steady Go!* By the summer of 1967 the light show was a standard part of the repertoire of most fashionable bands, and lighting engineers vied to produce the most spectacular and original effects. Many progressive musicians and clubs such as UFO and Middle Earth in London, and the Melkweg and Paradiso in Amsterdam, valued the blurring of the spectator/performer roles that the overwhelming light effects allowed, but this was perceived as a problem by groups and venues relying on the promotion of personalities. The first wave of light shows was not bettered until the advent of laser techniques during the mid-1970s, by which time the psychedelic ambience was out of favour. In the late 1980s the ACID HOUSE and INDIE POP movements reverted to the coloured wheels and oil-and-water approach to supplement the now commonplace high-tech laser and strobe displays and the computer-generated patterns known as 'fractals'.

- *We were using real liquids for the lights, which is impossible to do now unless you know what you're doing. The liquid wheels they use nowadays are a cop-out.*
  Liquid Len (Hawkwind's lighting man), Q magazine, August 1991

LIMBO BAR
In 1962 the 'gadgeteers' Rich Knerr and Spud Melin, founders of the prolific Wham-O corporation, attempted to emulate their success with the HULA-HOOP by launching a second fad inspired by North America's fascination with the exotic cultures on its doorstep. This time they chose to exploit West Indian limbo dancing by mass-producing the horizontal bar under which the acrobatic dancers pass. It failed to match expectations, however, and Wham-O had to wait for the FRISBEE for its next worldwide hit.

LINDY-HOPPING
A particularly exuberant and gymnastic form of swing dancing. It was incorporated into the JIVE repertoire in the 1950s, but ignored during the many subsequent revivals of Fifties styles until the early 1990s, when it was resurrected in London nightclubs and centres of DANCEFLOOR culture. The dance actually originated in the 1930s and was named after Lindbergh's flight – 'Lindy's hop' – across the Atlantic.

LIVE AID
See BAND AID.

LIVERPOOL SOUND

See MERSEY BOOM.

LOCKS

See DREADLOCKS.

LOLOBAL

The Lolobal was one of the trademark names for the plastic Saturn-shaped exercise balls that caught on among pre-teen children in 1987 and 1988 (Trimball and Disco-ball were the rivals). The balls had a surrounding platform allowing them to be gripped by the feet; their elasticity then permitted AEROBIC-exercise bouncing. The Lolobal was one of several consecutive ways of selling bouncing to the would-be fitness fanatic or playful child; the SPACEHOPPER, the POGO stick and the mini-TRAMPOLINE were others.

LOOK, THE

An amorphous term used in cultural and media studies since the 1970s, 'the Look' has three possible meanings. It may refer to the act of looking at an image (in this case invariably a human image) with the implication that the looker is indulging in voyeurism or the exercise of power over the object. Alternatively, the Look may be the passive or impotent, albeit knowing, gaze directed by the object at the observer. These difficult notions are often used in discussing the power relationships between male and female in two-dimensional visual representations and in everyday eye contact. A third sense of the Look has been used less theoretically by fashion photographers, cineastes and commentators on popular culture. Here 'look' means appearance, and 'the Look' means a particular, recognizable but indescribable quality or allure created by the features and expressions of certain human icons. Thus personalities as different as Louise Brooks, Billy the Kid, Rimbaud, Marilyn Monroe, and particularly Lauren Bacall could be said to personify the Look. It is a seductive, timeless and poignant something that strikes a chord in the beholder.

LOON PANTS

When the fashion for bell-bottomed trousers for both sexes began to go mainstream in the mid-1960s, demand outstripped supply, particularly for cheap, brightly coloured and durable versions. The fashionable young gravitated towards the north London Laurence Corner surplus shop; and stall-owners and traders in London's antique markets began to buy summer-weight naval-issue bell-bottoms, adapting them by narrowing the thighs and lowering the waists, but retaining the buttoned flap fronts. These trousers and later versions mass-produced in coloured velvet became part of the HIPPIE uniform, enduring from their modish appearance in 1966 to their disappearance after 1976, by which time they had become a ridiculed symbol of the fading PSYCHEDELIC era. 'Loon pants' was the name under which the style was marketed by mail order. The verb 'to loon', 'loon about' or 'loon out', meaning to disport oneself in an uninhibited, anarchically playful way, was briefly a vogue term in HIP hedonist circles.

LOW RIDERS

While the fashion among WASP car enthusiasts in the USA during the late 1960s and early 1970s was to jack up the suspension on automobiles, vans and trucks, the Hispanic PACHUCO and Chicano subculture of southern California took the opposite course. These young male gangs decorated their cars with metallic paint, chrome and KITSCH fur and plastic accessories and lowered the suspension so that during the ritual of CRUISING the cars lurched along close to the ground. Both the cars and their owners were known as 'Low Riders'. The fad persisted from the late Sixties into the Nineties and was emulated by a few CUSTOMIZERS in Latin America and Europe.

LOW TECH

Coined by analogy with HIGH TECH, Low Tech (sometimes spelt Lo-Tech) denoted the deliberate use of natural materials and minimal technology in order to solve environmental or construction problems. It was used particularly in connection with aid schemes for developing countries.

M

MACROBIOTICS

A vegetarian dietary system that claimed to be based on the
ancient Chinese notions of harmony and balance symbolized by the
complementary Yin (feminine) and Yang (masculine) principles.
Macrobiotics became a mainstay of the HIPPIE lifestyle in the late
1960s, when it was propounded by the Japanese-American Georges
Ohsawa, who in books such as *Zen Macrobiotic Cooking* offered a
seemingly systematic analysis of the correct proportions of Yin and
Yang to be found in certain foods and certain cooking practices.
However, the suggested connection to ZEN was spurious (that ascetic
Buddhist tendency in fact opposed any preoccupation with food),
and nor was the macrobiotic diet based on any known Chinese or
Japanese forerunners. Liberal dieticians criticized the strictures of
macrobiotics as unfounded and in extreme cases potentially harmful
(particularly when applied to carnivorous animals such as pet
cats), although macrobiotics did introduce brown rice to Western
palates. Nevertheless, macrobiotic restaurants flourished in the West
between 1967 and 1973, after which the movement subsided to
some extent. This fad triggered the new dietary consciousness of the
1970s and 1980s, introducing the concept of 'wholefood' (untreated
pulses, grains, nuts, etc.) and leaving a legacy of health-food shops
worldwide. In the early 1990s there were signs of a revival of interest
in macrobiotics by a younger generation of GREEN-issue enthusiasts
and NEW AGE FOODIES. Based on the Greek *macro,* meaning 'great'
or 'long', and *biotikos,* meaning 'of life', the quasi-scientific name
reflects the macrobiotic claim that by mirroring the order of the
cosmos within the body, a longer life (among other benefits) is
assured.

- *In another instance, I found a loaf of bread in a macrobiotic household, a bread with a beard – such a handsome beard that it made the members of ZZ Top look clean-shaven.*
    Julie Burchill, Sunday Times, *November 1984*

MAGIC REALISM

The term was first coined in 1925 by the German art critic Franz Roh, who was then referring to the unsettling atmospheric effects of the work of some of the Neue Sachlichkeit (New Objectivity or Matter-of-Factness) painters. In the 1970s it was resurrected as a categorization, this time describing a literary genre inspired by the work of the Colombian novelist and short-story writer Gabriel García Márquez. His seminal 1967 novel, *Cien Áños de soledad* (*One Hundred Years of Solitude*), blended reality and fantasy, history and myth in a style echoed in the writings of Mario Vargas Llosa, Isabel Allende, Carlos Fuentes and Italo Calvino, among others. In fact, the marvellous and the grotesque had been a feature of storytelling in South and Central America and the Caribbean for a hundred years before Márquez, reflecting the totalitarian regimes superimposed on the indigenous shamanistic and totemic cultures. Magic Realism became one of the most touted labels of the international literary scene of the 1980s, generally implying a political or historical allegory behind a narrative shot through with supernatural events. In Britain it was applied to the work of Salman Rushdie, and to the first novel by Tariq Ali, for instance. It was thought by some critics to form an important strand of literary POST-MODERNISM, representing as it did the merging of the real and the imaginary, and, in its later incarnations, promoting multiculturalism. In January 1992, however, *GQ* magazine declared that it was no longer a fashionable term to drop at intellectual get-togethers.

- *In Márquez's invented South American town of Macondo, a place isolated from the outside world, 'magic realism' rules . . . At one level, life is perfectly ordinary . . . but there is a second, irrational plane to ordinary existence.*
    Kenneth McLeish, Bloomsbury Good Reading Guide, *1988*

MAHARISHI

See TRANSCENDENTAL MEDITATION.

MAOISM

Mao Zedong's political philosophy was a mixture of Marxist-Leninist theories of social revolution, traditional Chinese pragmatism and (unacknowledged) Confucianism. The Chinese Cultural Revolution, inaugurated by Mao in 1966 with the help of the Red Guard youth movement and the ideological handbook, the *Little Red Book*, inspired many European leftists, particularly those involved in the student protests of 1968. Concepts such as the abolition of the past, the cult of youth and the idea of 'permanent revolution' were attractive to both militant and libertarian Marxists in Western countries who were seeking a radical alternative to Stalinism. The peasant/agrarian setting for Mao's theories and the realities of his repressions were both disregarded by some intellectuals in the early 1970s, particularly in France, where Parisian coevals of the SITUATIONISTS proclaimed themselves Maoists and expounded 'Maoist' views in literary and political journals and in other media, notably Jean-Luc Godard's 1967 film *La Chinoise*. Mao's Utopianist and absolutist failings began to be exposed in the later 1970s, and by the early 1980s Maoism had ceased to exert any influence except in the form of the Sendero Luminoso ('Shining Path') rural guerrilla movement of Peru and in similar groups in Bihar, India.

• *Maoist China, they say, is hermetic, suspicious, hostile to foreigners, yet the Maoist cell in Hampstead was as open as the laundromat where Mr Manchanda had been doing his smalls.*
Sunday Times *magazine, 8 December 1968*

• *. . . Maoism was the thing on the Left Bank, and [Julia] Kristeva was one of a group of writers who visited China in 1974 . . . They came home disillusioned . . . And so, because half a dozen egg-heads had been disappointed in their three-week holiday, the politico-economic climate of the Western world shifted.*
Lucy Hughes-Hallett, Independent on Sunday, *February 1992*

MARTIAN SCHOOL

A minor British literary genre of the 1980s named after a poem
by Craig Raine entitled 'A Martian Sends a Postcard Home'. The
poem describes everyday objects and activities from a standpoint
of supposed alien detachment, rendering the familiar unfamiliar. In
fact the poet subverts his own intentions by lapsing into knowing
sentimentality in the closing lines. The 'Martian' epithet has been
applied to the literary coterie comprising Raine, Andrew Motion,
Blake Morrison and other contemporaries who are said to share a
lofty and ironically alienated vision of modern – or POST-MODERN –
social reality.

MASCULINISM

See MEN'S MOVEMENT.

MAXI-SKIRT

A predictable reaction against the dominance of the MINISKIRT
towards the end of the 1960s, the maxi-skirt appeared at the end of
1968 along with the MIDI, and was promoted intermittently by the
fashion industry until 1971. It enjoyed a brief vogue among young
women in the USA and the UK, particularly in low-cost denim,
canvas and corduroy versions. The name maxi continued to be
used in the 1980s – though generally only by the fashion trade –
to describe any full skirt of ankle or floor length. The styles that
succeeded in dislodging the mini among the fashion-conscious were
in fact the retro-Forties calf-length flared skirt and the PENCIL SKIRT.

● *. . . the couturiers showed shorts merely as a sop to the big
American buyers who had such a disastrous season with midis and
maxis this winter.*
Sunday Times *magazine, 21 February 1971*

MBALAX

A dance music from Senegal sometimes blended with imported
REGGAE elements. It was adopted by European aficionados of WORLD
MUSIC at the end of the 1980s.

McLUHANISM

(Herbert) Marshall McLuhan (1911–80) left no systematized body of ideas or movement, but was probably the most important English-speaking cultural commentator of the 1960s and many of his ideas have been resurrected in the 1980s under the new guises of HYPERREALISM and CYBERPUNK, for instance. McLuhan was a Canadian professor of English literature who was inspired by the social historian Harold Innis to investigate the effects of new technology on culture and consciousness. As early as 1951 McLuhan was analysing the social implications of the popular press, TV and the automobile; later he developed his best-known theories, encapsulated in the much-quoted slogan, 'The medium is the message' (originally a chapter heading; McLuhan also at times substituted 'massage' for 'message'), and the phrase 'GLOBAL VILLAGE', which became a cliché of the COUNTERCULTURE.

What McLuhan was suggesting was that the means by which humanity communicates socially influences, determines, or even overwhelms the content of the communication. He suggested that electronic systems had rendered print obsolete and that traditional national and cultural boundaries were irrelevant in the face of instantaneous worldwide transmission of data – hence the global village, which also had Utopian overtones in its suggestion of a new sense of mutual understanding and community. McLuhan chose to distinguish between 'cold' media – such as TV or print that are of low definition and require effort by the recipient – and 'hot' media – such as radio and film that reflect, extend and heighten the human senses in a direct way. The categorization has not proved lastingly useful. The ideas of hyper-articulate McLuhan were eagerly embraced, if not always fully digested, by many progressives of the HIPPIE era. He was generally treated with disdain by traditionalist Anglo-American academics, who were disturbed by his provocative wordplay and flamboyant mixing of systematic deduction and inspired assertion. Leftists saw him as apolitical, or as an unwitting apologist for capitalist systems. After the mid-1970s, McLuhan was no longer widely quoted or referred to; by the Eighties the concepts of a post-literate society, self-referential media, instantaneous global communication, etc., had visibly come to pass and some of McLuhan's rag-bag of ideas seemed to have been validated.

- *Electric circuitry is orientalizing the West. The contained, the distinct, the separate – our Western legacy – are being replaced by the flowing, the unified, the fused.*
  Marshall McLuhan, quoted in Student *magazine, Autumn 1969*

- *The Bailey photograph and the Lichtenstein painting teach the same lesson: that the message is the material of which the message is composed is the medium in which it is transmitted. In other words the McLuhanite tautology.*
  Dick Hebdige, Hiding in the Light, *1988*

MEDIUM IS THE MESSAGE, THE
See MCLUHANISM.

MEN'S MOVEMENT

A relatively unfocused and inarticulate Men's Movement (known also as masculism or masculinism) gathered momentum in the USA during the 1980s. Primed by a prolonged uncertainty regarding the masculine role in personal relationships and in society in general, as well as by a backlash against the increasing assertiveness of women, men's support groups were formed. An amalgam of COMBAT GAMES, THERAPY, SURVIVALISM and NEW AGE mysticism found its focus in 1990 with the publication of the poet Robert Bly's fable, *Iron John: a Book about Men*, and Sam Keen's *Fire in the Belly: On Being a Man*. These and other texts encouraged the post-FEMINIST 'soft male' or NEW MAN, to locate the 'wild man' within; in other words to learn to communicate with the primitive father/warrior/protector that is the male essence. This attempt to reassert positive male values expressed itself in discussion groups, workshops, outdoor weekends and week-long seminars in which mainly middle-class males indulged in bonding and initiation rituals, role-playing, encounter groups, physical exercise and martial arts.

The need to reintroduce a heterosexual closeness between men, and to counterbalance a perceived oppression by mothers and partners, seemed to be a peculiarly American phenomenon, at least in its organized manifestations. In Europe, the invocation of a mythical and folkloric justification for masculinism, its veiled NEW RIGHT and militaristic overtones and the language in which these were couched were much ridiculed. Nevertheless, at the same time in Britain male-oriented CONSUMERISM had become firmly established and a new questioning of male roles, at least in a social and sexual sense, was being expressed by 'thirty-something' journalists such as David Thomas and Toby Young. In 1992 Robert Bly held his first 'Wild Weekends' in the English countryside.

- *The tough wimp. The loving hunk. The sensitive thug. The caveman was a moron; the Wild Man is an oxymoron.*
  Mark Lawson, Independent *magazine, 31 August 1991*

- *These men-only tribal gatherings use drumming, synchronised shouting and (bizarrely) vegetarianism to help men celebrate their masculinity and mourn their lost relationship with their fathers.*
  Time Out, *May 1992*

MERENGUE

A dance-music style from the Hispanic Caribbean, merengue enjoyed a local revival in the 1970s, and during the late 1980s formed part of the WORLD MUSIC crossover, helped by stars such as Juan Luis Guerra of the Dominican Republic. The music began in Haiti and Dominica; its name (pronounced 'mare-eng-gay') is a Spanish rendering of the French meringue.

MERRY PRANKSTERS

A group of pioneering hedonists who bridged the late BEAT and early HIPPIE subcultures, the Merry Pranksters were the companions of Ken Kesey, author of *One Flew Over the Cuckoo's Nest*. In 1964 the Pranksters, including Neal Cassady, Jack Kerouac's mentor and model for the Beat Generation, painted a second-hand school bus in PSYCHEDELIC patterns, named it 'Furthur' (sic), and drove across America, ritually ingesting hallucinogens as they went. The journey was celebrated in Tom Wolfe's reportage *The Electric Kool-Aid Acid Test*, and provided a first model for a mobile, tribal lifestyle carried on outside orthodox society that later encompassed the Manson family, among others. Various of the Merry Pranksters continued to be active in the COUNTERCULTURE until the mid-1970s.

MERSEY BOOM

As a cosmopolitan seaport with direct links to the USA and a local Irish/English tradition of folksong and poetry, Liverpool provided a springboard for the international pop-culture explosion of the early 1960s that accompanied the success of the Beatles. The music of the so-called Mersey Boom (also known as the Liverpool Sound and, when it encompassed musicians from other regions, as the BEAT BOOM), which peaked in 1963 and 1964, was a blend of the middle-of-the-road Anglo-American harmony pop song with harder, guitar-based ROCK 'N' ROLL and R & B as played by such American artists as Chuck Berry, Buddy Holly and the Everly Brothers. There were also echoes of Irish folk melodies in many of the first wave of Mersey songs. A network of clubs, coffee bars and dance halls (already providing a milieu for jazz and poetry), together with local showbiz impresarios, helped to launch the local 'beat groups', who included Gerry and the Pacemakers, Billy J. Kramer and the Dakotas, Freddy and the Dreamers, the Swinging Blue Jeans and the Merseybeats, along with an estimated 400 others.

Riding the same wave of media interest in Liverpool were the chanteuse Cilla Black (formerly hat-check girl at the Cavern Club) and the comedian Jimmy Tarbuck. Shortly after the first wave came the Liverpool poets Adrian Henri, Roger McGough and Brian Patten, whose HIP, sentimental style paralleled that of the music; they were followed by the pop/poetry ensembles of the Scaffold and the Liverpool Scene. Of the original Mersey groups, none but the Beatles progressed musically beyond the harmonized pop song, although some survived as crooners or novelty acts into the 1990s.

MICROSKIRT

See MINISKIRT.

MIDI

A skirt style that (re-) appeared at the end of 1968 with a new name, coined in reaction to the MINISKIRT and the MAXI. The midi failed to catch on in mass markets at the time and the name fell into disuse, although calf-length skirts did make a comeback after 1971.

- *Tricelon crêpe halter-neck midi dress has a deep neckline plunging down to its empire waistline, with a bold floral design in brilliant red, blue, yellow and black.*

19 magazine, January 1971

MIDS

See MODS.

MIND GYMS

A Californian concept of the early 1990s, the Mind Gym is the setting for mental AEROBICS, with or without the aid of SMART DRUGS. The idea is the result of the convergence of YUPPIE café culture, the Eighties' obsession with personal improvement, the NEW AGE concern with physical and psychic health, and the vogue for intellectualism, or at least pseudo-intellectualism, that emerged on both sides of the Atlantic after the demise of the 'enterprise culture'. It is a contrived salon at which ideas can be discussed, problems solved and information exchanged. Conversations may be stimulated by 'animators' or 'facilitators', by participants brainstorming and by so-called psychoactive drinks and drugs. A London version of the Mind Gym, the Ideas Café, was staged in an existing venue in Covent Garden in 1992. Meanwhile, style magazines promoted the new fashion for thinking, although generally confining themselves to lists of the 'brainiest people in London' or fashion spreads for the new intelligentsia.

- *. . . the previous Ideas Café was a bit of a disaster: Einstein hardly got a look in, because networkers would keep swapping business cards, and . . . the ideas people had too many ideas about what the Ideas Café should have ideas about.*

Polly Samson, Sunday Times, July 1992

MINIMALISM

A term applied in the world of fine art and sculpture to a tendency that arose during the mid-1960s and which flourished for about a decade. Minimalist works, whether in two or three dimensions, had in common a reduction to simple, abstract forms and a rejection of explicit message or narrative. They did not exalt the personality of the artist or his or her subject; nor did they intentionally seek to celebrate rational, bourgeois cultural values, although like most supposedly subversive avant-garde art, Minimalism's gestures were made within the constraints of the international fine-art market and gallery network.

Viewed in retrospect, Minimalism could be seen as a bridge between MODERNISM (including 'orthodox' abstract sculpture, HARD EDGE and POST-PAINTERLY canvases) and the CONCEPTUAL ART (including LAND ART) that dominated from the later 1970s. The original American Minimalists included Carl Andre (whose installation of 120 bricks, entitled *Equivalent VIII*, caused controversy when exhibited at the Tate Gallery, London, in 1976), Sol Lewitt, Robert Morris, Dan Flavin and Donald Judd. In Britain, exponents included Barry Flanegan and Richard Long, as well as the Art and Language Group. Minimalist art objects, which could include ready-mades and constructions made without the artist's hands-on involvement, tended more and more towards the intangible, finally encompassing ideas, texts or plans for unrealized works, thereby merging with Conceptualism.

The adoption of Minimalism as a fashionable term in art led to its application in other fields, notably in music, where it was used to denote both the avant-garde REPETITIVE MUSIC of Terry Riley, LaMonte Young, Steve Reich, Harold Budd, Philip Glass, Michael Nyman and others, and the deliberately simplistic three-chord ROCK of PUNK pioneers such as the Ramones. Around 1980 the Minimalist label was transferred to the fields of design, fashion and interior decoration, where it denoted a conscious austerity in forms and colours, often consisting of an emphasis on black, an imitation of supposedly ZEN motifs and/or an embracing of uncluttered, impersonal HIGH TECH effects.

- *Most marked is an exceptionally elegant minimalism, the deployment of lines, grids, dots in sensitive arrangements, at times so delicate as to be nearly invisible. It is a style stripped to the bone, down to the skeletal, elemental, visual structure.*
  Marina Vaizey, Sunday Times, June 1974

- *Minimalist art still offered some physical object for contemplation, but the 'information' it carried was as limited as possible.*
  Robert Hewison, Too Much, 1986

MINISKIRT

The 'Sloppy Joe' sweater favoured by female Beatniks (see BEAT
MOVEMENT) and EXISTENTIALISTS had descended past the thigh –
sometimes worn as a dress over leggings or leotard, belted or
otherwise – and the *haute couture* skirt had risen to the knee,
when Mary Quant, owner of the Bazaar boutique since 1955, seized
the initiative in promoting the short skirt previously worn by a
generation of pre-teenage girls as the fashion statement of 1964. It
quickly became an emblem of 'swinging London'. At the same time,
the Paris-based fashion designer André Courrèges was introducing
geometric MODERNIST-inspired ensembles for women that also
included belted hipster skirts ending several inches above the knee.
The resultant miniskirt was a potent symbol of female emancipation
and exhibitionism that also allowed physical freedom of movement.
Its ambiguity was compounded by the sexual vulnerability it
suggested, and the child-woman image it conjured up.

The miniskirt was pioneered by young women in the UK. In 1965
the English model Jean Shrimpton caused a stir when she wore
one at Melbourne racecourse in Australia. By 1969 it had become a
worldwide orthodoxy. Fashion evolution and the search for novelty
resulted in a prompt and short-lived backlash represented by the
MAXI and the MIDI in 1968 and 1969. In 1970, however, the mini
evolved into the microskirt, which was so short that it was usually
worn like a tunic over matching shorts, and in turn mutated into HOT
PANTS. PUNKS reintroduced the mini, often in leather or in the form
of a kilt, at the end of 1976. At first an avant-garde minority taste,
it grew in popularity, rivalling longer PENCIL SKIRTS and changing
from a flared to a figure-hugging shape. By 1985 the miniskirt was
back as the ubiquitous standard for younger women. Longer skirts
for everyday wear remained marginalized for the next seven years,
despite the attempts of designers to reintroduce them.

- *Of all the couturiers now working in Paris, Courrèges is the one
  whose designs are really revolutionary. He questions some of the
  basic conventions of women's dress: why should skirts go down to
  the knee?*

  Observer, 7 March 1965

- *. . . punk girls salvaged shockingly lurid lurex minis of the sort*

*worn in Italian 'jet-set' films of the mid-1960s . . . they also
reclaimed tarty fishnet stockings, black plastic miniskirts and, of
course, ski-pants . . .*
    Angela McRobbie, Zoot Suits and Second-hand Dresses, *1989*

MIXING
See SCRATCHING; RAP; REMIXING.

MOCKNEY
Mockney – a blend of 'mock' and 'cockney' – referred in the 1950s
to the often hilarious attempts of classically trained or upper- and
middle-class actresses and actors to render the London working-class
accent. The nickname was similarly applied to the upper-class
Bohemian habit of affecting some elements of cockney pronunciation.
This tendency of the two ends of the class spectrum to converge
in some vowel sounds and tricks of usage had been noted by social
commentators since the 19th century. Mockney was much heard in
the would-be classless 'swinging London' of the 1960s, sometimes in
the form of a parody, as adopted by Mick Jagger, the Rolling Stones
vocalist, who deliberately exaggerated his authentic outer-London
accent. The SLOANE RANGERS of the late 1970s generally adhered
to the so-called 'received pronunciation' or 'RP' of the traditional
public schools, but occasionally inserted the London 'glottal stop' –
the swallowing of the '-t' or '-tt' in 'got' or 'bottle', for example. This
tendency, which can be heard in the speech of the Princess of Wales,
in contrast with the pedantic muted RP of her husband, increased
among YUPPIE and educated media circles during the 1980s and
early Nineties. Although often derided, contemporary mockney
probably represents a genuine attempt to limit the ability of language
to define and maintain social differences in Britain.

MODERNISM
Modernism describes a general trend permeating all areas of cultural
expression from the turn of the century until the end of the 1950s.
Loosely, it was a reaction against the Christian bourgeois certainties
of the 19th century and a rejection of classicism and realism in
favour of experimentation with new forms. Modernism imposed

a self-conscious cult of the new in fine art, often characterized by abstraction and a moving away from familiar forms through Cubism, Futurism, Constructivism and Vorticism to the ABSTRACT EXPRESSIONISM and HARD EDGE schools of the post-Second World War years. Other avant-garde forms such as Dada and Surrealism fit less easily under the Modernist umbrella. Modernist architecture and design relied on stark, geometric forms, with the Bauhaus exporting its precepts from Middle Europe to the USA. In Britain, Modernist styles, particularly versions of the NEW BRUTALISM, dominated public architecture into the late 1970s. In music, it encompassed the very different approaches of Stravinsky, Schoenberg, John Cage and Stockhausen, the atonal, MUSIQUE CONCRÈTE and FREE JAZZ. In literature, the Modernist label is generally applied to writers such as James Joyce, Virginia Woolf, Ezra Pound and T. S. Eliot; more recently Beckett and the dramatists associated with the THEATRE OF THE ABSURD have been included.

By the Seventies many expressions of what can be described as Modernism were being perceived as sterile, clichéd and élitist, and the preoccupation with outmoded ideas of technological Utopias, the assumption of linear progress and the inaccessible debates on the special status of 'art' and 'artist' had alienated many. Ironically, the world itself took on overtones of a dated orthodoxy. As early as 1964 the American Marxist critic Fredric Jameson had coined the word POST-MODERNISM and, despite its being even more imprecise than its predecessor, by the 1980s this term was generally accepted as a description of the current Western cultural condition. Quite when in the various arts Modernism gave way to Post-Modernism is the subject of much debate. Movements such as POP ART and the NOUVEAU ROMAN are held by some to belong to the former tendency, whilst others ascribe them to the latter. In fact, they probably mark a transitional stage of the 1960s and 1970s, since when the old Modernist/traditionalist distinction has been swallowed up in the confusion of styles, forms and concepts competing in the so-called HYPERREALITY of CONSUMER capitalism.

MODS

The Mod movement flourished in Britain between 1962 and the end of 1966, when most remaining Mods metamorphosed into HIPPIES, or into the first SKINHEADS. Mod styles in a simplified or debased form were revived in 1976 at the time of the PUNK explosion, and a small number of self-styled Mods were in evidence throughout the 1980s. In 1962, some young people in London's East End and Soho (at first often the sons and daughters of Italian and Jewish families) were adopting Italian and French fashions in clothes, shoes and hair, displaying a most un-British obsession with style. In fact, the 'Italian look' – 'Roman' hairstyles for men, lightweight shiny suits, narrow ties, Vespa scooters – had been around since about 1958 among a small élite of art students and modern jazz (see FREE JAZZ; TRAD) aficionados. The spread of the new cosmopolitan look was the result of the new affluence and independence of working-class and lower-middle-class teenagers, and was a reaction against the prevailing drabness of the 1950s, an era when fashion, such as it was, was dominated by upper-class modes based on military styles for men and adapted from *haute couture* for women. The formality and sophistication of the growing trend also contradicted the hard-edged uncouth and now outdated Americanisms of the ton-up boys (see ROCKERS), ROCK 'N' ROLL enthusiasts and remaining TEDDY BOYS.

In 1963 this metropolitan movement, whose adherents called themselves 'Modernists', later shortened to 'Mods', spread beyond the city centre and first reached the attention of the press. In central London during 1964 and 1965, Mod trendsetters (referred to in their own circles as 'Stylists' or 'Faces') presided in discothèques, coffee bars and boutiques over a frantic succession of short-lived fads in clothing and dance. Elsewhere, less sophisticated imitators (less radical Mods were known as 'Mids', stragglers as 'Tickets') settled on a stereotype appearance of short bouffant hair for men, worn with brightly coloured Italian casual or American Ivy League styles, whilst their female counterparts favoured severely geometric cuts in hair and clothing, and heavy, contrasting make-up. In 1965 images adopted via art schools from POP and OP ART were added to the Mod repertoire. The Mod influence had polarized working-class and lower-middle-class youth culture by 1964, and for the press and many adults the most abiding memories of the period are the battles at seaside resorts between self-styled Mods wearing American army parkas and riding scooters, and motorcycle-riding Rockers who still held to the American 'rebel' uniform of leather jacket and jeans. These rival tribes also disagreed in their musical tastes, Mods dancing to American SOUL music or Jamaican BLUEBEAT and SKA, Rockers to white American Rock 'n' Roll. Pep pills and alcohol

fuelled the Mod lifestyle, as opposed to the cannabis smoked by their
BEAT contemporaries.

The Mod phenomenon marked the CONSUMERIST emancipation of
working-class teenagers and the end of the dictation of fashion by
High Society. It was narcissistic and apolitical, but subversive in its
implied contempt for class values and its absolute cult of novelty.
Once popularized, the movement quickly changed from an élitist
avant-garde statement to a conformist and eventually reactionary
gang subculture (Skinhead racism is ironic in the light of the Mods'
admiration for black music and style). The best-known pop groups
associated with Mod were the Who and the Small Faces, and in its
second incarnation in the 1970s, the Jam. In the 1960s, in the absence
of the affordable technology that later allowed INDIE record labels
and FANZINES, the only media outlet for Mod expression was the cult
TV music programme *Ready Steady Go!*

- *When we found out that Mods were just as conformist and
  reactionary as anyone else, we moved on from that phase,
  too.*
  Pete Townshend, Rave *magazine, February 1966*

MOHICAN

The hairstyle known in the USA as a Mohawk, and in the UK and
France as a Mohican, although identified with a particular period of
the 1970s, had been adopted as a gesture of individualism since the
1950s. First observed among groups of American servicemen during
the Second World War as a variant form of the crop or CREW CUT, it
surfaced periodically in newspaper reports in Britain throughout the
1950s as individual schoolboys partially shaved their heads in order
to outrage parents or teachers (in the USA, a female example was
reported in 1951). Probably the most radical hairstyle possible – a
bald head can be explained away, long hair can be tied back – the
Mohican was a logical choice for the extremist exponents of PUNK
anti-culture. Previous versions had tended to be shortish geometric
ridges; the Punks combined the bristling SPIKE-TOP look with shaved
sides and back to produce a high plume or series of pointed cones,
often lacquered and/or coloured. Outrageous in 1977, Mohicans,
now worn by both sexes, had become almost commonplace in parts
of urban Britain by 1981. They were frozen as a key element in the

iconography of Punk, and hence of modern folklore, appearing on postcards and in guidebooks.

The original Mohicans were an Amerindian people who inhabited the upper Hudson River Valley in the northeast of what became the United States. Like both the Mohawks, who lived in the area of modern New York State, and the Iroquois, they sometimes wore topknots as decoration, initiation symbols or for hygienic purposes, in common with other tribal societies worldwide. The modern image of the Mohican derives from the stories of James Fenimore Cooper (particularly the comic-book versions of the 1950s) and from the portrayal of Indian warriors in the DAVY CROCKETT films.

MONETARISM

Based on the 18th-century writings of the Scottish philosopher David Hume and propounded in the 20th century by the American economist Milton Friedman, the economic theories known as monetarism came to the attention of non-specialists in the industrialized West in the early 1980s. The views of Friedman and the Chicago School were the intellectual basis for the right-wing backlash against Keynesianism, and for the free-market ethos behind both the REAGANOMICS and THATCHERISM that dominated the decade.

Crudely put, monetarism proposes that governments should strictly regulate the money supply in a national economy, otherwise leaving market forces to bring about a healthy and dynamic equilibrium. One of the most controversial corollaries of a monetarist policy is its tolerance of a certain natural level of unemployment. The notion that the theory was associated with a lack of social compassion and with authoritarian political regimes such as that of post-Allende Chile, where it had been tried out, provoked hostility on the Left. The word monetarism began to be employed as a catch-all description for all radical Conservative supply-side economic policies but in both Britain and the USA a strict monetarist approach had in fact been abandoned by the mid-Eighties, and the term itself had ceased to be a buzz word by the time of the stock-market crashes of 1987. The moralistic element in monetarist and NEW RIGHT thinking, particularly among British exponents, re-emerged in Conservative criticism of the increased public spending of John Major's administration after 1990.

- *... the monetarist and explicitly authoritarian solutions to the national crisis which Thatcherism offered ... the essentially Hobbesian view of a self-interested and atomised society ...*
  Dick Hebdige, Hiding in the Light, *1988*

MONKEY BOOTS

Tough, lightweight rubber-soled ankle boots, laced almost to the toe, monkey boots enjoyed a brief cult status among late first-wave MODS in the 1960s. They were then adopted by proto-SKINHEADS as an alternative to the emblematic heavy BOVVER BOOTS before both were ousted by DMS in the early 1970s. Brightly coloured versions were worn by HIPPIES from 1971 to about 1974. In 1979 they were adopted as part of an anti-fashion female uniform (usually including blue jeans or overalls and short hair) favoured by FEMINISTS, leftists and social workers, amongst others. They were celebrated by the south London post-PUNK all-girl group the Gymslips in their anthem to the RENEES in 1980. Maintaining a low profile during the remainder of the style-conscious Eighties, the monkey boot reappeared as an essential component of the TRAVELLER and CRUSTY festival-goer's outfit as worn in 1992.

MONOBOARDING

See SNOW SURFING.

MOONIES

The nickname given to followers of the South Korean Reverend Sun Myung Moon, founder of the Worldwide Unification Church, a sect created in 1954. Moon, an industrialist and arms manufacturer, promoted himself as a religious messiah who had been entrusted with the task of uniting the world in one sinless family. The substitute family, group chanting, prayer and singing were the appeal of Moon's Christian-based ethos. His own family was claimed to be the perfect model and adherents were required to live communally and donate their worldly goods to the movement. The Moonies based themselves in the USA, where the Reverend's ideology accorded with local right-wing extremism. His vast wealth, overt espousal of ultra-conservatism and crusade against Communism, his rumoured links with the CIA and his brief imprisonment for tax evasion all provoked vitriolic attacks on his organization. Deprogramming agencies kidnapped some of his mainly young followers in order to reunite them with their natural families. In the early 1990s, in spite of sustained press criticism, the Moonies were covertly sponsoring political and social events in Britain and elsewhere.

MORPHIC RESONANCE

See NEW SCIENCE.

MOSHING

Moshing is dancing in a packed scrimmage to HEAVY METAL, HARD CORE or any other fast, loud ROCK music. This activity, which is more a form of energetic communal writhing than dancing, was adopted by fans of HARD ROCK during the late 1980s as a successor to HEAD-BANGING, SLAM-DANCING and the playing of imaginary guitars (see AIR GUITAR). As part of the experience, members of the audience will often climb on to the stage and then hurl themselves bodily into the crush, a practice known, predictably, as stage-diving. The word 'mosh' is an invention derived from such standard terms as jostle, mash, mass, squash, crush and thrust.

- *In front of the stage a herd of boys and girls . . . have commenced 'moshing': hurling themselves about with arrythmic abandon, slamming into one another and falling down . . . Behind them, slightly older teenage males are diligently headbanging.*
  Zoë Heller, Independent on Sunday, 6 September 1992

MOTHERFUCKERS

Taking their name from the anti-authority COUNTERCULTURE slogan 'Up against the Wall, Motherfucker!', the Motherfuckers were a street gang which evolved out of the Students for a Democratic Society movement and the New York dada activist group, the Black Mask. While the latter had disrupted artistic events, the new grouping attacked meetings of the non-libertarian NEW LEFT and campaigned against HIPPIE entrepreneurs who they accused of profiteering from the ALTERNATIVE SOCIETY. In 1968 they set fire to the accumulated garbage following a strike in New York City and attacked firefighters; in the same year they began a series of bomb attacks on business premises on the East and West Coasts of the US. The Motherfuckers, who also called themselves the Werewolves on occasion, were never more than a handful of extremists, some of whom were absorbed into the WEATHERMEN.

MOUNTAIN BIKES

The mountain-bike craze began during the late 1970s in California when backpackers and surfers bought rally bikes or CUSTOMIZED touring bicycles for use over rough terrain and sand-dunes, although this was a practice that had existed among teenagers since the 1950s or earlier. Manufacturers reacted to the trend, which had quickly spread to urban stylists and the ecologically aware, and the mountain bike, with its multigears, thick, deep-tread tyres and heavy, strengthened frame, became a middle-class fad of the mid-Eighties. In Britain the Muddy Fox company launched a relatively cheap version of the mountain bike deliberately marketed at fashion-conscious weekend bikers, who eagerly embraced the accessories (Lycra shorts, wraparound goggles, neckerchiefs, BUMBAGS, etc.) and the athletic pose. Although popular with city-centre couriers, the mountain bike was never comfortable or efficient for casual on-road use, whilst the less expensive versions were likewise unsuited to real mountainsides. In the early 1990s the vogue began to wane and in 1992 Muddy Fox went out of business, leaving the market to the American specialists and the downmarket mass-producers.

MUPPETS

The puppet characters created in the 1970s by Jim Henson for the American educational children's TV show *Sesame Street* became a favourite among pre-teen children in the tradition of earlier TROLLS, GONKS, WOMBLES and SMURFS. (In British slang usage the word itself was taken as an unaffectionate term for a retarded, incapacitated or grotesque person.) Following their worldwide TV popularity, the Muppets were merchandised exhaustively: feature films based on the same characters (including the seminal *Pigs in Space*) inspired a new tradition of increasingly sophisticated cine-animation.

MUSIQUE CONCRÈTE

In Europe, the word 'concrete' was widely used in a MODERNIST
artistic context from the 1930s (as in CONCRETE POETRY, for instance).
It generally indicated a rendering of an intellectual concept or notion
in a visible, tactile and/or audible form and usually implied an
element of abstraction, mathematical precision and impersonality.
Applied to music in the late 1940s, the term labelled an avant-garde
or experimental process whereby music was created using real or
'found' sounds, such as birdsong (used by Messiaen among others),
voices, traffic noise and machinery, which were then recorded and
processed. As the name suggests, the method was pioneered in
France, by Pierre Schaeffer, Jean Barraque, Edgar Varèse and others.
It was an influential and early form of electronic manipulation of
music. When the journalist Bernard Levin was thought to have
slighted the genre, the husband of a practitioner physically assaulted
him on air during the TV SATIRE show *That Was the Week That Was*.

MY LITTLE PONY

A craze among pre-teen girls in 1983, My Little Pony was a toy
designed especially to feature tactile attractions. The Pony's plastic
skin texture was chosen to provide maximum pleasure to the touch,
while the long silken mane and tail were for caressing and combing.
The miniature Pony was un-lifelike (some had detachable hooves),
but served as an idealized object of affection. As a 'promotional toy'
or manufactured and merchandised fad, the Ponies were a milestone
in 1980s mass-marketing.

NAMBY

See NIMBY.

NATION OF ISLAM

See BLACK POWER.

NEOCLASSICISM

Although the revival and reworking of classical forms has been a
recurrent feature of 20th-century architecture, the resultant styles
have varied greatly, from the urban office architecture of turn-of-
the-century New York and Chicago through to the 1930s totalitarian
neoclassicism of Italy, Germany and Russia. Since 1945, the
best-known examples of neoclassical architecture have come from the
more conservative wing of the POST-MODERN movement, including
Allen Greenberg in the USA and Quinlan Terry and Raymond Erith
in the UK. While many so-called Post-Modernist buildings mix
in classical components among the jokes, parodies and jumble of
references, in contrast Quinlan Terry, for example, has produced a
reinterpretation based almost completely on classical models, but
filtered through Palladian and 18th- and 19th-century English town
architecture, albeit highly coloured and with appended 'heritage'
effects such as cobbles and flint walls. His Richmond Riverside
development won praise from Prince Charles and other opponents of
HIGH TECH and MODERNISM, but was derided by others as a clumsy,
timid pastiche.

Neoclassicism proved to be the most accessible and publicly
acceptable form of Post-Modernism, in keeping with the romantic
conservatism and concern for heritage shared by YUPPIES, the NEW
RIGHT, YOUNG FOGEYS and NEW GEORGIANS during the early 1980s.

As such it permeated the whole field of decoration and design, manifesting itself in the use of framed architectural plans as wall decorations, the increased popularity of classical or reproduction busts, statuary and sculptures, and the inclusion of classical motifs in curtains and other textiles (typified by Timney Fowler's best-selling lines of 1985) and even in clothing and stationery. By the early Nineties, neoclassical had become a visual cliché, but the underlying identification with historical notions of geometric harmony and order, with their overtones of austerity, power and continuity, remained potent.

- *Recently in the news for the drubbing his design for the extension to the Tate Gallery received, Stirling's free-style classicism is manifested by conjugating the authenticity of the Roman amphitheatre into the clean-cut post-modernity of the walls. Quite!*
  Blitz, October 1987

NEO-FAUVISM

A name given by some to a trend in graphic design and illustration appearing in the early 1980s, particularly in Britain, where it was associated with nightclub and DANCEFLOOR cultures, as evoked in posters, record covers, magazines and clothing. Like the original Fauvism (from the French *fauve* meaning wild beast, referring to the artists rather than the subject-matter), the style depended on a vivid primitivism executed in primary colours. The new version was a reaction against the MINIMALIST and monochrome aspects of PUNK-era visuals, as well as the NEOCLASSICISM embraced by some designers and decorators. It incorporated currently fashionable African and Latin American motifs and influences.

NEO-GEO

A fashionable genre in New York painting of the 1980s, Neo-Geo was a simplistic abstract style using mainly vivid primary colours and, as the name suggests, geometric forms. The Neo-Geo artists were controversial not for the content of their work, but for the fact that much of it was painted to order, sometimes by anonymous helpers. The style was deliberately commercial and self-aware, rather than a pastiche or revival.

NEURONAUTS

A rather pretentious and probably ephemeral name adopted by the users of SMART DRUGS in the early 1990s to lend a science-fiction bravado to their activities. Through the analogy with cosmonaut and astronaut, neuronaut (from the Greek *neuron*, meaning nerve or sinew, and *nautes*, meaning sailor) conjures up an image of a pioneer experimenting with the acids that supposedly enhance the firing of electronic impulses between the synapses of the brain.

NEW AGE

A catch-all phrase encompassing the practices, concerns and beliefs of the 1980s incarnation of the 1960s HIPPIE culture, New Age refers to the belief held in the late Sixties that a new era of enlightenment, sometimes known as the 'Age of Aquarius', was beginning or had begun. The values of the earlier COUNTERCULTURE were maintained in Britain by the TRAVELLERS among others; in the US they became part of the self-improvement and consciousness-raising culture flourishing in particular on the West Coast, but adapted to a new CONSUMERIST, unalienated ethos. HOLISTIC MEDICINE, progressive THERAPIES, unorthodox healing techniques, occultism and interest in Oriental and tribal spiritual traditions were some of the ingredients of the New Age movement. The term began to be heard in the mid-1970s, in preference to the rather discriminatory 'fringe' and 'alternative'. In the early Nineties there were signs of a convergence between various strands of progressive adult and youth cultures, taking place in particular on the summer festival circuit, where Travellers, RAVERS and CRUSTIES met with the newly defined WESSEX MAN and the more libertarian members of the MEN'S MOVEMENT. Among the many pastimes indulged in were shamanistic drumming (see SHAMANISM), dowsing, TREE-SNIFFING, WICCA, worm-charming and casting the TAROT or RUNES.

- *Totnes in Devon has been called the Alternative Capital of Britain, but here New Ageism nestles rather uneasily against ordinary life, with the Arcturus alternative bookshop and crystal distribution centre tragically situated opposite the butcher.*
  Sunday Times, *3 May 1992*

NEW AGE MUSIC

So-called NEW AGE Music evolved out of the progressive instrumental
music of the late HIPPIE era, with recordings such as the best-selling
Tubular Bells and *Hergest Ridge* by Mike Oldfield, and the later
electronic compositions of Tangerine Dream, Vangelis, Jean-Michel
Jarre and Klaus Schulze. In Britain from 1976 Brian Eno popularized
a slightly more cerebral REPETITIVE MUSIC, published with similar
artists on his Obscure label and referred to by Eno as 'Ambient
Music'. In the USA these influences were blended with an admixture
of soft jazz, jazz ROCK and Indian, African and other 'ethnic' sounds,
and the resultant genre was marketed under the New Age banner.

A homogenized, soothing and subdued synthesis of earlier
more serious and subversive forms, New Age Music nevertheless
provoked strong reactions in many critics – in particular devotees
of Sixties Rock or PUNK, who pronounced it bland, 'easy-listening',
'wallpaper music'. The success of New Age Music in the 1980s, sold
on labels such as Windham Hill, Venture and Coda, accompanied
the increasing dominance of high technology – for example,
sophisticated electronic recording techniques and the vastly
improved sound quality of the compact disc. It was sold in the USA
as part of an affluent 'Californian' lifestyle of health food, personal
fitness and spiritual consumerism; a neo-Hippie hedonism, stripped
of its radical COUNTERCULTURE overtones. The music was designed to
contribute to an environment, rather than to agitate or narrate. Filling
a market niche between Adult-Oriented Rock (AOR) and WORLD
MUSIC, New Age Music sold well if not spectacularly in the UK,
appealing to an element of the 'thirty-something' generation of the
late 1980s and early 1990s.

- *Many is the article I have read, and indeed written, that looks in
  vain for new lusts, violence and social unrest and instead lights
  upon New Age Music in a condemnatory fury.*
  David Toop, The Face, February 1988

- *New Age Music proved that people can listen to quite boring
  material.*
  Brian Eno, interviewed on The Thing Is . . ., Channel 4, May 1992

NEW AGE TRAVELLERS

See TRAVELLERS.

NEW BRUTALISM

The origin of the phrase 'New Brutalist' is disputed. The Swedish
architect Hans Asplund claimed to have coined it in January 1950,
but other authorities ascribe it to the Smithson family (Alison
and Peter Smithson were among the main proponents of the style)
in 1954. The term contrasts with 'New Empiricism' and 'New
Humanism', two names for the moderate style that dominated
public architecture in England and Sweden at the beginning of the
1950s. The New Brutalism was an uncompromising promotion of
stark, monolithic structures expressing their functions and locations
without ornament or façade. The seeming anti-aesthetic of the
approach was actually based on an ethos influenced by the postwar
industrial wasteland coupled with EXISTENTIALISM and earlier
influences such as 18th-century classicism, 19th-century engineering
projects and 20th-century rationalist and functionalist architecture.
The term New Brutalism was later generalized to refer to any
undecorated MODERNIST or concrete building, from the shoddily built
residential tower blocks of the 1960s through the city skyscrapers of
Colonel Richard Seifert and some of the less sensitive works of Sir
Basil Spence to the National Theatre complex designed by Sir Denys
Lasdun.

- *... it is hard to define it as architecture at all. It is a formalist
  structure which will please only the architects, and a small coterie
  concerned more with satisfying their personal design sense than with
  achieving a humanist, functional architecture.*

  Architects' Journal, *1954*

- *There is no doubt in my mind that anyone who suggests people
  should actually have to live in a building whose style is described as
  New Brutalist is a danger to society.*

  Reader's letter, Independent, *18 February 1992*

NEW GEORGIANS

A mid-1980s phenomenon in Britain, the New Georgians were a
disparate group of fairly affluent aesthetes (overlapping with the
YOUNG FOGEY tendency) who renovated late 18th- and early 19th-
century houses with meticulous attention to authenticity. The New
Georgian pose (perhaps prompted in some cases by reading David
Watkin's *Architecture and Morality*) was taken to extremes by some
revivalists, who affected a version of archaic costume in keeping with
the period and eschewed electric light, central heating and 20th-
century plumbing. This stance was partly based on practicalities: the
opening up of east London had revealed the existence of unreclaimed
and affordable town houses of this most sought-after period, but
total modernization would have been prohibitively costly, as well
as offensive, to these conservative- and heritage-conscious design
enthusiasts. Individuals categorized as New Georgians at one time
or another included John Martin Robinson, Gavin Stamp, Stephen
Calloway and Quinlan Terry.

NEW LAD

See NEW MAN.

NEW LEFT

A blanket term applied to the many strands of leftist thinking
that appeared in Europe and the USA during the late 1950s and
which differed from or challenged traditional Labour-movement or
syndicalist socialism and doctrinaire Leninist–Stalinist versions
of Marxism. The disillusion with Russian-dominated Communist
ideology and practice triggered by the invasion of Hungary in
1956 was compounded by a growing libertarian spirit that led to
re-examinations of Marx's earlier writings and to the ideas of Hegel,
Trotsky, Bakunin, Gramsci and Freud, amongst others. In the USA
the New Left encompassed the radicals involved in the Civil Rights
Movement and the later anti-Vietnam War activists, as well as the
gurus of the new libertarianism, notably Herbert Marcuse.

In Britain, however, the phrase New Left specifically denoted an
intellectual tendency that was crystallized by the founding in 1960
of the magazine *New Left Review* (from a merger of two little-known

journals, *The University and Left Review* and *The New Reasoner*)
under the editorship of Stuart Hall. Apart from Hall, prominent
figures in the New Left included Raymond Williams, E. P. Thompson,
Richard Hoggart, Juliet Mitchell and Tom Nairn. The highly educated
middle-class historians, sociologists, writers and critics who were
central to the New Left were a small élite, but the indirect influence
of their precepts and assumptions was powerful in the social
sciences, the arts and media, and especially in the field of education
during the later 1960s and 1970s. Even if they were without a
coordinated stance (the progressive Left was always prone to feuds
and factionalism) and lacked popular support and the glamour
of their French contemporaries (among whom Louis Althusser
probably exercised the most influence in the Anglophone world),
these thinkers did establish left-wing philosophies as the dominant
intellectual fashion of the time, inspiring the student activists of
the late Sixties as well as making the practice of cultural and media
studies academically respectable in Britain for the first time.

As a force for overt social change, however, the British New Left
was ineffectual. In the early 1960s it was hampered by innate British
conservatism and by its own diffuse nature; in the late Sixties it
failed to come to grips with the arrival of hedonistic, apolitical
HIPPIE ideals. In the early 1970s its approaches were circumvented
by the new issue politics of FEMINISM, GAY LIBERATION and, slightly
later, the GREEN MOVEMENT. At the end of the 1970s the increasingly
belligerent 'enterprise culture' of the new CONSUMERIST and populist
Conservatism was ready to dismiss the ideas of the Left without
engaging with them. The failure of successive Labour Party election
campaigns further diminished the vestiges of New Left influence.

- *These young people, unlike the supernumeraries at the 'Black
  Dwarf', were not wearing the costumes, hair styles and fashion
  accessories of the pace-setting New Left. They were dressed in plain,
  ordinary clothes . . .*
  Sunday Times *magazine, 8 December 1968*

- *The historical context of the Old Left was the abundance of
  poverty: that of the New Left, the poverty of abundance.*
  John Patrick Diggins, The Rise and Fall of the American Left, *1991*

NEW LONDON SCHOOL

See SCHOOL OF LONDON.

NEW LOOK

The 'New Look' was the name bestowed by the American press on a revolution in women's *haute couture* that took place in 1947. The sensational change in style was ascribed to Christian Dior, whose collection (originally known as the 'Corolle Line') abandoned the relative austerity and simplicity of wartime fashions in favour of an extravagant and artificial romantic effect that emphasized the female figure and was achieved by natural shoulder lines, accentuated waists, full skirts and lavish use of expensive materials (the latter was seen as an act of provocation by some British commentators). In fact Dior's move was a reintroduction of a tendency begun by Balmain, Balenciaga and others in Paris during the late Thirties but abandoned due to the exigencies of the war. The élitist opulence of the New Look dominated high fashion until 1955, when Dior introduced the more severe A-LINE. In mainstream female fashion full skirts with figure-hugging tops continued to be worn into the early 1960s. Detached from its original dressmaking context, the phrase New Look became a reusable catch phrase for the Fifties and Sixties.

NEW MAN

Originally a concept in Nietzschean and Marxist philosophy and a phrase used (by Fidel Castro among others) to describe the unalienated, reinvented ideal human being (not necessarily male), the idea of the New Man was adopted by FEMINISTS in the 1970s. This New Man was an ideal reconstructed from a woman's perspective: he was sensitive and non-exploitative, and 'househusband' and 'role-reversal' were the buzz words associated with him at the time. The New Man label became a cliché of the mid- and late 1980s, when it was picked up by social commentators, the mass media and, perhaps most significantly, by marketing and merchandising experts.

Having first appeared in the USA, chiming with NEW AGE ideals after the demise of the aggressive and competitive YUPPIE role model, the New Man was promoted, then questioned and subsequently ridiculed by many in Britain, not necessarily from a sexist standpoint, but from a suspicion that outside fashionable or leftist circles the changes in men's behaviour did not extend beyond a new willingness to use cosmetics (a tendency that in any case dwindled in a recession). Upper-middle-class male commentators such as the youngish journalists David Thomas and Toby Young confirmed that in their milieux at least traditional male stereotypes had been upset. Meanwhile, other style writers coined the term New Lads to describe a generation of young men who adopted a New Man veneer for opportunistic motives, and informal studies suggested that sport, ownership of consumer durables and a predatory interest in women remained the priorities of a majority of men under forty-five. In 1992 the four UK men's magazines abandoned the New Man to stage a circulation war based on a revival of machismo. Meanwhile, in the USA the concept of the New Boy had been invoked: the male child unconditioned by older masculine stereotypes.

- *Judging by the number of words which spew forth on the subject in everything from teen mags to worthy sociological journals, it would appear that there are earnest young men all over Britain looking for a way to bring themselves into being as new men, reconstructed to be turned on only by erotica, never by porn, and to know for sure which is which.*

  Geraldine Bedell, Independent, *October 1990*

NEW ROMANTICS

The most enduring name among those given to the 1980 fashion phenomenon first known as the CULT WITH NO NAME and originated by the BLITZ KIDS. Before it subsided into the general, eclectic jumble of Eighties youth styles, this movement had evolved a near-uniform of ruffled shirts, wide belts and breeches or leggings worn with spats, pumps or PIXIE BOOTS. It was this look, as worn by pop stars such as Adam Ant and Spandau Ballet, that spread beyond the metropolitan originators and was referred to as New Romantic.

- *. . . the New Romantics, a new generation of fops and would-be pop stars (as many of them now are – Boy George of Culture Club most prominently). Fops, but working-class fops, whose response to Thatcherism certainly doesn't make left-wing sense, but which isn't simply escapist either.*

  Simon Frith, Mother Jones, *1983*

NEW RIGHT

First used in the USA during the late 1970s to characterize
conservative commentators such as William Buckley and puritan
activists such as Anita Bryant, in the following decade New Right
came to define a fashionable pattern of thinking rather than merely a
reaction against left-wing orthodoxies and supposed permissiveness.
In the 1980s the term usually referred to the intellectual proponents
of free-market conservatism taking their cue from the MONETARIST
school of economic theory and the writings of John Locke and Adam
Smith. In Britain 'New' was sometimes used to distinguish these
Conservatives from earlier 'one-nation' Tories, sometimes to indicate
relative youth, as in the case of the philosopher Roger Scruton,
the journalists Charles Moore, Dominic Lawson and Christopher
Monckton, and some members of those think-tanks propagating the
new policies, such as the Adam Smith Institute and the Centre for
Policy Studies. Others to whom the categorization was applied –
Professor Norman Stone and Richard Oakeshott, for instance – were
of an older generation.

The New Right flourished under the patronage of the Reagan (see
REAGANOMICS) and Thatcher (see THATCHERISM) administrations. In
the field of economics, its adherents, following mentors such as
Friedman and Hayek and vindicated by the mid-Eighties consumer
boom and the collapse of Communism, enjoyed tremendous
influence. In the British and American press, but not the broadcast
media, the voice of the New Right went virtually unopposed. More
extreme versions of the accepted wisdoms, including the radical
individualism of the American Robert Nozick – who was against all
State intervention to the extent of disapproving of income tax – and
the calls of British Young Conservatives to privatize the police and
legalize drugs, brushed up against right-wing anarchism.

NEW SCIENCE

A term loosely applied to scientific developments since Einstein, the
New Science has particularly denoted science that has moved beyond
traditional certainties into areas where to the lay person it appears
to shade off into the paranormal, and to the scientist to move further
towards a unifying theory that will reconcile current understandings
of subatomic physics, quantum mechanics and cosmology. The

phrase encompasses a number of ideas which during the 1980s have caught the imagination of non-specialists and filtered into their vocabulary, including the UNCERTAINTY and ANTHROPIC PRINCIPLES, the CATASTROPHE and CHAOS THEORIES, the GAIA HYPOTHESIS and more outré concepts such as 'morphic resonance', the proposal by Rupert Sheldrake that species generate a field in which their past and present interact. The spread of these notions has come about through popularizing works by writers such as Carl Sagan, Stephen Hawking, Peter Medawar, Martin Gardner and, in particular, Frijtof Capra, who, with his *Tao of Physics* and *New Paradigm Thought* has attempted to draw parallels between ancient Oriental wisdom and post-relativity Western science, suggesting that a new consciousness is coming about as a result.

● *Relativity, quantum physics, cosmology and chaos theory reveal the style of the so-called 'new science'. At the very heart of the matter, in that extraordinary and mysterious world of quarks and leptons, our notions of determinism and causality are being ruthlessly exposed as inadequate.*
　　　　　　　　　　　　　　　Anthony Clare, Sunday Times, 10 May 1992

NEWTON'S CRADLE

Originally designed to demonstrate laws of motion, but now an icon of 1970s KITSCH, Newton's cradle consists of a row of steel balls suspended under a wooden or metal frame. When swung against each other the balls transfer motion and kick out the balls on either end. This novelty item, reminiscent, at least in its characteristic clattering, of the CLACKERS children's craze, was one of the best-known executive toys. Intended to provide avant-garde decoration, these objects of contemplation were also meant to inspire creative thought. Originating in the US, they were emblematic of the executive culture that began to be both imitated and parodied in the UK and elsewhere from the mid-1970s.

NEW WAVE

A translation of the French *nouvelle vague*, a phrase coined by the critic Françoise Giroud, New Wave refers to a group of French cineastes who revolutionized Western film-making at the end of the Fifties, many of whom were also film critics writing for the journal

Cahiers du Cinéma, founded by André Bazin in 1950. Despite their differences in temperament and technique, New Wave directors such as François Truffaut, Jean-Luc Godard, Eric Rohmer, Claude Chabrol and Chris Marker (the categorization was sometimes extended to include Robert Bresson, Louis Malle, Agnes Varda and Alain Resnais) had in common a knowing intellectualism and a commitment to the AUTEUR THEORY, whereby a film was the creation of the director rather than the studio. New Wave films were perforce low-budget and often employed techniques then considered avant-garde, such as hand-held cameras, the mixing of still and moving images, jump-cuts, actors addressing the camera and ad-libbing, private jokes and interrupted narrative.

The high-energy, generally upbeat and slick yet improvisational look of these films became a landmark of early Sixties pop culture. The French cine-renaissance, paralleled to some extent by the activities of Pasolini, Antonioni and Fellini in Italy, was followed by a similar phenomenon in Czechoslovakia between 1965 and the Russian invasion in 1968. In Britain the New Wave was a minor influence on the mix of social realism and frivolous pop films being made by younger directors at the time. The New Wave also helped to introduce the concepts of CINÉMA VÉRITÉ and FILM NOIR to an English-speaking audience, conferring high-art status on some earlier Hollywood movies (to the bemusement of Hitchcock, for one) and influencing a generation of American directors – Arthur Penn, Peter Bogdanovich and Brian de Palma in particular.

Once established, the phrase New Wave became a reusable cliché, heard for instance in connection with post-Philip K. Dick science fiction written in English, and most notably when it was briefly applied by the would-be SITUATIONIST impresario Malcolm McLaren to the birth of PUNK ROCK music. This usage was taken up by the pop-music press and the music industry as a useful generic term for the diverse musical styles and poses that appeared alongside hard-core Punk. Thus New Wave could also refer to a wide spectrum of progressive musicians flourishing in 1977 and 1978, from the Jam, Nick Lowe and later Joe Jackson at the melodic end to the Cure, Wire, Cabaret Voltaire on the experimental wing. As the label fell out of use in the music context during the early 1980s, it was applied to new developments in graphic design.

- *One of the new wave boys . . . same old thing in brand new drag.*
  Lyrics to 'Fashion' by David Bowie, 1980

NEW YORK SCHOOL

See ABSTRACT EXPRESSIONISM.

NIMBYS

A Nimby is someone who opposes controversial legislation (typically on environmental or social issues) only in cases where he or she is directly affected. The word is an acronym for the slogan or catch phrase 'Not In My Backyard!', coined in the USA during the 1980s to describe a syndrome whereby a person who in principle supports a potentially harmful move or policy, opposes it in practice for selfish reasons. The American expression entered British usage in about 1986 and was used to deride opponents of nuclear installations, planning-permission laws and the Channel Tunnel rail link, amongst others. By extension, a person in unqualified opposition to the same issues is known as Namby, from 'Not in Anyone's Backyard!'

- *He thinks working motherhood is a jolly good thing, but he's also a nimby ('by all means let mothers work, so long as it's not in my office').*
  Sarah Jane Evans, Sunday Times, 18 March 1989

NIPPLE-PIERCING

One of many forms of body decoration verging on self-mutilation (compare the SAFETY PIN and TATTOOING), nipple-piercing has been practised by members of the gay community (see GAY LIBERATION), devotees of sado-masochism, post-PUNK fashion followers and NEW AGE occultists. The underground film of the 1980s, *Robert Having his Nipple Pierced*, helped to publicize the practice. As well as a form of quasi-tribal ornamentation logically following on from ear- and nose-piercing, the insertion of rings, bars and studs in the secondary and primary sex organs is claimed to increase pleasurable sensitivity in these areas. It is also an optional sideline of tattoo parlours, in many cases catering to bravado and exoticism rather than sexual intentions.

NORTHERN SOUL

A movement that began at the end of the 1960s in the dance halls
of the North of England (the best known being Wigan Casino), just
as the fashionable interest in American SOUL music pioneered by
the MODS began to wane elsewhere in the face of progressive ROCK
and PSYCHEDELIA. Northern Soul enthusiasts collected and danced
to rare imports from Detroit, Philadelphia, Chicago and Cleveland,
eventually founding their own independent record labels to reissue
the music. Characteristically favouring a clothing style evolved
from Mod (short hair, later mutating into a WEDGE, Oxford bags and
loafers for both sexes), Northern Soul devotees kept black American
dance music alive in Britain until it was taken up in the DISCO boom
of 1976 and by southern SOUL BOYS. As American Soul in the US
itself became another branch of middle-class showbiz, the British
underground continued to revive obscure Sixties classics, prefiguring
the 1980s explosion of black-inspired dance culture and the RARE
GROOVE and DANCEFLOOR vogues.

NOUVEAU ROMAN

The French term *le nouveau roman*, meaning 'the New Novel', was
the name given to a self-consciously avant-garde literary genre that
began in the mid-1950s. Its main proponents were the author and
critic Alain Robbe-Grillet, who suggested the term in his essay 'Pour
un nouveau roman' in 1963; Nathalie Sarraute; Michel Butor; and,
according to some categorists, Marguerite Duras and Claude Simon.
In fact, the sources and concerns of their writing varied greatly, but
critics perceived a common tendency. The *nouveau roman* rejected
bourgeois conventions of fiction such as linear plots, characterization
and the reinforcement of social values; it also avoided political
or moral messages. The resulting works were based on meticulous
descriptions of environments and objects and accounts of thought
processes and dialogues without commentary; they often resembled
arid film scenarios, and were probably more admired than enjoyed by
readers. In fact some critics claim that the most satisfying expressions
of the ideas and aims of the *nouveau roman* actually occurred on
film – in Robbe-Grillet's own *Trans-Europe Express*, and in Alain
Resnais' *L'Année dernière à Marienbad* and *Hiroshima mon amour*
(scripted by Duras).

In their exploration of the dislocation between internal and external realities, in their attack on the conventions of the novel and, in retrospect, in their interest in cultural differences between East and West and colonial and metropolitan, the *nouveau roman* writers, whose real influence outside France was small, formed a bridge between literary EXISTENTIALISM and MODERNISM and the later POST-MODERNIST reflexive novel or 'metafiction' that questioned assumptions of literature but knowingly exploited its ability to entertain or excite. In his *roman à clef*, *Femmes*, published in 1983, the critic and former friend of the *nouveaux romanciers*, Philippe Sollers, dismissed the movement as an 'old gimmick for profs'.

NOUVEAUX PHILOSOPHES

A term which translates as the 'New Philosophers', used to describe a group of young writers and thinkers celebrated in the French media during the late 1970s. The core of the group consisted of Bernard-Henri Levy, Pascal Bruckner, Andre Glucksmann and Alain Finkielkraut. They put forward theories that criticized revolutionary Marxism and leftist orthodoxies and which anticipated in many ways the free-market conservatism of the 1980s, as well as the calls to 'collaborate' with CONSUMERISM by POST-MODERNISTS such as Baudrillard. Contemporary disapprovers on the Right accused them of cultivating a glamorous image, while they were dismissed by the Left as 'mere journalists'.

NOUVELLE CUISINE

During the mid-1970s, concern at the unhealthiness of traditional French cooking, with its overuse of rich sauces, together with the currently fashionable MINIMALIST aesthetic combined to prompt a revolution in gourmet eating. Chefs and restaurateurs such as Paul Bocuse, Jean and Pierre Troisgros, Roger Vergé and Paul Haeberlin had been moving towards a new approach since the late 1960s, but it was the restaurant-owners and critics Gault and Millau who gave the tendency its name (which translates as 'New Cooking'). The resultant *cuisine nouvelle* or *nouvelle cuisine*, as it finally came to be known, demanded top-quality ingredients, emphasizing their natural flavours and textures. A secondary concern was with the arrangement of the food on the plate: components were meticulously thin-sliced and fanned, juxtaposed and colour-coordinated. Key features included the use of exotic fruits (the omnipresence of the kiwi became a joke among consumers), miniature vegetables, warm salads and *coulis*, purées of fruit or vegetables. A simultaneous move to small portions and non-fattening ingredients was given the name *cuisine minceur* ('Slimming Cooking'), and was pioneerd by Michel Guerard at his restaurant in southwest France. By the early 1980s versions of *nouvelle cuisine* had become an orthodoxy in Western restaurants, but by the end of the decade there were signs of a backlash against its limitations and pretensions.

- *Of course the appeal of* nouvelle cuisine *is that the sauces are all based on condensed milk, thus allowing sophisticates to eat baby food without revealing their true, insecure colours: you have to be very rich and in the advanced stages of anorexia to properly appreciate* nouvelle cuisine.
  Julie Burchill, Sunday Times, *November 1984*

- *Perrier was the 'designer water' of choice in restaurants offering 'designer food' – nouvelle cuisine – more for looking at than eating; the less there was, the more it cost (appropriate for a period when you couldn't be too rich or too thin).*
  Vogue *75th Anniversary Issue, 1991*

NOUVELLE VAGUE

See NEW WAVE.

Named after the inarticulate chant or rallying cry of its devotees, Oi was a neo-SKINHEAD movement of the early 1980s formed around several ROCK bands – including Skrewdriver, the Four Skins, Infra-Riot and the Gonads – who played post-PUNK MINIMALIST anthems and espoused an extreme right-wing ethos. The first inspiration for this tendency came from the Punk group Sham 69, whose singer, Jimmy Pursey, had promoted a politically ambivalent proletarian pride hysteria in 1978 and 1979. It began by including supporters of the Left as well as the Right – the RANTING poet Attila the Stockbroker and the poet Garry Johnson, for instance – but galvanized the racist thug element that had always existed on the margins of the Punk scene, and, helped by the weekly music paper *Sounds* and the fascist British Movement, promoted itself as a viable youth cult. From 1982 to 1985, Oi survived as a minority phenomenon, its FANZINES indistinguishable from neo-Nazi propaganda and many of its exponents becoming involved in organized racist or political violence. In the second half of the 1980s it dwindled as a music-based craze and merged with the international far-Right alliances stretching from London to Prague.

- *Of course it was hideous macho bullshit, perpetrated by junior thugs taking time off from the football terraces, and of course the music hasn't stood the test of time: it was a short, sharp cretin hop. But it was so perfectly anti-authority that for a short time it exuded appeal.*

  Andy Darling reminiscing in Blitz, *September 1991*

OP ART

A style of painting exploiting the illusions of depth and movement created by geometric shapes and colours on a two-dimensional canvas, Op, or Optical, Art was an attempt at a non-figurative, non-referential pure art, influenced by the earlier abstraction and Constructivism of such artists as Jesus Raphael Soto, Josef Albers and László Moholy-Nagy. Two of its best-known exponents were the Hungarian-French artist Victor Vasarély and the British Bridget Riley. Op became a craze in 1966, moving from the gallery to T-shirts, coffee mugs, BADGES and other mass-produced graphics. It was briefly adopted by the MOD subculture, and helped to influence the PSYCHEDELIC visual style that appeared the same year. By 1969 it was considered *passé* in popular circles, unlike its contemporary POP ART, but in the early 1990s there were signs of a positive reassessment of OP's significance.

- *Bridget Riley's merciless concentration of her own eyesight into a painting that affects other people's eyesight was phenomenal in 1961 and is phenomenal today.*
  Tim Hilton, Guardian, February 1992

ORANGE PEOPLE

The epithet applied to the mainly American and European followers of the Indian Bhagwan Sri Rajneesh, characterized by their orange clothing, their devotion to their spiritual leader and by a philosophy of sexual liberation. First operating from an ashram in Poona, India, and later from a stronghold in Antelope, Oregon, the Bhagwan was one of many manipulative and fraudulent Eastern religious gurus of the 1970s who flourished in spite of vilification by sections of the press (the British satirical magazine *Private Eye*, for example, campaigned against the self-styled mystic they dubbed the 'Bagwash' throughout the late Seventies and early Eighties) and investigation by law-enforcement agencies and tax authorities. Rajneesh's followers were encouraged to deify their leader (his name translates as 'Blessed One', with Shree as a respectful title), to surrender their wealth to the movement (their mentor owned forty-three Rolls-Royces) and to practise free love with other members of the sect and, on occasion, with the Bhagwan himself. This last feature of his otherwise incoherent philosophy was especially responsible for the sect's notoriety, which was compounded by the prevalence of venereal disease and the advent of Aids. In the mid-1980s, under pressure from the US Internal Revenue and disaffected followers, the Bhagwan delegated executive leadership of his movement to a female assistant, Sheela. Tensions between the Orange People and the inhabitants of Antelope resulted in the collapse of the centre, the jailing of Sheela and the flight of the Bhagwan, who died in 1990, at the age of fifty-nine. Two years before the Bhagwan's death, a former disciple, Paul Lowe, founded a sect known as Khumara in Switzerland, charging 5000 Deutschmarks for six-week enlightenment seminars to applicants who could furnish evidence of a recent Aids test.

ORBITAL RAVES

See RAVES.

OREOS

See WANNABES.

ORGANIC ARCHITECTURE

A movement in international architecture that attracted attention during the 1980s, organic architecture – also known as natural Architecture – consists mainly of the work of one exponent, the Hungarian Imre Makovecz. The style is influenced by Frank Lloyd Wright, Gaudi, the ideas of Rudolf Steiner, and mythological and folk symbols. Buildings are constructed from natural materials, particularly wood (Makovecz uses whole trees as support columns, turf or wooded tiles as roofing), and follow natural forms. Makovecz's own evolution as a designer was a reaction against the MODERNISM of the Bauhaus and Bolshevism. His move towards a pan-European, ecologically aware architecture was criticized as 'wilful individualism', but seemed set to trigger widespread imitation in the 1990s. Typical of organic architecture is his 1977 anthropomorphic mortuary chapel in Farkasret, Budapest, made in the form of a human ribcage, with the bier in place of the heart.

OUTING

See GAY LIBERATION.

OUTSIDER ART

Outsider Art is the term usually applied in Anglophone countries to the Art Brut defined by the French artist Jean Dubuffet in the 1940s. The term refers to art produced by individuals outside the influence of normal society, the innocent or the disturbed working without precedent or tradition. Many Outsider artists have been certified as mentally ill; all have been untutored and creating, at least initially, without commercial intentions. In Britain the Outsider tradition (as distinct from primitive or folk art, which it sometimes resembles) encompasses the 19th-century canvases of Richard Dadd and the increasingly bizarre illustrations of Louis Wain. Internationally the genre has been most popular in Western and Central Europe and North America. Its best-known exponents include Adolf Wölfli, Martin Ramirez, Scottie Wilson, the mediumistic Madge Gill, and in the 1990s the young British obsessive Vonn Stropp (a nom de plume among 120 others). Outsider Art has been promoted as a subversive and deviant alternative strain of expression by the critics Victor Musgrave and Roger Cardinal, particularly following the major exhibition at the Hayward Gallery in London in 1979. In Lausanne a permanent collection was established in 1947.

- *What is 'different' is also enriching, and where autistic attitudes mean an aggravation of individualism and the consequent concentration of creativity . . . they produce an effect of such 'high-voltage' that it would be cowardice not to try to experience them.*
  Roger Cardinal, Outsider Art, 1972

PACHUCOS

A synonym of the later Chicano, Pachuco was the nickname given to members of the Hispanic ghetto street culture of southern California during the 1950s and 1960s. Pachucos contributed to postwar style by wearing the ARGENTINE DUCKTAIL and ZOOT SUITS, and by inventing LOW RIDING. The word is of obscure origin, but may derive from Pachuca, the name of a city in east Central Mexico.

PAGANISM

See SHAMANISM; WICCA.

PAINTBALL

See COMBAT GAMES.

PATAPHYSICS

A 'science of imaginary solutions' proposed by the French absurdist (see THEATRE OF THE ABSURD) Alfred Jarry, pataphysics was to be to metaphysics as metaphysics was to physics. This surreal science was propounded by Jarry – best known as the author of the play *Ubu Roi* – in *Les Gestes et opinions du Docteur Faustroll*, published posthumously in 1911, and in his only novel, *Le Surmale* (*The Super-male*). Jarry, although little known to the middlebrow public, continued to exercise a powerful underground influence on the Western avant-garde throughout the century, and a Pataphysical Society was established to celebrate and extend his thinking. Pataphysics was the outcome of a collision between a childlike fascination with the outer reaches of mathematics and early 20th-century science and a profoundly subversive anti-authoritarian and anticlerical vision.

PATCHOULI OIL

Of all the essential oils and perfumes that formed part of the HIPPIE paraphernalia of the late Sixties, patchouli was the most pungent and the most emblematic of the COUNTERCULTURE. It was also the most persistent, not only in its short-term effects but as a long-term favourite of post-Hippie TRAVELLERS and some CRUSTIES in the early 1990s. Sold in small phials, the exotic essence was highly concentrated and thus highly economical. Often mistaken by the un-hip for the smell of marijuana, the heady perfume is derived from the Indian pacculi plant.

PC

The so-called Political Correctness movement was a phenomenon that first appeared on North American campuses in the late 1980s. Taking its name from a phrase used in prescriptive authoritarian regimes (notably the People's Republic of China during the MAOIST era), the tendency combined FEMINIST, anti-racist and other liberationist doctrines to create a new post-Marxist leftist orthodoxy. The beginnings of PC go back to the work of the POST-STRUCTURALISTS, in particular the DECONSTRUCTION of Jacques Derrida, which during the 1970s took a firm hold in many university departments in the US, where the application of those ideas to literature was later extended to subjects such as history and anthropology. One of the notions contained in Deconstruction, and in the provocative theories of the psychologist Michel Foucault, is that cultural messages are not free of ideology, assumptions of power relationships or the reinforcement of orthodoxies, all of which are expressed unwittingly through choice of language. Feminists, for instance, had already begun to identify the sexism inherent in language in the early 1970s, and by the end of that decade many supposedly masculinist terms – those ending in -man for example – were taboo.

Political correctness expanded this taboo to cover terms reinforcing racial or heterosexist stereotypes, Euro-centrism in historical studies or discrimination against the physically or mentally disadvantaged. In this controversy of euphemisms, 'handicapped' became 'disadvantaged', which in turn was rejected as discriminatory in favour of 'differently abled' or 'challenged'. It was this nominalist purification of the lexicon that attracted most attention internationally, but PC also attacked the teaching of the 'Canon', the body of learning that bolstered a system designed by and for 'DWEMs' – Dead White European Males. By the early 1990s the strictures of PC were being set out in handbooks, dictionaries and, in California, even in local legislation, and teachers and others who offended against them, even with a joke or a look, risked ostracism or, in some cases, dismissal, a situation that provoked an anti-PC backlash by some conservatives and liberals.

By 1992 PC in the USA was spreading beyond the campus, while observers in the UK and Australia speculated on its future overseas. In Britain, despite ridicule in the media, there were signs of PC making headway, particularly among feminists, educationalists and those involved in ethnic issues and social work. In spite of its excesses and illiberalism, PC in the USA opened up the difficult issues of 'cultural relativism' (the idea that value judgements about art, literature, language, etc. are dependent on the viewpoint of one's own culture, not on absolute standards); of the role of language in exercising power; and of society's attitude to those with difficulties (in this context, disapproval of ageism was followed in the US by defence of the rights of the fat, and then the ugly). The Establishment seemed unable to react decisively to these questions; meanwhile PC's promoters seemed to be replacing one oppression with another.

- *One does not wish to be apocalyptic – though thoughtful and honest teachers may be forgiven for thinking their world is coming to an end . . . the force is with the extremists, who ride roughshod over the opposition by intimidating it with accusations of 'racism'.*
  Wall Street Journal, *31 July 1991*

PEACE CONVOY

See TRAVELLERS.

PENCIL SKIRT

A tight, tapering, calf-length skirt shape introduced by Dior in 1950 as an alternative to the triangle silhouette of the NEW LOOK, the pencil skirt later became a mainstay of Fifties (slightly Bohemian) chic. The style was revived briefly by British teenagers in 1973, and more lastingly in 1979. The original 'pencil' appellation was one of a bewildering number of images conjured up by the frenetically competitive *haute couturiers*; 'tulip', 'pumpkin', 'pipe' and 'trumpet' were others.

PERFORMANCE ART

Performance Art is essentially live art in which the actions of performers replace conventional art objects. Between the 1960s and the 1980s it moved from being an obscure, avant-garde approach to become a major movement taught in colleges of art and forming the basis of many progressive gallery and theatre shows, to the extent that in 1991 the British Arts Council appointed a Live Arts Officer. Performance Art can be seen as a logical development of one aspect of the MODERNIST tendency in that it aims to move art further into everyday life, breaking down barriers between audience or consumers and artists or producers, and pushing beyond the constraints of traditional artificial forms of presentation in two or three dimensions. It is also a logical step from KINETIC or installation art or interactive theatre. Critics have traced the roots of Performance Art back in some cases to medieval public miracle plays, in others to the many examples of gestures, events and provocations carried out by earlier 20th-century avant-garde movements. Alfred Jarry (see PATAPHYSICS), Dada cabaret, the Futurists and Constructivists, the Surrealists and Artaud's Theatre of Cruelty, have all been cited.

The first important post-Second World War performances were the HAPPENINGS staged in the USA at the very end of the 1950s. These were followed in the 1960s by a merging with other genres such as modern dance, FRINGE and community theatre, jazz, ROCK and PSYCHEDELIA. Quintessentially COUNTERCULTURE examples such as the People Show or the Welfare State were followed in the 1970s by mixed-media groups like Coum, who mutated into the PUNK and occult-tinged Throbbing Gristle and Psychic TV. In the fine-arts field Performance Art achieved notoriety during the 1970s and 1980s through its ability to involve spectators in controversial or shocking – and, to the uninitiated, usually incomprehensible – situations. The Viennese Rudolf Schwarzkogler died following a public self-mutilation, a tactic also practised by the French artist Gine Pane. The Australian Chris Burden had himself shot in the arm in the course of a performance, and in 1972 Stuart Brisley sat in a bath with decaying meat for two weeks. Lesser shocks involving nudity and bad language were commonplace. Some artists performed in their own homes; the more light-hearted Japanese expatriates, the Frank Chickens, however, staged theatrical classics in London at other peoples' homes, using toys to play the roles.

It could be said that Performance Art suffers from its lack of norms and limitations, and from the impression of personal, private concerns made public yet still inaccessible; its challenging of inhibition assumes the complicity of a knowing audience. By the 1990s it was still mainly confined to the élite milieux of galleries or theatres.

- *This week's three-day festival of performance art at the Serpentine Gallery promises more subdued dare-devilry: a man will shed his clothes by torch-light and two women will dangle on a trapeze suspended from a crane. It's enough to highlight the real danger with performance art: that on paper it just seems silly, if not pretentious.*
  Independent, *19 July 1991*

PET ROCKS

Created by the Californian Gary Dahl, the pet rock was a cross between a ZEN object of contemplation – perhaps partly inspired by the rock and sand garden of Ryoan-ji in Japan, or by the water-eroded rocks prized by the Chinese as evocative decoration – and an executive toy. The novelty item was marketed in the USA in the 1970s as a trouble-free household pet; others saw it as a glaringly decadent example of disposable CONSUMERISM.

PHOTOREALISM

See HYPERREALISM.

PHREAKING

See HACKERS.

PIRATE BROADCASTING

The pop culture of the early and mid-Sixties lacked a dynamic outlet in the press or broadcast media as the BBC monopolized domestic airtime and followed an implicit policy of disapproval of progressive popular music or fashions. Only Radio Luxembourg provided American-style commercially funded broadcasts, avoiding the restrictions on record time imposed by BBC agreements with musicians' unions, but its signal was of variable quality. In March 1964 the entrepreneur Ronan O'Rahilly started Radio Caroline, broadcasting from a ship anchored outside UK territorial waters in the North Sea. This was followed by Radio London and several others, some located on abandoned offshore defence platforms.

These new stations played Top Forty hits, record requests, adverts and jingles, and promoted themselves with T-shirt sales, sponsored concerts and discothèques on land. After a year of operation they had attracted an audience of over fifteen million. A generation of disc jockeys including Johnny Walker, Emperor Rosko, Dave Lee Travis and Kenny Everett began their careers as pirates. The dual support of listeners and the music industry kept the offshore pirates in business for three years, prompting the BBC to introduce Radio One, and the Government to pass and finally enforce the Marine Broadcasting Act in 1967. Radio London closed down immediately. Other pirates attempted to defy the Act over the next few years: the authorities made ready to board them and close them down by force, but it was rough seas that finally defeated Radio Caroline and Radio Laser.

Although the later licensing of local and commercial radio in Britain partially removed the rationale for pirate broadcasting, illegal stations reappeared in the early 1980s. The new versions of pirate radio relied on the increased availability of relatively cheap equipment that could be easily dismantled and moved. Many pirates were now young club habitués promoting minority music styles, principally black SOUL and REGGAE (as parodied by the comedian Lenny Henry in his character Delbert Wilkins), jazz and the sub-genres making up DANCEFLOOR culture. Others were simply operating an illegal offshoot of the fashionable enterprise culture of the time. Some of the broadcasters, including Kiss FM, the London black music station, were offered and took the opportunity to take up legal franchises in 1987; once again legislation was brought in to curb the rest. In 1986 there was an attempt to start a pirate TV station, Network 21, which succeeded in broadcasting over a limited area in London, but was short-lived. Like CB RADIO, KARAOKE, home video and audio-taping, pirate radio in both its incarnations was an attempt to force a reluctant monopoly to yield to consumer choice.

- *With the words 'Radio London is now closing down' Big L went off the air on Monday . . . Over the weekend the DJs had been signing off as their programmes went on the air for the last time.*
  Melody Maker, *19 August 1967*

- *The pirate stations controlled the world they created: they made records, hyped them in the clubs and promoted both over the air-waves. Snappy, iconic visuals helped to sell their adverts and club admission tickets.*
  Cynthia Rose, Design After Dark: The Story of Dancefloor Style, *1991*

PIT BULL TERRIERS

See FIGHTING DOGS.

PIXIE BOOTS

Quasi-medieval or 18th-century ankle boots with doubled-over tops that were fashionable for both sexes in the UK from 1981. They were originally theatrical costume footwear bought by NEW ROMANTICS from wardrobe specialists such as Anello & Davide in London's Covent Garden.

PLASTER DUCKS

See KITSCH.

PLATFORM SOLES

An unforgettable symbol of the excesses of 1970s GLAM ROCK fashion, platform soles (and heels) mutated out of the stacked-heel coloured boots fashionable for both sexes (but an essential component in

the modish male HIPPIE wardrobe) during the late 1960s. As Art
Deco influences began to merge with the late-Hippie style from
1968 onwards, the narrow, low shapes of boots and shoes gave way
to a heavier, more rounded look. Platforms on women's shoes had
already been a vogue in the late 1930s; and in the Forties the Italian
shoe designer Salvatore Ferragamo had consolidated the look with
built-up cork and wood bases, which conveniently replaced scarce
leather. In 1971 platform shoes for women became high fashion, some
with wedge soles (the heel and sole in one), some recalling the sports
look of the Forties in gingham, canvas, raffia, rope and cork. Part of
mainstream fashion by 1974, they were outmoded by 1976.

Meanwhile, in the music business male performers such as Slade,
Gary Glitter and Elton John adopted the platform boot as a key
item of GLAM and GLITTER display. Often worn with appliqué stars,
the soles and heels became more and more exaggerated until they
reached the limits of wearability. By 1975 the style was played out,
persisting only in the outfits worn by black American FUNK bands.
For men the platform never made a comeback, except as part of
short-lived outbreaks of Seventies parody such as that accompanying
the 1980s RARE GROOVE fad, whereas there have been minor revivals
for women, in 1987 in club and DANCEFLOOR fashion, and again, this
time in designer collections, in 1992. The platform look as seen by
interpreters is an interesting contradiction: the height enhancement
and weightiness of the style is said to reinforce an image of power
and assertion, whilst the instability involved supposedly emphasizes
sexual vulnerability.

- *Paula Murphy, the Fastest Woman Drag Racer in the World, as
  garishly decorated as her machine, was surrounded by admiring
  teenagers in tight jeans, silver battle-tops and high, platform-
  soled boots.*

  Nova *magazine, January 1975*

- *My platforms were orange with a star in the tongue, the soles were
  three inches high; topped by my afro I was about nine feet tall and
  looked like Herman Munster.*

  Lenny Henry, Sunday Mirror *magazine, 8 December 1991*

POGO

A dance consisting of leaping up and down with arms motionless at one's sides, the pogo (named after its similarity to the movements of Pogo-stick users) was characteristic of PUNK audiences and partygoers reacting to their chosen music. Said to have been invented by Sid Vicious in his days as a fan before he joined the Sex Pistols, the pogo was a minimalist, deliberately autistic pose, convenient for stage-front crushes. Colliding pogoers gave rise to the later vogue for SLAM-DANCING. Among the confusion of retro styles making up the DANCEFLOOR and INDIE POP scenes of the early 1990s, the pogo made a limited and self-conscious comeback.

POLITICAL CORRECTNESS

See PC.

POMP ROCK

A derogatory nickname applied to the ponderous, overblown style of music and stage performance that by 1975 had evolved out of the PSYCHEDELIA and progressive ROCK of the late 1960s. While one strand of electronic Rock mutated into the cruder, albeit still bombastic, HEAVY METAL genre and a slightly younger generation introduced the camp parodies of GLAM and GLITTER, some British musicians, notably Pink Floyd, Rick Wakeman, King Crimson, Genesis and Yes, mounted ever more extravagant performances featuring multi-instrumentation and orchestration, pretentious, often ludicrous quasi-mystical lyrics, and expensive, but tasteless costumes and lighting displays. It was this trend, in which performers became more and more remote from audiences and the sound more and more difficult to reproduce outside the recording studio, that helped to trigger the back-to-the-basics PUB ROCK movement and provoked the contempt of PUNKS for what they saw as HIPPIE culture. The Pomp Rock genre did not go away, however, and the nickname was transferred at the end of the Seventies to HARD ROCK groups such as the Scorpions and Iron Maiden, whilst the internationally successful group Queen continued in the classic Pomp Rock vein into the Nineties.

PONYTAIL

First popularized at the end of the 1940s by the BOBBYSOXERS
and their emulators in Europe and Australia, including the less
wholesome Teddy Girls (see TEDDY BOYS) and WIDGIES, the ponytail
was the exclusive province of the female until the end of the 1960s,
when some long-haired males, particularly American bikers (see
HELL'S ANGELS), back-to-nature HIPPIES and backpackers, began to
tie back their hair. Out of fashion from around 1974 to the end of
the Seventies, except among residual Hippies and TRAVELLERS, the
ponytail for men made a comeback in the late Seventies among
French and Italian playboys and during the early 1980s in the
UK and USA, first in the form of a miniature pigtail worn with
an otherwise short hairstyle, and subsequently as a full ponytail
favoured by style-conscious males typically working in the fashion
industry, advertising, design or the music business. The attraction
of the ponytail for men (known pejoratively in the later Eighties as a
'dork-handle') was that it was 'acceptably radical' – both flamboyant
and controlled, wearable with jeans or suits. For women the ponytail
was briefly popular during the ROCKABILLY fad of the early 1980s, but
apart from occasional revivals of the *fausse-ingénue* Brigitte Bardot
look it has remained out of favour except amongst schoolgirls and
horsewomen.

- ... LA is regarded by many ... as the seventh level of Hell, where
  pony-tailed junior demons are developing major script options while
  they wait tables in Japanese-Ecuadorian restaurants ...
      John Diamond, Sunday Times Book Review, May 1992

POP ART

The Anglo-American movement in painting and sculpture that
characterized the later 1960s and which ousted MODERNIST
abstraction once and for all as the dominant progressive style in
postwar art. The defining term was coined by the British critic
Lawrence Alloway around 1952 when referring to the ideas and
ideals of a small coterie calling itself the Independent Group, based
at the Institute of Contemporary Arts in London. The group included
the painter and sculptor Eduardo Paolozzi, the painter and teacher
Richard Hamilton, the artists John McHale and William Turnbull and

the art historian Reyner Banham. They had in common an interest
in mass culture and new technology and a fascination with the
artefacts of American consumer society. It was Richard Hamilton who
actively promoted the concept of Pop Art at the time of the 'This is
Tomorrow' exhibition at the Whitechapel Gallery in 1956. His own
work shown there, a photomontage of a body-builder posing among
consumer durables, entitled *Just what is it that makes today's homes
so different, so appealing?*, is generally accepted as the first example
of the new genre. At the same time this novel, colourful, KITSCH-
influenced figurative style was being paralleled in the USA – where
the labels New Realism and Neo-Dada were considered – by painters
such as Robert Rauschenberg, Jasper Johns and Robert Indiana, who
were using collage and traditional canvas techniques to reproduce
folk and consumerist images partly inspired by European Dada and
American primitive art.

By the early 1960s a generation of artists was converging under the
Pop umbrella. In the USA Roy Lichtenstein was creating enlarged
comic-strip images, Andy Warhol was combining commercial-art
techniques with Duchampian gestures, Claes Oldenburg was
producing soft sculptures of household objects, and Tom Wesselmann
was painting highly coloured assemblages that prefigured
Photorealism (see HYPERREALISM). British Pop artists tended to
combine a detached view of everyday images with personal narratives
and cultural cross-references. Hamilton continued in a cerebral
experimental vein, as did the American expatriate Ron Kitaj; Allen
Jones produced glossy fetishist images of women; David Hockney
moved towards a type of decorative hedonism; and Peter Blake
combined elements of folk art with sentimental portraiture. Outside
the Anglo-American ambit there were few Pop artists.

Following major exhibitions in 1964 and 1965, Pop Art was an
international success: it was upbeat and accessible, and it overturned
the hermetic, élitist mystique of previous avant-garde styles. Pop was
knowing and confident, confronting photography for the first time
by assimilating and reproducing it. Pop icons and imagery were by
definition easily transferable back into the fields of graphic design,
packaging and advertising. With hindsight Pop may be considered
one of the first genuinely POST-MODERN genres. Its central problem
for observers looking for commitment – a concept much discussed at
the time of retrospective exhibitions at the end of the Eighties – was
its intellectual emptiness and its cool re-presenting of the surfaces of

commodity capitalism without deciding whether its own stance was ironic detachment or fetishistic celebration.

- *The inclusion of every image could be explained, but you do not need to know. Kitaj himself quotes approvingly Wittgenstein's words about an Austrian poem: 'I don't understand it, but its tone delights me.'*

  Observer *magazine, 27 March 1966*

- *Asked about his own contribution, [Peter] Blake is unhesitating. 'I invented Pop Art, if one is being arrogant, along with Jasper Johns and the Independent Group. Yet in this Royal Academy show my pictures would fit into a quarter of Warhol's picture of Mao.'*

  Sunday Times, *15 September 1991*

POSITIVE PUNK

See GOTHS.

POST-MODERNISM

Many people's most direct experience of so-called Post-modernism has been with the architectural style that appeared under this name at the beginning of the 1980s. This tendency in architecture and design consisted of a mixing of historical references, particularly classical, 'Egyptian/Babylonian' and modern, in a joky pastiche, often with pastel- or primary-coloured KITSCH decoration and a blurring of the inside/outside distinction – trees in the atrium, pipes and ducts on external walls, the street inside the shop, for instance. The approach began in the USA in the late Seventies. First examples often looked like visual parodies or rectangular MODERNIST buildings with triangles and spheres added as an afterthought, but by the mid-1980s a recognizable range of Post-Modernist structures was appearing worldwide, welcomed by many consumers as the first confident rejection of Modernist Brutalism (see NEW BRUTALISM). Leading exponents were Robert Venturi, Michael Graves and Charles Moore in the USA; Ricardo Bofill and the designer Javier Mariscal in Spain; and in the UK the NEOCLASSICIST Quinlan Terry and the promoter of a 'city of signs' (inspired by SEMIOLOGY), Nigel Coates.

The term Post-modernism was in fact coined in 1964 by the American Marxist critic Fredric Jameson. It has come to encompass a whole collection of notions that together seem to represent a new phase in Western culture; one where truths and values have all become relative, and where the barriers between high and mass culture, art and CONSUMERISM and between artistic genres are disappearing. In the Post-Modern world, notions of linear history, of constant progress and the opposition of avant-garde/traditional and real/imaginary have ceased to apply. The result is a chaos of competing styles and cross-references transmitted by a free-market consumerist system that creates its own reality for its own ends. The clearest proof of this HYPERREALITY is probably the case of youth subcultures, where the linear progression of fashions and fads from 1945 to the end of the 1970s collapsed at the beginning of the 1980s, leaving a confusion in which all the styles and poses of the past are simultaneously recycled and restaged in an ideologically empty display. Youth culture is also typically 'Post-Modern' in its multi-ethnic cosmopolitanism, epitomized by such trends as WORLD MUSIC and NEW AGE spiritual inquiry.

Other products of the Post-Modernist age are the heritage industry, with its rebuilding and rewriting of the past, which chimes with the American historian Francis Fukuyama's claim that in the West history as we knew it has come to an end. In literature the Post-Modern novel combines MAGIC REALISM and an awareness of Semiology. In the world of business, economics and commerce, the key associated terms are 'post-industrial capitalism', 'the information society' and 'third-stage consumption' (consumers having graduated from products through services to information and experiences). Justification for all these theories is found in the NEW SCIENCE and in technology-based innovations such as CYBERPUNK and VIRTUAL REALITY. Writers who have reported and defined Post-Modernism include the French POST-STRUCTURALISTS and DECONSTRUCTORS Derrida, Lyotard and Baudrillard, the Italian Umberto Eco, and the Palestinian-American Edward Said, among others.

● *Post-Modernism, which deals with the past like one huge antique supermarket, looks very relevant indeed. Pastiche and parody is just an uncomfortable transition to a time when period references will be used without any self-consciousness.*
Peter York, Style Wars, *1980*

● *Depending on your aesthetics, Post Modernism is either a freakish charade, a mere diversion from the Modernist mainstream, or the saviour of twentieth-century design, deliverance from all those boxy shapes.*

The Face, *October 1987*

● *Postmodernity is modernity without the hopes and dreams which made modernity bearable. It is a hydra-headed, decentred condition in which we get dragged along from pillow [sic] to post across a succession of reflecting surfaces, drawn by the call of the wild signifier.*

Dick Hebdige, Hiding in the Light, *1988*

POST-PAINTERLY ABSTRACTION

A term coined in 1964 by the influential American critic Clement Greenberg (who also originated the category ABSTRACT EXPRESSIONISM) in order to describe a tendency in fine art that was moving away from a preoccupation with the act of painting, the texture of paint and canvas and the personality of the artist, towards a cool, geometric, abstract style using flat planes of colour. Artist considered to belong to this movement include Morris Louis, Larry Poons, Jules Olitski, Kenneth Noland, Frank Stella and Ellsworth Kelly, some of whom had previously been referred to by the HARD EDGE label. The form of abstraction stripped to essentials they practised was a step towards MINIMALISM.

● *Younger painters associated with this tendency, for example Kelly, Stella, have recently begun to experiment with shaped canvases, moving towards a breaking-down of the barriers between painting and sculpture.*

Observer *magazine, 27 March 1966*

POST-STRUCTURALISM

Post-Structuralism – a tendency, not a theory – was one of the most potentially subversive forces in postwar thought, but it remained embedded in arguments and dialogues among literary and social theorists from its inception in the late 1960s. Whereas STRUCTURALISM and SEMIOLOGY suggested that the surface signs and symbols generated by society were representing some deeper realities, Post-Structuralism, triggered off by the French philosopher Jacques Derrida's systematic DECONSTRUCTION of literary texts, suggested that beyond 'signs' – in practice usually words and images – were simply more signs coexisting in a fluid state of relativity, and that there were no underlying truths or certainties – 'meanings' – to a text that could ultimately be revealed by an 'objective' or 'dispassionate' observer. These insights, embraced by academics in France and the USA in particular, were condemned by other liberals and traditionalists, most notably in the UK, as intellectual nihilism.

The implications of Post-Structuralism gave a rationale to the idea, observable in 'late-capitalist' Western society, that traditional ideologies and categories, whether of the Left or the Right, the avant-garde or the traditionalists, had ceased to operate, giving way to a new POST-MODERN culture. Post-Structuralism was as controversial in the English-speaking world as its predecessor had been. In 1981 a junior lecturer at Cambridge University, Dr Colin McCabe, was the centre of an acrimonious dispute when he was ousted by the English Department for holding Post-Structuralist sympathies. In 1992 the acrimony resurfaced when Derrida was proposed for an honorary degree by the university.

POWER DRESSING

A term that will forever be identified with the YUPPIE era of the mid-1980s, when it was used to refer to the fashion amongst ambitious professionals of both sexes (although it was applied most often to women) for expressing assertiveness through choice of clothing styles and accessories. In practice, power dressing consisted of wearing severely cut or exaggeratedly geometric jackets, skirts and suits with jewellery, watches, shirts and scarves that were bold in design, size or colour. It is significant that the underlying styles favoured were essentially part of the traditional business uniform: power-dressing had little to do with the avant-garde. It was a move away from the pre-1980s custom of deferential dressing by subordinates and restraint by the truly powerful. By about 1987 the most obvious elements of the power wardrobe – shoulder-pads and high heels for females; braces, garish ties and heavy watches for men – had become mainstays of the high-street retailing boom. The term itself, which appeared in the USA during the early Eighties, was probably based on the notion of the 'power breakfast' at which the driven super-executive concluded high-level deals before the traditional white-collar worker had arrived at the office. A joke almost as soon as it was coined, the expression disappeared around 1990.

POWER POP

An ill-defined sub-genre forming part of the post-1977 musical NEW
WAVE, Power Pop was the relatively apolitical, melodic end of the
PUNK spectrum. The phrase was invented by the music press –
probably coined by the newspaper *Sounds* – and promoted by the
music industry, who applied it to British musicians and groups
such as Nick Lowe, Elvis Costello, Eddy and the Hot Rods, and the
Corgis, sometimes to MOD revivalists the Jam and the Chords, and
to American groups including the Cars, the Knack and the Shoes.
The appellation, which suggested that the songs in question were
lightweight but relied on 'power chords', lasted from 1977 to 1979
only and was rarely acknowledged by the musicians themselves.

● *The idea of power pop was the essence of pop, the People's music,
all those twinkling, twangy bright guitars and melodies, that 1964
sound; and boys in suits. It was a low camp haberdashery idea with
no wind in it at all.*

                      Peter York, Style Wars, *1980.*

PREPPIES

The Preppie (also spelt with a terminal 'y') was the first of the
middle-class – as opposed to alternative – youth subcultures to be
identified and anatomized, coming before JAPS, SLOANE RANGERS,
YUPPIES, VALLEY GIRLS and UHBS. The nickname, whose currency was
given a boost in 1976 by its use in the best-selling novel and film *Love
Story*, refers to a student or ex-student of an American preparatory
school. American prep schools (as opposed to the British version,
which educates boys from eight to thirteen in preparation for entry
to public school) are prestigious private secondary schools preparing
students for college. Being a Preppie implies subscribing to the
values, manners, jargon and dress codes (for males the equivalent of
the Ivy League look) of conservative upper-class white America. The
Preppie is thus the American counterpart of the British Sloane Ranger
or the French BCBG (for *bon chic/bon genre*). The *Official Preppy
Handbook*, published in the USA in 1980, was a tongue-in-cheek
guide to Preppie mannerisms, etiquette and 'how to be top-drawer'.
The Preppie version of casual dress (polo shirts and button-down
Oxfords, canvas trousers and skirts, deck shoes and loafers, etc.) was

marketed worldwide to a predominantly YUPPIE clientele by the
American designer Ralph Lauren.

- *The charmed life of the Preppy leads to a disproportionate use of*
  superlatives, expressing a seemingly limitless enthusiasm. For girls
  especially 'cute' is the supreme accolade.
                                        The Official Preppy Handbook, *1980*

- *He [the Preppie] might be viewed as an American Hooray Henry,*
  except that he is quietly spoken, excessively polite, and never throws
  muffins.
                                        Independent, *12 March 1988*

- *. . . Talking Heads' chilly preppieisms – on songs like 'No*
  Compassion' – now grate after fifteen years of the New Right . . .
                                        Jon Savage, England's Dreaming, *1991*

PRIMAL SCREAM

One of the first psychotherapy techniques to promote rebirthing
(re-experiencing the trauma of birth whilst under supervision), Primal
therapy was developed in the USA during the late 1960s by Dr Arthur
Janov, and became particularly fashionable in COUNTERCULTURE and
progressive circles from about 1970. John Lennon and Yoko Ono
were among the celebrities who experienced and recommended the
process. Primal therapy assists the patient to regress to a childlike
state in which unresolved conflicts and 'primal' neuroses can be
dissipated by acting out or reliving traumas. The most spectacular
aspect of the treatment is the cathartic screaming that accompanies
the experiences of being rebirthed and confronting parents or siblings
while in an inarticulate state. Janov's notions and practices were
paralleled and expanded upon by many other therapists, particularly
by those of his followers who broke away from him before 1973 to
set up the International Primal Association. Almost any uninhibited
release of emotion, as practised for instance by MEN'S MOVEMENT
workshops, is now referred to as Primal screaming, while Primal
therapy and rebirthing have become standard components in NEW AGE
healing and consciousness-raising.

- *There are basically four techniques in use to bring you to a primal*
  or rebirthing experience: hypnotic age regression . . . psycholitic

> *methods using psychedelics such as LSD . . . simulation of the birth experience, or breathing.*
> Brian Inglis and Ruth West, The Alternative Health Guide, *1983*

● *Dr Janov, holder of UK trademark registration B1 020-326 for the word Primal would like to make it clear that nobody trained by him is practising in the UK. All other advertising employing the word Primal is fraudulent misrepresentation.*
> Announcement in Time Out, *3 June 1992*

PRINGLES

An alternative nickname for the youth cult also known as the CASUALS. Heard in the early stages of the movement, Pringle was taken from the brand name of expensive casual pullovers and cardigans worn as part of the uniform. Pringles of both sexes belonged to a working-class milieu that overlapped with early 1980s football hooligan gangs.

PROCESS, THE

A sinister quasi-religious sect operating in London at the end of the 1960s and inspired in part by SCIENTOLOGY. Followers of the Process were recognizable by their uniform of black robes worn with pendants of silver crosses. The cult's leader, de Grimston, was accused by critics of practising mind-control techniques and a blend of fascism and occultism. The Process was one of many enlightenment movements that practised communal withdrawal from society and demanded submission from its devotees, offering a new rigour to dilettantes and refugees from the COUNTERCULTURE alike. In 1992 the Process was reported to be active in California.

PROCESS MUSIC

See REPETITIVE MUSIC.

PROTEST SONGS

Protest songs were a subcategory of FOLK and pop singing that became a HIP fad and then a commercial cliché between 1965 and 1967. They originated in the work of late 1950s folk singers such as Woody Guthrie, Pete Seeger, Cisco Houston and Mahalia Jackson,

whose songs explicitly attacked social injustice and promoted
civil rights. In the early 1960s Joan Baez and Bob Dylan brought
the politically committed or anti-Establishment ballad to a younger
and wider audience for whom mainstream pop, jazz and ROCK 'N'
ROLL were failing to take account of the important issues of the day:
the nuclear threat, pacifism, racial equality and personal liberty.
By 1965 the music industry had belatedly embraced the concept of
the protest song as a marketable category: second-wave imitators –
including Dylan's British shadow, Donovan, who recorded the anthem
'Universal Soldier' – and commercial opportunists were climbing on
the bandwagon (now embarrassing hit-parade examples include the
hit 'Eve of Destruction' and the right-wing counterblast, 'Dawn of
Correction') and the English-speaking world's press was promoting
the term. By 1967, when the 'Summer of Love' introduced HIPPIE
values on a large scale, the protest song no longer had a separate
identity. Protesting – now more than anything against the Vietnam
War – had become incorporated into a lifestyle whose music took it
for granted. The protest-song label was not heard again, except when
applied briefly to the socialist songs of the British post-PUNK singer
Billy Bragg in the early 1980s.

- *There is now a protest song protesting against protest singers. It
  has been written by a London advertising man, Mike Margolis,
  and recorded by a twenty-one-year-old music student who uses the
  professional name Micha.*
  London Life, *16 October 1965*

PROVOS

The Provos – from the French *provocateur* – were the first European
COUNTERCULTURE activists to organize themselves. They were
libertarian anarchists who carried out public provocations of the
authorities, organized community housing and shops, and published
a newsletter – the 'White Paper' – in Holland from 1965. The Dutch
Provos – not to be confused with the terrorist Provisional IRA –
became famous for their White Bicycle scheme whereby free bikes
were left in the streets of Amsterdam to provide environment-friendly
transport for anyone requiring it. The Provos, with their successors
the KABOUTERS, succeeded in occupying whole districts of Amsterdam
in their effort to found an 'Orange Free State'. The Dutch experiments,
carried out in the face of an extremely liberal Establishment, were not

(perhaps unfortunately) adopted as a blueprint for later movements in the US and UK, although in the latter their pioneering of SQUATTING was influential.

- *Whenever headmasters will not listen to the demands we make under the White School Plan, we shall be forced to press them home by means of large-scale actions such as school strikes, boycotting of teachers, sit-ins, sitdowns (with or without smoke bombs), inflammatory leaflets, etc.*

Provo manifesto, 1966

PSYCHEDELIA

The term 'psychedelic' was an invention coined in the mid-1960s derived from the Greek noun *psyche*, meaning soul, and the verb u*deloun*, meaning to show. It is often translated, however, as 'mind-expanding'. It was used to refer to the effects of hallucinogenic drugs such as LSD, mescaline and psilocybin, whilst 'psychedelia' was used to describe the variety of graphic and musical styles that tried to reproduce or evoke these effects, as well as the devices and paraphernalia – posters, textiles, LIGHT SHOWS, TRIP GOGGLES – that embodied them. Dr Timothy Leary, the guru of the early HIPPIE drug culture, popularized the word in his journal, the *Psychedelic Review*. The psychedelic mixed-media shows that began on America's West Coast in 1965 involved dense, complex visual and aural effects, using projected marbled-coloured patterns produced on oil and water slides, stroboscopes and multitracked swirling sounds. By 1967 these techniques, together with the use of the wah-wah pedal and the wearing of floral and Paisley designs, scarves and Eastern regalia, had converged to create a 'psychedelic look' that was incorporated into the repertoire of progressive ROCK bands all over the English-speaking world.

By 1973 the concept was outdated, except among the remains of the COUNTERCULTURE. It went underground until a brief revival in Britain during 1981, when, stripped of its drug connotations, it became a confused fashion stance for some NEW ROMANTICS and GOTHS. Psychedelia took on a new significance – the word itself is now usually used with a sense of self-parody – following the 1988 ACID HOUSE craze, when youth culture staged a second 'Summer of Love' and again turned to LSD and ECSTASY for inspiration. Devotees of Acid House and the RAVE movement, as well as TRAVELLERS and

CYBERPUNKS, grafted elements of Sixties psychedelia on to a new high-technology version based on TECHNO music and computer-generated light effects.

- *Four million Americans took LSD, a psychedelic drug, last year. Dr Timothy Leary, leader of the Psychedelic Revolution who operates from a New York mansion, claims that those who 'turned on' were mainly university and middle-class people.*
  Sunday Times *magazine, 1 January 1967*

PSYCHOBILLY

A subdivision of the early Eighties ROCKABILLY movement, Psychobilly was inspired by the eccentric American group the Cramps, who had revived a strain of obscure, macabre and frenetic ROCK 'N' ROLL songs of the 1950s and written their own 'psychotic PSYCHEDELIC' pastiches during the PUNK era. Appearing in London around 1981, Psychobilly, also known as 'Mutant Rockabilly', involved frenzied, outlandish, often acrobatic stage acts and a visual style that combined spectacular QUIFFS, black leather, pseudo-occult and voodoo insignia and Rockabilly work clothes. Led by the Meteors, these groups played electric guitars, acoustic double bass and snare and tom-tom stand-up drum kits. The genre, already a parody of a parody, was itself parodied by the group King Kurt (who assaulted their audiences and each other) before it subsided in 1984. Obscure Psychobilly groups continued to perform to a small number of devotees into the 1990s.

PUB ROCK

The musical genre that immediately preceded and helped to create PUNK ROCK in the UK, Pub Rock was named after its environment. In reaction against the bombast and expense of POMP ROCK and the empty, camp posing of GLAM, an underground network of small venues, unrivalled in the USA or France, grew up all over Britain, allowing amateur and low-paid professional musicians to perform to small, local audiences. Many of these venues were underused rooms in pub or hotel premises; in London the best known were probably the Nashville Rooms in West Kensington, the Greyhound in Fulham Palace Road, and the Hope & Anchor in Islington. The music played under the heading of Pub Rock encompassed R & B, revivals of 1960s British pop, 1950s ROCK 'N' ROLL and American Country music. The unifying factor was that the music was raw and basic, usually based on a simple guitar and drum ensemble without synthesizers or orchestration. Pub Rock bands dressed down, favouring scruffy street clothes and Fifties and Sixties Rock poses.

One of the first groups to take to the pub circuit was Brinsley Schwarz (which included Nick Lowe), followed by Dr Feelgood, Bees Make Honey, Ducks Deluxe, Kilburn and the High Roads (containing Ian Dury and the founders of the Punk group 999) Dave Edmunds and Rockpile (credited by John Lennon with keeping Rock 'n' Roll alive in the early 1970s), the Motors, Eddy and the Hot Rods and scores of others. American GARAGE bands and Sixties revivalists such as the Flaming Groovies and Chris Wilson arrived to play to the same audiences. Small-time entrepreneurs began to manage the groups and to organize the concerts, as well as founding independent record labels such as Chiswick and Stiff. When the Punk phenomenon arrived in London from New York it began in London clubs, but the Pub Rock circuit provided the NEW WAVE with a training ground (Elvis Costello, Joe Strummer of the Clash, Poly Styrene of X-Ray Spex and many others all first performed in pubs) as well as a nationwide network of venues later adopted by the cabaret and ALTERNATIVE COMEDY circuit.

PUNK

In 1975 the Bohemian milieu of New York City had thrown up a new generation of would-be intellectual rebels whose writings appeared in December of that year in a ROCK-music FANZINE called Punk. These individuals, who included the poets Patti Smith and the poets/musicians Richard Hell and Tom Verlaine, adopted a pose inspired by the bourgeois-baiting shock tactics of the French poet Rimbaud and the nihilism of Nietzsche. At the same time, some GARAGE-band musicians were evolving a new style and attitude in reaction to the decadence of the mainstream Rock scene, which was still dominated by post-HIPPIE POMP ROCK. The pioneers of the new sound were the Ramones, a New York group who took the melodies of Sixties BEAT BOOM ballads and stripped them down to a repeated three chords, then speeded up the rhythm to a maximum. The Ramones wore the uniform – black leather jackets, dark glasses, torn jeans – and affected the inarticulate, brattish manner of a street gang.

At the same time in London, a disaffected generation made up of the self-consciously seedy tail-end of the GLAM ROCK movement, PUB ROCKERS and Hippie-despising teenagers was waiting for something to happen. The catalyst was the group the Sex Pistols masterminded by the boutique-owner Malcolm McLaren, who was familiar with the New York scene and who had ambitions to stage spectacular subversions on SITUATIONIST principles. The Sex Pistols began to play at private parties at the end of 1975; between then and the following September, when they headed the Punk Rock Festival at the 100 Club in Oxford Street, the new movement gathered pace. By the end of 1976, when the press had seized on the trend and denounced it, Punk had spread across the UK in less time than it took for it to cross the US to the West Coast, which led many later commentators to label it as a 'British' cult.

The British devotees of what became known as 'dole-queue Rock' added a stylized anger and despair to the American rebel-urchin pose. They imitated the adopting of '*noms de guerre*', introduced the rituals of GOBBING and POGOING and refined the Punk uniform with SAFETY PINS and SPIKE-TOP and MOHICAN hairstyles. The do-it-yourself ethos of the movement was propagated by fanzines and INDIE record labels. Punk was not a ground-swell expression of the angst of the working-class unemployed, but rather the emancipation of the nervous adolescent; the sensitive misfit taking on the adult world by adopting an extremist parody of nihilism. Punks were non-violent; their aggression was staged and symbolic. They pretended to sniff glue, and incorporated the imagery of sexual perversion into their look, but the drug they favoured was the artificial booster, speed, and they famously declared their disgust at sex ('three minutes of squelching noises') and love ('something you have for pet animals').

The first London Punk bands included the Damned, Siouxsie and the Banshees, Chelsea, Generation X, Subway Sect and the Clash, who were quickly joined by hundreds of provincial groups such as the Buzzcocks, Penetration and the Rezillos. In America the first wave of Punk Rockers – Television, Richard Hell and the Voidoids, Blondie, Talking Heads – stayed close to the 'art Rock' image; a second generation would imitate the British desperation pose. After its peak year of 1977, Punk continued as a musical force, taking with it the disparate strands known as NEW WAVE and spinning off the first ELECTRO pop, RANTING and INDUSTRIAL MUSIC, as well as the OI movement and the GOTHS, but by the end of the decade, it had run out of momentum and lapsed into self-parody. As early as 1978, in their book *The Boy Looked at Johnny – The Obituary of Rock 'n' Roll*, the music critics Julie Burchill and Tony Parsons had announced the demise of the movement, dismissing all its exponents as flawed or worse, with the exception of the political activist Tom Robinson Band and the ingenue X-Ray Spex. Nevertheless, new generations of teenage Punks continued to appear on the streets until the 1990s. The Punk uniform entered British folklore as the TEDDY BOY outfit had before it, and a sanitized version of the black Punk ensemble became the fashion standard of the Eighties.

- *Punk Rock is the sickest, seediest step in a rock world which thought it had seen it all.*
  Daily Mail, *August 1976*

- *God save the Queen – She's not a human being . . .*
  There is no future – In England's dream . . .
  We are the flowers in the dustbin . . .
  We are the poison in the machine . . .
  We are the romance behind the screen . . .
  Lyrics to 'God Save the Queen' by the Sex Pistols, 1977

PUSSY-POWER

See THEME DISCOS.

PYRAMIDS

It was the HIPPIE culture of the late 1960s that seized on older occult traditions in order to revive the myth of the power of pyramids. The proportions of the Great Pyramid of ancient Egypt supposedly gave it supernatural powers. Miniature replicas were said to have the same properties of focusing cosmic energy, and were bought by enthusiasts at the end of the Sixties as some of the first NEW AGE decorative conversation pieces, or with the more practical intention of keeping razor-blades sharp. At the 1971 Glastonbury Free Festival in England, the stage was dominated by a huge pyramid designed to attract positive vibrations, emanations from the earth and aerial powers. In 1991 pyramids were the subject of media attention when it was discovered that the Duchess of York had been visiting a New Age healer who treated her patients under a room-sized pyramid.

QUIFF

A plume of hair worn over the forehead by men, the quiff was an
integral part – along with the DA – of the 1950s ROCK 'N' ROLL and
TEDDY BOY look exported from the USA. It had the advantage of
being luxuriant and provocative while not offending the taboos of
the time against long back and sides. Quiffs, including the elaborate
ELEPHANT'S TRUNK version, were abandoned by the fashionable during
the 1960s, but enjoyed a brief revival by the retro-ROCK band Sha-na-
na and the proto-GLAM Roxy Music in 1971. During the PUNK era in
1977 and 1978 a new generation of Teds surfaced wearing versions
of the quiff that were restrained in comparison with those sported by
the Revillos parody group of the same period. The major resurrection
of the quiff took place in the early Eighties in the context of the
ROCKABILLY and PSYCHOBILLY crazes. The émigré American Stray
Cats popularized it, but the fashion-conscious young flirted only
briefly with quiffs before opting for the more manageable UNICORN or
FLAT-TOP.

R

RAËLIAN MOVEMENT

Raëlians are named after a Monsieur Raël, a French sports journalist who in 1973 witnessed a UFO landing in the Perigord and was instructed in the secrets of human existence by an alien dressed in green. According to Raël's teachings, extraterrestrials created humankind and supplied the planet Earth with its great religious leaders and philosophers, who will be brought back at some future date to establish an embassy. The international movement claims 27,000 members and assets of at least $2 million and hopes to welcome our creators once terrestrial problems have been overcome. Raëlians promote a sort of cosmic consciousness based on a reinterpretation of traditional religious beliefs combined with so-called 'sensual meditation'.

RAGGA

An alternative name for Dancehall Reggae, Ragga is a Jamaican musical style involving a REGGAE sound stripped of its African and political 'roots' overtones and combined with SAMPLING and TALKOVER by star DJs. Some critics inside and outside Jamaica vilified Ragga, which developed in the later 1980s, for its suggestive, sexist, amoral lyrics and its identification with ghetto gangsterism and drug subculture (it may take its name from 'ragamuffin man', an expression meaning a street-smart 'wide boy', and also the origin of 'Reggae'). In spite or because of this aspect of the music, the fame of the leading exponents of Ragga, who included Shabba Ranks and Ninja Man, spread beyond Jamaica to Britain and the USA, where non-RASTAFARIAN Jamaican culture had been taking hold since the late Seventies. The original Ragga and its local Caribbean references merged with local HIP HOP culture in both its new homes, mutating into American Ragamuffin RAP and British Hip Hop Reggae.

- *Reggae has always been the music of struggle, but ragga has tended to avoid issues.*
  Black record producer Mikey Bennett, Sky Magazine, *August 1991*

RAI

Rai is a version of traditional Algerian music played on 'Western' electronic instruments. It combines Arab and Berber melodies with pastiche ROCK and Latin sounds, more recently adding elements of FUNK and HOUSE music. Rai emerged among émigrés in Paris during the late 1970s and was sold and broadcast in Algeria, where it faced continuing disapproval from conservatives and Islamic fundamentalists. The music achieved a crossover into fashionable white club culture in France and to a lesser extent in Britain and Germany during the early 1980s, in keeping with the vogue for WORLD MUSIC and eclectic DANCEFLOOR styles. By the end of the Eighties it had penetrated the American market for exoticism via the New York club the Harem. Rai's best-known male exponent is probably Cheb Khaled; among its many female singers Chabba Fadela is the most famous.

- *Rai, a music in which singers are paid upfront cash on a no-royalty basis and sing the vocal tracks before the music is laid down, and in which a 16-track studio and a Roland 808 drum machine are the apex of technology, can only be a diversion in the non-Algerian world.*
  David Toop, The Face, *February 1988*

RAM-RAIDING

A criminal fad that attracted British media attention during 1991 in conjuction with the HOTTING craze. Carried out by youths operating in a delinquent underclass based on council housing estates, ram-raiding consisted of using powerful cars stolen to order to ram shop fronts in smash-and-grab raids. The cars used were generally destroyed and abandoned at the scene, the gang escaping in a second, accompanying car, also stolen. The perpetrators of ram-raiding often achieved hero status within their communities. Within a year ram-raiding had been adopted by professional criminals all over the UK. A variation on the original technique was to use stolen earth-moving equipment to wrench cash-dispensers from walls.

R & B

A musical label that has been applied to many different styles, Rhythm and Blues generally suggests an electric guitar-based, speeded-up and hence danceable version of the traditional black American blues. In the 1940s the two words were first combined to describe the fast swing music played by 'jump bands' and recorded for young all-black audiences under the umbrella heading of 'race music'. During the 1950s electric guitarists evolved a version of this orchestral music with a strengthened beat and rhythm and strong simple lyrics and melodies. The frenetic gospel-tinged end of this spectrum of sounds evolved via Little Richard and Chuck Berry into the predominantly white ROCK 'N' ROLL genre. The electric blues styles of John Lee Hooker, Muddy Waters, B. B. King and Johnny 'Guitar' Watson formed another strand, which heavily influenced the purist blues underground in post-TRAD Britain during the early 1960s. From those enthusiasts – Cyril Davies, John Mayall, Alexis Korner – and from record imports a younger generation, including the future Rolling Stones, Beatles, Animals and Them, for example, took R & B and used it as a basis for the British BEAT BOOM. Even the then progressive groups who inspired PSYCHEDELIA and later HARD ROCK and HEAVY METAL, among them the Yardbirds and the Who, all began by playing what they referred to as R & B.

Meanwhile in the USA during the early to mid-Sixties the term was being used indiscriminately for any commercial black music that was not jazz. The record charts published at that time under the heading of R & B (to distinguish them from mainstream pop) were filled with groups who would now be thought of as SOUL or gospel acts. (In the 1990s R & B continues to be used in the music press and among black Americans as a synonym for Soul, FUNK, Gospel and some elements of DISCO.) From the late 1960s to the mid-1970s, R & B was swamped by more flamboyant and complex versions of Rock. It surfaced again as the mainstay of British PUB ROCK between 1974 and 1978, and in the 1990s is still being played, but maintains a low and unfashionable profile in an age of electronic DANCEFLOOR and WORLD MUSIC.

- *R & B artists who kicked off '65 with tremendous success have been the Impressions, the Marvelettes, who made a tremendous comeback with 'Too Many Fish in the Sea', Marvin Gaye, the Drifters and Ben E. King.*

Rave *magazine, February 1965*

- *Once, rock drew its transgressive power from flaunting the body, celebrating the 'raw truth' of desire. The directness dirt and insistence of R 'n' B was the dangerous energy in pop.*
  Simon Reynolds, Against Health and Efficiency, *1986*

RANTING

One of the first alternative performance arts triggered off by the PUNK phenomenon (and inaugurating the pub cabaret and ALTERNATIVE COMEDY movements) was Ranting. This was a short-lived style of politically conscious hectoring poetry characterized by an exaggeratedly aggressive, quick-fire rhythmic delivery using the nasal sneer of hard-core Punk songs. Its best-known proponents were Steven 'Seething' Wells, a SKINHEAD poet later to become a music journalist for the *NME*, and Attila the Stockbroker. Ranting (the word, defined as 'to declaim excitedly', is from Old Dutch) was inspired by the original Ranters, an extremist Puritan sect active in the 1640s, whose adherents advocated freedom from moral constraints for the elect and the overthrow of the social order. Their apocalyptic preachers, who included Joseph Salmon and Abiezer Coppe, sometimes stripped naked to deliver hysterical and obscene sermons. (The Ranter epithet was later also applied to so-called Primitive Methodist preachers of the early 1800s.) The 20th-century incarnation lapsed into obscurity by about 1983.

RAP

Rap is the quick-fire spoken monologue over musical backing that, along with GRAFFITI and BREAK DANCING, formed the basis of the black HIP HOP culture of the 1980s and 1990s. In its current form, Rap was born in the housing projects of New York's South Bronx around 1974, when local disc jockeys presiding over open-air parties began to imitate the Jamaican custom of TALKOVER or TOASTING (declaiming an improvised rhythmic chant through a microphone while playing ready-made records on turntables). It may have been the Jamaican Kool DJ Herc who introduced the technique while visiting New York;

Jamaican immigrants were in any case playing recordings of REGGAE exponents such as U-Roy and Jack Ruby MC to their neighbours.

Not only did Rap not require any instruments or professional expertise, it also fed into a long tradition of public poetry and oratory in Afro-American culture, from the tribal storytellers of Africa through the Caribbean Creole oral historians via the pre-Second World War bebop JIVE-talk monologues of Cab Calloway and the talking blues that had been emulated by ROCK and SOUL musicians from Bo Diddley to James Brown. The 'Godfather of Hip Hop', Afrika Bambaataa, distinguished other forms of 'proto-Rap': the seductive love talk of the FUNK singers Barry White and Isaac Hayes; the late 1960s performances of the Last Poets; the gospel-influenced harangues of Malcolm X and the boxer Muhammad Ali; and the onstage banter of the singer Millie Jackson.

In New York, the Rap artists, now using the MC label and imitating the colourful pseudonyms of the Jamaicans, formed 'posses' or 'crews' that competed among themselves in Rapping contests. In 1979 the Sugarhill Gang had the first hit record featuring Rap, 'Rapper's Delight'; this was followed by Grandmaster Flash and the Furious Five's 'The Message' and 'Planet Rock' by Afrika Bambaataa and the Sonic Soul Force. Teenagers emulated the DJs and girls joined in as the underground novelty became an adolescent craze in the inner cities. Small independent record labels such as Sugarhill, Winley and Enjoy were founded, and Rap unwittingly revolutionized performing and recording techniques with its amateur 'quick mixing' (blending snatches from existing records into a kind of collage). Mixing evolved the SCRATCH technique, which in turn developed into SAMPLING.

The music chosen to back Rap was originally defined as 'anything funky' and could include Rock, jazz and SOCA as well as Soul, Funk and DISCO. Around 1982 the first generation of Rap stars, who had promoted themselves with a flashy showbiz visual style, were overtaken by newer sub-genres, including the brash, streetwise B-BOYS, the mock-futuristic ELECTRO, and the controversial Gangster Rap. Rap lyrics had always concentrated on strutting bombast and ritualized macho boasting as well as social comment, but to critics Gangster Rap consolidated the movement's reputation as sexist, racist, homophobic and potentially dangerous. Often using obscene lyrics, this form of Rap – represented by performers such as Ice-T, NWA, the Geto Boys and 2 Live Crew – seemed to celebrate the drive-by shooting and drug-dealing subculture that had taken over

American ghettos, as well as treating women with a fearful contempt. The ambivalent attitude to hoodlum mythology among Rappers was reflected in the early 1990s by films such as *Boyz 'n' the Hood* and *New Jack City*, which veered between social conscience and exploitation.

Not all Rap adopted this hard-core stance: WASP, Hispanic and some Asian Rappers, as well as international hit performers such as MC Hammer, widened the appeal of the mainstream style from 1987, whilst in 1988 groups such as the Jungle Brothers and De La Soul proclaimed the HIPPIE-tinged 'Daisy Age' by throwing flowers at audiences. By 1992 Rap was being practised in schools, in the broadcast media, in TV ads for Pepsi, and beyond the English-speaking world. There were more and more examples of Rap and Hip Hop combining with other musical forms in crossover fusions such as Ragamuffin Rap, Hip-Hop Reggae and Hip House.

- *. . . When they said kill I felt chill, man . . . But once I pulled the trigger then things got ill, man . . . My homeboys dipped out the back fast . . . Left me alone in the echo of the gunblast . . .*
  Lyrics to 'The Hunted Child', Ice-T, 1990

- *Though rap regularly namechecks peace and God, that great MC in the sky, it is really built on dumb machismo and grasping materialism.*
  Tony Parsons, Weekend Telegraph, *May 1991*

RARE GROOVE

So-called Rare Groove was one fashion among many making up London DANCEFLOOR club culture in the mid-1980s. It began in 1983 as a DJ-led revival of 1960s SOUL music and early 1970s Soul and FUNK and was based on rare or obscure imported records as well as better-known classics, particularly James Brown, on sometimes illicit reissues, and local live groups, the most prominent being the Brand New Heavies. Rare Groove music was accompanied by its own mini-subculture who broadcast it on PIRATE radio and also made an attempt, peaking in 1987, to reintroduce fashions of the Seventies, including flared trousers, caps, tartan and lamé clothing and PLATFORM boots.

RASTAFARIANISM

Derived from 'Ras Tafari', one of the titles of the late Emperor of
Ethiopia, Haile Selassie, Rastafarianism is a liberationist philosophy
and religion of the oppressed which is native to Jamaica. It is a recent
manifestation of an older tradition, combining the idea of a messianic
black liberator with a cult of 'Ethiopianism' based on biblical
references and more recent legends of fabulous Abyssinian kingdoms,
and repatriation to Africa. Rastafarianism began as an underground
movement of the 1940s among sympathizers of the pre-war political
leader Marcus Garvey, and until 1965 its main support was among
poorly educated slum dwellers. In 1966 Ras Tafari himself, considered
a living deity, visited Jamaica and addressed his followers, advising
them to liberate themselves in their own country before thinking of
returning to Africa. Over the next few years the religion attracted more
widespread support, drawing in ex-Christians and, most importantly,
because they represented folk heroes in local youth culture, a number
of RUDE BOYS. A Rastafarian offshoot called the People's Democratic
Movement was set up in Notting Hill, London, in 1966, but it was the
merging of Rastafarianism with REGGAE subculture that gave it a new
impetus and spread its trappings beyond the Caribbean (DREADLOCKS,
'tam' berets and emblematic colours of red, green, gold and black) and
its 'soul talk' (patois terms like 'I and I' for 'we', and the notion of
blacks in exile in a white 'Babylon', yearning for an African 'Zion').

While Bob Marley and others spread the image, if not the substance,
of Rasta, first to the remains of the COUNTERCULTURE, then to the
international music scene and finally to political establishments in
the developing world, in Britain and the USA during the later 1970s
'white Rastas' (sympathizers and women married into the faith)
appeared in the inner cities. Some critics of Rastafarianism – not
all of them white supremacists – disapprove of its systematic use of
'ganja' (herbal marijuana) as a sacrament; others are disturbed by what
they see as a demeaning role for women in the movement. In the US
alleged links with drug dealing in the 1970s and 'Yardie' gangs in
the 1980s led to the arrest and harassment of New York Rastafarians.
In Jamaica itself, the decline of purist 'roots' culture and the rise of
political and criminal violence in the late Eighties accompanied a
lessening in the influence of Rastafarianism.

RAVE GRANNIES

An ephemeral nickname used in some youth circles in Britain during the early 1990s to define a category of female to be found in the RAVE and CRUSTY subcultures. The counterpart of the male SOAP-DODGER, she is characterized by a neo-HIPPIE or post-PUNK appearance, typically wearing a loose black dress over heavy boots – hence the comparison with an archaic peasant/grannie.

RAVES

The terms 'rave' and 'rave-up' were first used to describe wild parties or occasions of abandoned behaviour in Bohemian circles in Britain during the late 1950s. In the early 1960s the words were briefly adopted by the MODS, and shortly thereafter were picked up by the media and the older generation. Among the fashionable young, 'rave' became a comic archaism until the 1980s, when it was simultaneously revived by two separate strands of youth culture. Students and middle-class teenagers, evoking the Sixties spirit semi-facetiously, began to use the word again when referring to large-scale parties; meanwhile black SOUL music enthusiasts took up the word – probably from Jamaican usage – to describe their own network of private parties and amateur DISCOS. When the ACID HOUSE movement began to operate WAREHOUSING in the late 1980s, the mobile underground mass celebrations – inspired by Ibizan models and featuring non-stop frenzied dancing – were known as Raves or, if strategically located for the M25 motorway ringing London, as Orbital Raves. The subculture that coalesced around Acid House expanded to encompass other musical genres, including TECHNO and INDIE POP, while the ECSTASY-influenced hedonism, clothing (a mixture of BAGGY and neo-PSYCHEDELIC) and poses that accompanied it became known as the Rave Scene, peopled by stereotypes known, in addition to Ravers, as RAVE GRANNIES and SOAP-DODGERS. In the early Nineties Rave enthusiasts joined forces with TRAVELLERS and CRUSTIES to reinforce the summer open-air free-festival circuit. Like those subcultures before them, they began to operate in tribal groupings with names like Spiral Tribe, the Electro-people, Shiny Protein, bringing with them HIGH TEC accoutrements (in some cases mobile phones and faxes) and entrepreneurism, as well as their militant hedonism.

REAGANOMICS

A term first heard in the USA in 1981 to describe the economic policies and ideology of the Ronald Reagan administration (1980–1988). A collection of notions and practices, rather than a coherent philosophy, Reaganomics encompassed elements of MONETARISM, TRICKLE-DOWN THEORY, tax-cutting, welfare cuts, the reduction of central government intervention, and increased defence spending. Like its contemporary, THATCHERISM, Reaganomics at first resulted in job creation and increased economic activity, but by the end of the administration its most noticeable legacy was a huge budget deficit. Reaganomics seemed to be born of a combination of negligent right-wing populism and an underlying assumption of a confrontational foreign policy, neither of which could sustain the Bush administration that followed.

REBIRTHING

See PRIMAL SCREAM.

RECREATIONAL SHOPPING

An extreme manifestation of mid-1980s consumer culture, recreational shopping was shopping pursued as a hobby or competitive sport – the ultimate illustration of 'conspicuous consumption' and 'commodity fetishism' as defined by sociologists. The term was coined in the USA to describe a phenomenon that was briefly reported in the British media in 1987 before the worldwide stock-market crash of 'Black Monday' signalled the end of the boom years of the enterprise culture. Whereas in Britain recreational shopping was a self-conscious pose by YUPPIES, fashion followers and CONCEPTUAL ART pranksters, in the US it was merely a retitling of the habits of JAPS, VALLEY GIRLS and other habitués of shopping malls and designer stores. In Japan the practice was so commonplace as to be taken for granted. Recreational shoppers planned their forays meticulously, vying with one another to spend more, to amass more purchases, or to display more prestigious labels on their return. Their activities were celebrated on BADGES and postcards by slogans including 'Shop till you Drop', 'I Shopped for England', and 'I Shop Therefore I Am'. As practised by some devotees, recreational shopping was a form of self-aware offensive CONSUMERISM, extolled by the French POST-MODERNIST critic Jean Baudrillard as a positive response to the HYPERREALITY of modern society. In the early Nineties recreational shopping reappeared in the teen market in the form of computerized board games such as Barbie Goes Shopping, Girl Talk, Mall Madness and Pretty Pretty Pretty Princess.

RECYCLED FASHION

See JUNK ART.

REFLEXOLOGY

Reflexology concentrates on the soles of the feet, which are seen as providing a map of the whole body. The technique, which comprises massage and pressure, uses the concept of body 'meridians' employed in ACUPUNCTURE. As an alternative healing technique, reflexology makes spiritual and medical claims that are disputed by some orthodox practitioners, but it is certainly effective in the treatment of stress.

REGGAE

Reggae is the slower, more textured and refined musical style that evolved directly from ROCKSTEADY, SKA and BLUEBEAT in Jamaica at the very end of the 1960s. During the Seventies Reggae quickly adopted synthesizers and multitracking DUB techniques in place of the tinny, spare, amateur sound of its forerunners. The rise of RASTAFARIAN culture and the conversion or decline of the RUDE BOYS gave the new genre a political and religious underpinning as well as an African leaning in its lyrics, sounds and accompanying dress. Reggae moved from being a local subcultural curiosity to become an internationally famous musical movement after the white Jamaican impresario Chris Blackwell, owner of the Island record label, gave Bob Marley and the Wailers £4000 to record *Catch a Fire*, their first album, in 1972. Other original Reggae stars included Toots and the Maytals and Peter Tosh. 'Toots' Hibbert actually coined the name of the music in 1968 (it is a patois rendering of 'rags' or 'ragamuffin man', a term of disapproval used by respectable citizens of the Rude Boys) and it first appeared in the song title 'Do the Reggae'. Johnny Nash introduced a sanitized form of Reggae into the US in the mid-1970s via his hit 'I Can See Clearly Now'; this was later reinforced in the American ghettoes by Jamaican immigrants' sound-system parties, which contributed to the RAP and HIP HOP musical movements of the 1980s.

Reggae music as promoted by Bob Marley became strongly identified with the struggle for emancipation in the Third World during the late 1970s, combining a new international political status with commercial success in terms of record sales. Different varieties came and went in Jamaica, where ethnically conscious 'roots' Reggae was followed by heavy, minimalist Dub and then ROCKERS, while in Britain local blacks formed their own Reggae groups (Aswad, the Cimarons and Steel Pulse being the most prominent), as did musicians in South Africa, France and elsewhere. Reggae rhythms and melodies affected the indigenous dance-music styles of many African and Caribbean regions. White PUNKS and leftists also embraced the sound and ethos of Reggae and its associated street style, and mainstream SOUL and ROCK musicians recorded with Jamaican rhythm and horn sections. The early death of Bob Marley left Reggae without an international figurehead and in the 1980s the bastardized RAGGA ousted traditional Reggae as the ghetto favourite in Jamaica itself. In the jumbled European DANCEFLOOR culture of the late Eighties and early Nineties, Reggae and Ska elements, sometimes performed by 'purist' local groups, but often now merging with Rap and Hip Hop, could still be heard.

REICHIANISM

Wilhelm Reich began as an intimate of Sigmund Freud in Vienna and died in 1957, imprisoned by the US Federal Food and Drug Administration. He posthumously became a hero of the UNDERGROUND and was celebrated in the 1968 film *WR – Mysteries of the Organism* by the Yugoslav director Dusan Makaveyev. Reich claimed to have discovered a natural force he called 'orgone energy', made up of electrochemical 'orgone' particles from outer space. He based all his theories on the idea that the psychic and political repression of the individual is brought on by sexual repression, and that sexual liberation is a revolutionary process. Not surprisingly, Reich was hounded out of Austria and Germany by the psychiatric and political authorities. In the USA he constructed 'orgone boxes' in which patients could be treated. By the late 1950s Reich showed signs of delusion beyond mere eccentricity, but was prosecuted for infringing drug laws by selling his boxes. Although his pseudo-scientific claims were discredited, his liberationist ideas continued to influence radicals through the 1970s and 1980s. In the Nineties NEW AGE devotees began again to promote the benefits of the orgone box.

REMIXING

Like SCRATCHING and SAMPLING, the technique of remixing originated in DUB and became associated with the rise of the producer and DJ and the loss of status for the recording artist in the world of 1980s DISCO and DANCEFLOOR music. Remixing involved electronically manipulating, enhancing and augmenting an original studio production to produce new versions. The practice began with the creation of instrumental versions of hit singles in order to provide instant B-sides, 12-inch singles (as opposed to 7-inch) and album-fillers. Longer 'dancefloor versions' of standard-length hits were engineered in the late 1970s for use by live DJs who vied to play novel mixes; fans proved willing to buy several incarnations of the same record, and earlier hits could be updated and re-released. It became controversial when producers reworked music without the permission of the original artists or copyright holders. Remixing should be distinguished from mixing (see RAP), a HIP HOP technique in which sounds are blended by using twin turntables.

RENEES

The Renees, or 'Reens', were a social group identified by the all-girl post-PUNK band the Gymslips in London in 1980. In their album *Rocking with the Renees*, and also in their anthem 'We're the Reens', they satirized earnest proletarian pride as promoted by earlier groups such as Sham 69 and the fascist OI movement, while celebrating a genuine local subculture of hard-drinking, fun-loving south London women, characteristically wearing short hair and MONKEY BOOTS. The nickname they chose was the working-class pronunciation of the (originally French) girl's Christian name, thought to be quintessentially KITSCH.

REPETITIVE MUSIC

Also known as Process Music, Ambient Music and sometimes as
'wallpaper music', this is a genre of progressive electronic music
inspired by the compositions of Erik Satie, cyclical Indian ragas, and
the earlier avant-garde works of John Cage, Stockhausen and others.
Without lyrics or traditional climaxes and resolutions, Repetitive
Music reflected the impersonality and MINIMALISM of much art of
the late 1960s to the mid-1970s. Its major exponents during the Sixties
were LaMonte Young, Steve Reich and Terry Riley, whose album
containing 'Rainbow in Curved Air' and 'In C' was the first example
of this type of music to achieve a crossover into the collections of
non-specialist record-buyers.

Repetitive Music came into its own in the mid-1970s, represented
on the progressive wing by Philip Glass and Harold Budd, and on
the commercial by Tangerine Dream, Vangelis, Jean-Michel Jarre
and Klaus Schulze. In a central role was Brian Eno, the British
manipulator of electronics and promoter of what he called Ambient
Music – a sort of cerebral muzak or sound environment. Eno,
formerly a member of the GLAM band Roxy Music, had helped to
gather disparate strands of the British and American art ROCK scene,
including Nico, John Cale, Kevin Ayers and Robert Wyatt, to perform
together; he followed this by creating the Obscure record label to
release his own recordings and others by experimental composers
in sympathy with his ideas. Eno thus brought Repetitive Music to
the attention of a wider pop and jazz audience; the result was to
trigger a new commercial genre of NEW AGE MUSIC, which appealed
particularly to Americans enthused by the increased sound quality of
the compact disc. By the mid-1980s repetitive electronic music was
established, particularly for soundtracks for cinema films, as in Philip
Glass's *Koyaanisqatsi* and Michael Nyman's work for the director
Peter Greenaway. A little later it was also established for British
TV drama, a development partly pioneered by the BBC's Electronic
Workshop.

- *. . . my own pleasure in 'gradual processes' prevented me from
  attempting to create surprises and less than predictable changes in
  the piece. I was trying to make a piece that could be listened to and
  yet could be ignored . . .*
      Brian Eno, sleeve notes to Discreet Music, 1975

RHYMING SLANG

Rhyming slang appeared in the rich argot of the working-class subcultures of London's East End in the mid-19th century. Probably first used by criminals and street traders as a secret code, it consisted of taking an everyday term or catch phrase as a rhymed substitute for the term to be communicated. The system worked as well for innocent terms – 'whistle and flute' for 'suit'; 'Barnet Fair' for 'hair' – as for taboo words, for example 'raspberry tart' for 'fart' and 'Berkshire' or 'Berkeley Hunt' for 'cunt' (then meaning 'fool'). As the rhyming formulations became more widely known in the community they were abbreviated, giving the modern 'whistle', 'barnet', 'raspberry' and 'berk' – the latter two often used in innocence of their origins. For most of its existence rhyming slang has remained within its original social and geographical milieu, although it was exported to Australia, where native examples were coined, for example 'Noah's' (Arks) or 'Joan of Arcs' for 'sharks'. In the 1950s the disdain of the fashionable for working-class culture ensured that London slang remained marginalized; in the late 1960s slang itself became fashionable, but it was the American HIP TALK variety that prevailed all over the Anglophone world. It was not until the late 1970s that middle-class British Bohemia began to employ rhyming slang. Others too adopted it with enthusiasm, for example the drug subculture, which coined terms such as 'Uncle Mac' (a children's radio presenter of the Fifties) for 'smack' or heroin, and university students, amongst whom at the end of the 1980s there was a vogue for rhyming-pun equivalents for classes of degree: 'Douglas' (Hurd) for Third, 'Patty' (Hearst) for First. By the early 1990s rhyming slang was thriving in a number of milieux, with adolescents, pub habitués, journalists and the homeless coining their own neologisms. Meanwhile, in its place of origin inventing new rhymes was a point of pride among street traders in particular, so that in one market the till or cash register might be the 'Buffalo Bill', in the next the 'Benny Hill'.

ROCKABILLY

After PUNK subsided, British fashion and youth culture cast around for new influences to feed the need for novelty and excitement. Among the rag-bag of visual styles experimented with at the very end of the 1970s was a parody 1950s hillbilly/Country and Western look.

This set of images meshed with the cowboy stereotype chosen by some gays (see GAY LIBERATION), the appeal of second-hand American work clothes imported by such stores as Flip, and the continuing fascination with Fifties ROCK 'N' ROLL that had created retro-Teds (see TEDDY BOYS) in 1976, but which had been submerged by Punk. The musical genre around which all these influences coalesced was Rockabilly, a fast, lightweight dance style based on the music of Johnny Burnette, Clyde McPhatter and Mac Curtis, amongst others, and using piano, minimal guitar sound and stand-up bass. It was a sub-genre that had been waiting its turn since around 1974, sustained by an underground network of purist record collectors. Like the SKIFFLE of the late 1950s, to which it was related, Rockabilly could be played on cheap instruments by inexperienced musicians, and was suitable for busking. It was music without a message, but with an accompanying stance of swagger and energy that appealed to teenagers, art students and former Punks. A new generation of groups, including the Stray Cats, the Polecats and the Shakin' Pyramids, re-created the sound – now usually speeded up – and the image, which settled into a uniform of work shirts, T-shirts and blue jeans, worn with a QUIFF or a FLAT-TOP if male, and a PONYTAIL if female.

The Rockabilly boom, supported by the music press and by a few radio DJs such as John Peel, lasted from 1979 to the middle of 1984, by which time it had generated the parody sub-genres of PSYCHOBILLY, represented by the American Cramps, who had been playing a manic form of Rockabilly since 1977, and the Meteors, and Countrybilly, represented by such transient names as Yip Yip Coyote, Tex and the Horseheads, and the eccentric Scot, Champion Doug Veitch. The high-fashion scene also took note: Vivienne Westwood's Hobo and Buffalo Girl collections of 1982 were part of the same matrix. Rockabilly also swept France and Japan, while in the USA less derivative musicians such as Los Lobos and the TEX-MEX bands were playing new forms of Country and Rock.

ROCK AGAINST RACISM

A left-wing pressure group formed in 1976 by a number of journalists, musicians and political activists to combat the threat of right-wing extremism then being manifested by attacks on blacks and Asians and in the resurgence in the streets and at the polls of the National Front and British National Party. RAR's secondary aim was to counter the tendency within ROCK music itself towards forms of fascism. David Bowie, the most influential product of GLAM ROCK, had given a Hitler salute before fans at Victoria Station; Eric Clapton had pledged support for the views of Enoch Powell; and in addition, the less sophisticated wing of the PUNK movement showed signs of emulating SKINHEAD racism and violence. The political initiative behind RAR came largely from the the Socialist Workers' Party, which had succeeded the International Socialists and the more militant Trotskyite Socialist Labour League and International Marxist Group as the leading group on the revolutionary Left. RAR used concerts to raise money and to provide public platforms from which to denounce the far Right; they also published a FANZINE-format newsletter called 'Temporary Hoarding', which featured interviews with pop music celebrities.

In April 1977 riots involving 4000 demonstrators attempting to prevent 1000 members of the National Front from marching through Lewisham in south London galvanized the movement and triggered mass meetings of RAR in the form of free public carnivals (100,000 gathered at Victoria Park in east London in March 1978 to watch the Tom Robinson Band, the Clash, Steel Pulse and X-Ray Spex) as well as the formation of the Anti-Nazi League to carry on non-musical campaigning. Rock against Racism's tactics were successful. By mobilizing fans of Punk, PUB ROCK and REGGAE, they demonstrated that they could consistently swamp the racist minority movements, even in areas thought to be their strongholds. They firmly established the solidarity between white and black musical subcultures, as well as the libertarian credentials of a generation of musicians. The National Front never repeated its electoral successes, but the Anti-Nazi League, disbanded in 1980, was resuscitated in 1992 in the face of increased activity by the British National Party and other European extremists.

ROCK DOUBLES

A series of novelty musical acts appearing in Australia at the end of the 1980s, ROCK doubles, also known as clone bands or tribute acts, were parodies or pastiches of real stars, living or dead. Beginning as homage by besotted fans or as jokes mounted by amateurs, the idea caught the imagination of pop and Rock audiences and lovers of camp and KITSCH. Rock doubles toured Australia, coming to the notice of the British media in 1991. The best known of these performers were probably Bjorn Again, a tongue-in-cheek but faithful re-creation of Abba; the Australian Doors and the Australian Cure, both also straightforward imitations of the originals; and Elton Jack. More eccentric versions of the genre included the Village Girls, a parody of the all-male Village People, and a trio of gay male impersonators of Kylie Minogue. U2, the Eurhythmics, Madonna, James Brown and many others were also being presented by doubles in Australia. In Britain the White re-created Led Zeppelin hits at fan conventions in 1992, while the Counterfeit Stones gigged on the London club and pub circuit.

Although there was a tradition of mockery by imitation in the Rock world – for instance the Beatles-imitating Rutles, Elvis look-alikes and the comedy REGGAE band Dread Zeppelin, among many others – this new explosion of impersonators may have been more than a joke. One element was the WANNABE phenomenon whereby admirers, no longer content only to dress as their idols, were determined to live out their roles in full; another was the determination of audiences to have live performances of their favourite songs, even if the originators were dead, jaded or unwilling (although U2, the Cure and the B-52s met and endorsed their clones). To these two manifestations of 'audience power' could be added the simple profit motive: Rock double acts were 'market-led' and lucrative.

- *'I think its a sad, crappy idea, but criticising them is like picking on little fluffy animals – they're just giving the public what it wants.'*
  John Casmir, Sydney music journalist, quoted in The Face,
  January 1992

- *. . . those groups are an open jive, a kind of post-modern joke at the expense of those original trailblazers to whom they pay a kind of irreverent lip-service in the form of low-camp kitsch.*
  Time Out, *17 June 1992*

ROCKERS

Rockers were the British bikers of the 1960s, although without the outlaw ethos and glamour that that word suggests. First known in the late 1950s as Ton-up Kids from their obsession with 'doing the ton' (reaching 100 mph) and later, occasionally, as Leather Boys (the title of an exploitation film of 1964), these mainly working-class, white teenagers and young men (women were involved, but usually in a

secondary role) based their lifestyle around 1950s ROCK 'N' ROLL music
– hence their nickname, which only became established after about
1962. With this lifestyle went an American 'rebel' look of greased hair,
black leather and denim, substantially different from the dandified
TEDDY BOY ensembles of a slightly earlier era. Rockers covered
a narrow part of the spectrum of youth subculture, incorporating
speed-obsessed delinquents on the one hand, and traditional, fairly
innocuous motorcycle enthusiasts on the other. (There were also some
Rockers who did not own motorbikes: this group favoured ice-blue
drainpipe jeans, luminous socks and WINKLE-PICKER shoes, confining
themselves to a fanatical devotion to Rock 'n' Roll.)

The rebellious and individualistic public image of Rockers belied
their usually conservative attitudes to drugs, music, race and even sex.
They were authentic daredevils, however, congregating at strategic
points such as the Ace Café on London's North Circular Road, the
Busy Bee on the Watford bypass and Chelsea Bridge before staging
a race or 'burn-up' (riding at top speed), which might end in a fatal
crash. Some Rockers formed their own clubs; others were recruited
into anti-delinquent motorcycle youth clubs such as the 59 Club by
'Ton-up Vicars' like the Reverend Bill Shergold. The relatively small
numbers of Rockers active in 1963 and 1964 provoked the derision of
the scooter-riding working-class wing of the MOD movement, which
saw them as hopelessly outdated and unsophisticated. Rockers in
turn despised the Mods' conformism, effeteness and Europeanized
obsession with style, as well as their preferred music of SKA and SOUL.
The two groups fought running battles at seaside resorts on the south
coast of England during 1964, continuing to clash sporadically until
1967, when the remaining Mods mutated into HIPPIES or SKINHEADS.
The Rockers, known to their enemies as 'Greasers', metamorphosed
into middle-aged anonymity, into bikers, or, in a few cases, into HELL'S
ANGELS.

The word Rockers was used in a quite different context in 1976,
when it was applied to a heavy, ethnic variety of Jamaican REGGAE
music, a near relative of DUB.

● *. . . what mostly characterised the Rocker era was innocence.*
'Perversion' was unsuspected, or at any rate never spelt out. For
most Bike Boys, involvement with machines was and is part of an
adolescent trip on the way towards the marriage that brings normal
conformity.

Johnny Stuart, Rockers, *1987*

ROCKET COCKTAILS

A combined novelty drink and style accessory of 1991, the Rocket
Cocktail was an exotic cocktail, high in alcohol content and packaged
in a capsule or ampoule. Like the JELLO SHOT of 1990, it was typical of
attempts to re-present stimulants using high technology and/or NEW
AGE overtones, partly in order to emulate or compete with the SMART
DRUGS craze. Multicoloured Rocket Cocktails contained permutations
of blue curaçao, vodka, Cointreau, Bacardi and amaretto.

- *The . . . Rockets, which it is claimed contain 24 per cent pure
  alcohol, deliver a large shot of potent liqueurs directly on to the back
  of the throat through an outsize plastic syringe.*
  Evening Standard, *25 March 1992*

ROCK 'N' ROLL

A musical craze that erupted in 1954, quickly spreading from
high-school and college dances in the USA to Britain, Australia and
then beyond. Its first manifestation was via the no longer youthful-
looking dance band Bill Haley and the Comets, whose fans rioted
at live concerts and in cinemas where *Blackboard Jungle* or *Rock
Around the Clock* were shown. The words 'rock' and 'roll' are black
American euphemisms for sexual movements, although they had
been innocently combined as early as 1934 in a song title referring to
the motion of a ship; the phrase is usually ascribed to the American
disc jockey Alan Freed, who hosted a Cleveland radio show called
'Moondog's Rock and Roll Party' in 1951.

The first wave of Rock 'n' Roll was a blend of black JIVE and R & B
with Southern white Country music, played on electric guitars,
piano and optional saxophone and double bass. Its runaway success
probably owed much to the fact that the postwar youth culture
belonging to the newly defined 'teenager' was in need of a new form
of music to call its own, the jive and the JITTERBUG being essentially
hangovers from a prewar swing style. The new music was subversive
enough to provide a soundtrack for would-be rebels. From the
beginning it was promoted as 'crazy' and 'wild', and the *Blackboard
Jungle* soundtrack helped to fix its association with delinquency in
the public mind. The Southern white-trash image of its performers
was consolidated by the more sinister second wave, which included
Elvis Presley, Eddie Cochrane, Jerry Lee Lewis and Gene Vincent.

In Britain, imitators of the American trend graduated from the SKIFFLE world or were invented by impresarios. Tommy Steele, Cliff Richard, Adam Faith, Billy Fury and Marty Wilde all combined crooning with Rock and featured in the hit parade, but the broadcast media in the UK virtually boycotted the music, and the press vilified it, appalled at its perceived primitivism and at the threat of Americanization and showbiz vulgarity it posed. In Britain thereafter, Rock 'n' Roll always referred to a specific 1950s musical style, traditionally accompanied by jiving and practised by TEDDY BOYS and ROCKERS. In the US, for want of terms such as the UK's 'pop' or 'beat' (see BEAT BOOM), the phrase continued to be used for all loud, fast, white electric music. At the end of the 1960s the shorter form 'Rock' came to be used in Britain in the same way, referring to the forms heard from 1967 onwards, which included progressive Rock, FOLK Rock, boogie, HARD ROCK, HEAVY METAL, GLAM ROCK, POMP, PUB and PUNK Rock. However, the original Rock 'n' Roll, which had introduced the first mass fashion to flout bourgeois conventions openly, had contributed a pose, an ethos and a look so potent that it was revived and recycled constantly in the following decades, despite the rise of DISCO and HIP HOP. The most recent return to the early forms was the ROCKABILLY fad of 1979 to 1984.

- *Did you ever hear a tenor sax . . . Swinging like a rusty axe?*
  Honking like a frog . . . In a hollow log . . .
  Baby, that is rock and roll.
  You say that the music spoils the verse . . .
  But you can't understand the words . . .
  But baby if you did . . . You'd really blow your lid:
  Baby, that is rock and roll.
  Lyrics to 'That is Rock and Roll' by Leiber and Stoller,
  recorded by the Coasters, March 1959

ROCKSTEADY

A Jamaican musical form of the late 1960s that was an interim stage between BLUEBEAT, SKA and the better-known REGGAE. The differences between these genres is minimal, but Rocksteady was characterized by a slower, more hypnotic beat than Ska, whilst its feel was 'poppier' and its instrumentation cruder than that of Reggae. It was identified with the culture of RUDE BOYS rather than RASTAFARIANS.

ROLFING

Also known as structural integration, Rolfing is an alternative
therapy technique based on mysterious – and mystic – principles.
It involves stretching, massage and pressure applied to the human
body, especially the sinews and muscles. It is designed to combine
a 'liberation of the physical structure' and a 'restoration of elasticity
and gravity' with the release of emotional tensions. The manipulation
system was developed in the 1940s by the biological chemist Dr Ida
Rolf. In the mid-1960s Dr Rolf became attached to the Esalen Institute
in California, where her method became famous in fashionable
COUNTERCULTURE circles. In the Seventies she opened her own
institute, training therapists, or 'Rolfers', and propagating Rolfing to a
worldwide clientele of 'Rolfees'. It quickly established itself, helped
perhaps by its intriguing name, as one of the mainstays of the NEW
AGE repertoire.

ROLLERBLADING

A non-competitive high-technology sport of the early 1990s,
rollerblading is based on ice-skates fitted with a line of wheels,
first used by figure- and speed-skaters practising on concrete in the
absence of ice. Like the earlier SKATEBOARDING, STREET HOCKEY and
ICEBALL, it is an amateur activity, although by 1992 there were signs
of commercialization and promotion in the form of a magazine.
The sport originated in the USA and has been picked up by a small
number of British enthusiasts.

- . . . *a market that is threatening to overtake bikes as a fast and
  eco-friendly way of getting around.*
                                                  The Face, *January 1992*

ROLLER DISCO

The combining of roller-skating for adults with DISCO music was
a craze at the end of the 1970s. Roller-skating, particularly when
practised outdoors, had made a comeback on America's West Coast
as part of the new obsession with fitness and healthy recreation. The
sport was taken up in New York and elsewhere by exponents of black
street culture, fashion-conscious clubgoers and members of the gay

(see GAY LIBERATION) scene; it then spread to teenagers in general, leading to a worldwide fad. Part of the novelty of the boom involved skating in public places, skating to and from work and school, and an increase in the number of skating waitresses, waiters and messengers. The trend then moved back indoors to large-scale rinks and the floors of discothèques. Acrobatic and circular skating to Disco sounds stayed fashionable among teenagers until about 1982, then faded as spin-offs like ROLLERBLADING and STREET HOCKEY and rival activities such as SKATEBOARDING and cycling (see BMX) took over.

ROOF-RIDING

See URBAN SURFING.

ROTTWEILERS

See FIGHTING DOGS.

RUBIK'S CUBE

A plastic puzzle that became a worldwide craze, the cube was invented by the Hungarian teacher Dr Erno Rubik. A sophisticated elaboration of earlier two-dimensional brain-teasers, Rubik's cube consisted of four faces, each made up of nine coloured squares. The object of the puzzle was to restore all the sides to their original configuration by rotating the squares. The cube sold in millions to all age groups during the late 1970s and early 1980s – a period when puzzles took 30 per cent of the toy market – and Rubik continued to create portable puzzles marketed under his name. They sold well, but understandably failed to repeat the runaway novelty success of the cube.

RUDE BOYS

Rude Boys or Rudies were the Jamaican HIPSTERS and would-be or actual gangsters who frequented the dance halls of Trenchtown and listened to BLUEBEAT, SKA, ROCKSTEADY and the first REGGAE. These young males, some of whom were drop-outs from middle-class families, dressed in a raffish imitation of North American jazz musicians or pimps with shiny clothes and snap-brim hats, joined gangs, smoked ganja and communicated in patois. They were the local anti-Establishment folk heroes, and it was when some of them converted to RASTAFARIANISM after 1965 that that movement and the later African-leaning 'roots' culture gained street credibility. Rude Boy style was revived and the nickname heard again at the time of the British TWO TONE fad of 1980.

RUNES

The original runes were a pre-Christian Germanic alphabet used in northern Europe by the Vikings and Anglo-Saxons, among other peoples. The twenty-five runic letters were incised into wood or stone and each of the letters was endowed with mystical significance in addition to its function as a linguistic sign. The lost magical attributes of the runes fascinated antiquarians and occultists in the 19th and early 20th centuries; in the 1970s a version of the alphabet carved on stones was sold as a NEW AGE divinatory system on the lines of TAROT or the I CHING. Users draw the rune stones from a pouch and 'cast' or arrange them before reading them for a personal prediction. The modern system's claim to tap prehistoric wisdom may be treated with some scepticism.

RURALISTS

With the waning of the COUNTERCULTURE in the UK in the early 1970s there was an exodus from the cities of artists, writers, designers and musicians, many of whom withdrew to the West Country and Wales. From 1974 this trend generated its own short-lived fashion in painting: the so-called Ruralism. This nostalgic, often mysterious figurative style, using rich, lush colours with echoes of primitive art and Surrealism, was one of the first signs of the gentrification of the POP and PSYCHEDELIC visual styles of the 1960s, and of the increasing dominance of traditional English country themes and motifs on middle-class taste during the Seventies. Leading exponents of Ruralism were David Remfry and Peter Blake, both settled near Bath, who, in 1975, proclaimed the setting-up of the 'Brotherhood of Ruralists'.

SABBING

The nickname given to sabotage activities by the British Hunt
Saboteurs Association and other ANIMAL RIGHTS activists. The Hunt
Saboteurs formed in 1963 when a group decided to go beyond the
lobbying of the League Against Cruel Sports and take direct action
to prevent stag-hunting on Exmoor. Since then the Saboteurs have
dedicated themselves to saving the lives of all animals, birds and
fish killed for sport. They have become associated with VEGANISM,
vegetarianism and anarchist and leftist politics, but their ranks
include professionals as well as students and the unemployed.
The Association is made up of local groups whose main concern
is to follow, harass and obstruct fox-hunt meets. In practice this
often results in violence, but unlike the Animal Liberation Front,
the Association is officially pledged to non-violent methods. In
the 1980s the campaign against fox-hunting led to an unresolved
running fight and continuing stalemate of litigation and counter-
litigation by hunters and sabbers. Meanwhile efforts to ban blood
sports repeatedly foundered in Parliament. By the early Nineties
autonomous sabbing groups existed in Italy, Germany, Holland, the
USA and France.

- *More than 80 sabs, mostly from the north, but also from as far
  afield as Norwich and Middlesex piled onto Crowden Moor
  near Holmfirth early in the morning. The area's history of shoot
  cancellations in the face of sab activity . . . did not dampen their
  determination to ensure that the shooters did not get a look in.*
  Howl, *the Hunt Saboteurs Association magazine, Autumn 1986*

SAFETY PINS

The safety pin was the symbol *par excellence* of the PUNK
combination of do-it-yourself style and extremist gesture. Pins
were inserted in ears and noses – and in a few cases in lips –
as body decoration, and were also used as brooches or to hold
together tattered or deliberately torn clothing. The Sex Pistol's
singer John 'Johnny Rotten' Lydon slashed a suit with a razor
before safety-pinning it together for use as a stage costume in 1977.
For the same group's single 'God Save the Queen', their graphic
designer, the SITUATIONIST-inspired Jamie Reid, produced a collage
photograph of Elizabeth II wearing a safety pin through her nose,
an image subsequently much reproduced on T-shirts and postcards.
Some writers have commented on the deeper symbolism of the safety
pin: its association with babies and young children, and therefore
with innocence, yet at one remove from pins and needles and their
overtones of sado-masochism, self-mutilation and drug use.

● *In 1979 . . . singer John Foxx – skeletal and pretty in his burned
blue suit, and wearing a shirt which was held together with safety
pins – advanced to intone 'I want to be a machine' . . . a hostile
spirit with a thick Mancunian accent shouted from the bar, 'Fuck
off, yer crap!'*
        Michael Bracewell reminiscing in Blitz, September 1991

SALSA

A Caribbean Latin dance music originating in Puerto Rico and
Cuba, Salsa takes its name from the Spanish word for (hot) sauce.
This lively music is based on Afro-Hispanic rhythms mixed with
elements of jazz and ROCK. At the end of the 1970s, Salsa crossed
over into fashionable non-Hispanic circles, helped by exponents
such as the jazz musician Ray Baretto and the American HIP HOP
youth culture DJ, Jellybean Benitez. Salsa remained a mainstay of
Hispanic-American street and DANCEFLOOR culture and was picked
up by European DISCO and nightclub devotees. By 1991 local
practitioners – 'salseros' – had appeared in many countries, including
Japan, although the most authentic Salsa was still being performed in
Cali, Colombia, Havana, Cuba and by Celia Cruz in New York.

SAMPLING

The dominance of the DJ, the record producer and the recording engineer over the old performer/audience relationship was compounded in the recording studios during the early 1980s by the development of sampling. This is the removal of snatches of an existing recording for use in a new one. It follows logically from the primitive SCRATCHING techniques of HIP HOP's amateur DJs, who manipulated other people's records to create their own sounds. At first just a trick of the engineer, sampling became a vogue among progressive 'composers' such as the avant-garde Art of Noise around 1985. By the time HOUSE music boomed in 1987, sampling had become an essential part of the sound, and instrumental breaks, musical phrases and chorus lines of SOUL, DISCO, ROCK and earlier DANCEFLOOR hits were extracted and seamlessly spliced into the new records. In the 1970s George Harrison had been sued for plagiarism after including a melody from the Chiffons' 'He's So Fine' in his hit 'My Sweet Lord', yet by the Eighties the idea of using an aural 'ready-made' or 'found object' seemed acceptable. Often the sample in question was no more than a couple of bars; if longer the original artists were usually paid for the use, as in the collage hits of Jive Bunny. Sampling was a sort of commercial APPROPRIATIONISM, suggesting that in POST-MODERN pop all sounds have equal value and all past musical culture may be plundered for recycling in the market-place.

- *Three years ago a similar device would have cost thousands; now for under £100, the Casio SK-1 brings digital sampling to the teen market. It takes any sound source and puts approximately 90 seconds of it at the command of a two-and-a-half octave keyboard.*
  The Face, October 1986

- *The music for De La Soul's ground-breaking 'Three Feet High and Rising' was entirely made up of samples. De La Soul were sued by Sixties group the Turtles for the use of a Turtles original, 'You Showed Me'. The case was eventually settled out of court.*
  Sunday Times *magazine, 24 November 1991*

SATIRE

The British satire boom of the early Sixties in fact took its impetus
from a tendency in American humour that began in the early 1950s.
Nightclub stand-up comedians led by Mort Sahl and Lenny Bruce
used the HIPSTER Bohemian milieux of Greenwich Village and San
Francisco to introduce an element of social comment and political
irreverence into their performances. The sardonic piano songs of
Tom Lehrer converged in the later Fifties with the college tradition of
lampoon and parody against a background of increasing agitation for
civil rights, a pervasive fear of nuclear apocalypse and the first overt
protests against the values of Middle America. (An offshoot of the
cynicism of the time was the SICK HUMOUR fad of 1959 and 1960.)

In the UK, in the meantime, the anti-Establishment disaffection
surfacing in the ANGRY YOUNG MAN phenomenon was blending
with the strain of Surrealist whimsy present since the 19th
century to create a new synthesis. This was manifested (via the
Cambridge University 'Footlights' student review) in the Beyond
the Fringe theatrical review of Alan Bennett, Peter Cook, Dudley
Moore and Jonathan Miller. The irreverence of this generation
and the indulgence of its audience were boosted by the scandals
compromising the still patrician Tory administration of Harold
Macmillan. In October 1961 a group of former public-school boys
founded the fortnightly magazine Private Eye, exposing scandals,
ridiculing public figures and introducing a formula of schoolboy
in-jokes and parodies of the mainstream press that has survived into
the 1990s. One of the backers of Private Eye, Peter Cook, started the
Establishment nightclub in London's Soho specifically as a venue
for satire beyond the reach of the censorship exercised by the Lord
Chamberlain's office.

Satire – the name bestowed by the media, from the Latin satira,
meaning a sarcastic poem or musical medley – became a household
word in Britain when BBC television launched That Was the Week
That Was, a topical late-Saturday-night show produced by Ned
Sherrin and presented by David Frost, which went on air on 24
November 1962. By the end of February of the following year it
was attracting a regular audience of twelve million. Apart from
its controversy and novelty, TW3, as it became known, derived its
strength from bringing together the disparate talents of stars from
the fields of journalism, theatre, cabaret and television comedy in a

way that consciously drew on the un-British café-theatre tradition of prewar Middle Europe. These first performers established a vein of satire that became a standard feature of British TV and magazine journalism for the next thirty years. It has been said that, at least until the Nineties, satire in Britain, operated by a small clique in intimate contact with its targets, served more as a safety-valve for the Establishment and Fleet Street than as any form of subversion. Nevertheless, observers from the USA and Canada have often expressed envy at the ability and willingness of British satirists to attack anyone and anything with impunity. Satire filtered into the arts to such an extent that many of the most successful films, novels, and dramas produced in Britain from the late 1960s onwards could be said to exemplify it.

- *Like so many satirists in such an insecure age, he [Mort Sahl] obviously fears a cult of negation and talks about what he believes in as if to show his satire is really a positive attempt to achieve it.*
  W. J. Weatherby, Guardian, *October 1961*

- *And in satire [in the 1980s] schoolboy sniggering replaced the restrained hyper-realism that had always been essential to proper practice of this black art which, along with sarcasm, is the highest form of humour.*
  Julie Burchill, Sunday Times *Book Review, 24 May 1992*

SCALLIES

Scallie – a shortening of 'scallywag', originally meaning 'scurvy rogue' – was the term applied in the early 1980s to the specifically male youth subculture of Liverpool. Scallie denoted a semi-mythical, cheeky, fast-talking ne'er-do-well, typically unemployed and moving between the pubs, football matches and street markets of the depressed inner city, living on his wits. The notion reflected the particular defiance and local pride among Liverpool's underclass that showed itself in the city's thriving black economy and in the community initiatives, official and unofficial, that established themselves in the recession of 1981 and 1982, and which also formed the background to the Toxteth riots and the Heysel stadium tragedy. The word Scallie was associated in the late 1980s with the BAGGY TENDENCY.

- *Scallies exist now only in the minds of media commissioners who sense a good tale and writers who want to sell it to them. All they were is boys with wedge haircuts who followed Liverpool and Everton football clubs in the mid- to late Seventies.*

  Kevin Sampson, The Face, *October 1987*

SCHOOL OF LONDON

A school of painting of the 1950s. The School of London, or New London School – as distinct from the so-called London Group of 1913 that included Sickert and Wyndham Lewis – was made up of five of Britain's most influential postwar artists whose reputations, temporarily eclipsed by abstraction and POP ART, were firmly re-established in the 1980s. The five central figures were Frank Auerbach, Francis Bacon, Lucian Freud, Michael Andrews and Leon Kossof. In spite of their different mannerisms and techniques, they had in common a detailed, figurative, empirical approach quite unlike that of their North American contemporaries, the ABSTRACT EXPRESSIONISTS. The London painters' work stressed an often pitiless observation and description rather than painterly gestures or aesthetic ideologies. The School of London was the product of a social setting as well as a geographical coincidence, Bacon, Freud and Andrews all taking part in the Soho Bohemia of the late 1950s, which revolved around the Colony Rooms drinking-club and the French Pub.

SCIENTOLOGY

A mind-control cult founded by the American best-selling science-fiction writer L. Ron Hubbard, Scientology has continued to excite controversy throughout its expansion from 1952 onwards. The Church of Scientology (a trademark name) is based upon the notion that human beings can realize their full potential and become 'clear' – that is, freed from restricting memories from this and other lives. This is achieved by the 'science' of Dianetics, which is a mixture of science fiction, mysticism and psychology, influenced by the earlier writings of Gurdjieff and Aleister Crowley. Potential members, known in insider jargon as 'raw meat', are invited to undergo 'auditing' sessions to rid them of negative mental 'engrams'.

Scientology was one of the first and most efficient of the

many quasi-religious self-improvement programmes to adapt the marketing techniques of big business to the credulous HIPPIE milieu worldwide. Hubbard's religion has continued to attract celebrity converts, from the Incredible String Band in 1967 to John Travolta in 1990 and Tom Cruise and Nicole Kidman in 1991, in spite of hostile rulings from courts and governments in many countries, and despite campaigns by relatives of members objecting to the movement's alleged brainwashing and dirty tricks, for which some senior officers were jailed in the US. In May 1988 the US Supreme Court ruled that Scientology was a profit-making organization, not a religion, whilst in Britain the activities of its East Grinstead headquarters have regularly been criticized by *Private Eye* (see SATIRE) magazine. Hubbard himself supervised a secret information and power network from seclusion. Senior acolytes accompanied him on his yacht the *Sea-Org* – where visitors to the ship had to take an oath of confidentiality lasting five lifetimes – and the rich and famous continued to be fascinated by his machinations until his death in 1986.

- *Carol Reiss of the church wrote to the* East Grinstead Courier *to sing the praises of what the church has done for humanity. The reason there were no riots in Soweto this year was that a quarter million copies of L. Ron Hubbard's* Way to Happiness *booklet had been distributed there. Absolutely, Carol.*

Private Eye, *8 July 1988*

SCOOBIDOO

Highly coloured strands of plastic woven into swatches, wristbands, key-fobs and so on, the Scoobidoo (spelt Scoubidou in the original French) was a pre-teen craze of 1960 throughout British schools. As a CUSTOMIZED fetish object, the Scoobidoo formed part of a series of highly organized fads for teenagers and pre-teens in France that went on to include key-rings and transfers. In Britain more strictly seasonal and cyclical fads had been a school tradition since the conkers and marbles of the 19th century and the pre-Second World War cigarette cards. As a 'token', the Scoobidoo parallels the later FRIENDSHIP BRACELET.

SCRATCHING

A technique used by disc jockeys, usually working with twin turntables, whereby the operator drags the needle manually across the surface of records or moves the record back and forth under the needle to repeat and distort the pre-recorded sounds. The resulting rhythmic stop-and-start effects – produced using DISCO or FUNK records – and the mixing of more than one music source formed the backdrop to HIP-HOP and RAP culture. Scratching started among the black ghetto sound-system parties of New York in the late 1970s and soon gave rise to virtuoso scratching performances, competitions between DJs and, eventually, automatic methods of producing the effect. In 1983 the craze took off in the UK and France, helped by the success of groups such as Grandmaster Flash and the Furious Five during the previous year. Like TOASTING, scratching marked the ascendancy of the MC or DJ over the musician, and the ascendancy of the record manipulator over the songwriter or singer.

SCROTES

A synonym for CRUSTY, Scrote is a humorous British slang term for a squalid or despicable person.

SEMIOLOGY

In the first decade of the 20th century, Ferdinand de Saussure, the French-Swiss father of modern linguistics, posited a new science that would interpret the underlying patterns of meaning expressed by the signs and symbols used in all aspects of human communication. Saussure's notions gave rise to Semiotics, the study of systems of contrasts in human or artificial languages. In sociocultural disciplines such as anthropology, sociology and literary criticism, Saussurean ideas were developed by Lévi-Strauss and others into STRUCTURALISM, a movement of immense influence in academic circles on the Continent. In 1957 the French critic Roland Barthes published *Mythologies*, in which he applied Saussurean principles concerning hidden signs and messages interpreted by the observer rather than intended by the communicator, to aspects of popular culture such as food, hairstyles and advertising. Barthes propounded the quasi-science and named it Semiology. It is also known loosely as Semiotics (the terms derive from the Greek *sema* or *semeion*, meaning sign or token), particularly in the USA, where the word had been used independently of Saussure by the philosopher Charles Sanders Peirce.

Unlike its Anglo-Saxon contemporary MCLUHANISM, Semiology has endured as an intellectual movement, merging with or influencing the DECONSTRUCTION of Derrida and the POST-STRUCTURALISM of Lyotard and others. In the 1980s it continued to be propagated, principally in the Latin countries and particularly through the influential *Semiotextes* containing the writings of Guattari, Deleuze and others. In the English-speaking academic world, on the other hand, it has had less influence, except in specific areas such as film criticism, particularly in the late 1960s, and literary criticism and media studies during the 1970s and 1980s. In hip non-academic circles, however, Semiology has become a buzz word and its concepts have to some extent penetrated middlebrow consciousness via the fiction of Umberto Eco and David Lodge, parodies in Garratt and Kidd's Biff cartoons, and, to a lesser extent, through translations of essays by Jean Baudrillard.

The work of Semiologists has been dismissed by positivists and empiricists as unsubstantiated rantings, and by scientists as lazy cultural relativism, and it is certainly difficult to sustain Semiology's claim to the status of a science. Nevertheless, if its insights are regarded as a critical approach focusing on relationships rather than bogus 'facts', and on cultural cross-reference rather than bourgeois assumptions, then Semiology probably deserves its central role in the diffuse POST-MODERNIST tendency in critical debate and the arts.

- *In short, in the account given of our contemporary circumstances I resented seeing Nature and History confused at every turn, and I wanted to track down, in the decorative display of what-goes-without-saying, the ideological abuse which, in my view, is hidden there.*

  Roland Barthes, Mythologies, 1957

- *What Semiotics has discovered is that the law governing or, if one prefers, the major constraint affecting any social practice lies in the fact that it signifies; i.e. that it is articulated like a language.*

  Julia Kristeva, Times Literary Supplement, October 1973

SHAMANISM

One of the mainstays of NEW AGE paganism and the MEN'S
MOVEMENT of the early 1990s, shamanism is an attempt to
re-create the spiritual bond with nature supposedly enjoyed by the
doctor-priests of North Asian or Native American tribal societies.
In ancient semi-nomadic Ural-Altaic societies, the shaman (the
word comes via Russian from the Tungus language) communicated
with an unseen and omnipresent spirit world by entering trances –
sometimes induced by hallucinogenic drugs. Knowledge and magic
power gained in this way enabled the shaman to practise healing
and divination. Neo-shamanism first appeared in the USA as part of
a late COUNTERCULTURE identification with the Amerindian heritage.
The more innocuous aspects of the cult include ritual drumming and
TREE-SNIFFING. In Britain in 1992 a revolutionary shamanist group
named Evolution advocated the use of ECSTASY and promoted anti-
capitalist RAVE culture and mass SQUATTING. Meanwhile, an American
believer in shamanism, Terence McKenna, used his book *Food of the
Gods* to extol the virtues of hallucinogenic mushrooms as an antidote
for modern society's CONSUMERIST obsessions.

SHAMBLING

A half-serious music-press categorization of the mid-1980s,
Shambling was applied to earnest, introverted, self-consciously
clumsy, usually drably dressed INDIE POP musicians, the best known
of whom were the Scottish Jesus and Mary Chain. These bands
played a PUNK- and PSYCHEDELIA-inspired ROCK music with little
energy. A similar stance at the end of the Eighties was known as
SHOE-GAZING.

SHELL SUITS

These brightly coloured ensembles made of shiny man-made
synthetics were an American successor to the tracksuits and leisurewear of the 1970s. Like the TRAINER, they emerged from underclass
street fashion to become an ubiquitous part of the mainstream casual
look of the early 1990s. Worn by both sexes and all ages, the shell
suit became an icon of KITSCH, continuing to be worn despite the fact
that it was easily inflammable.

- *An American biochemical company claims to have isolated a substance that may be the key to human sexual attraction, a chemical that could induce females to fall for the most repulsive-looking men – even those wearing shell suits or flared trousers.*
  Observer, 31 May 1992

SHIATSU

An alternative healing and therapy technique involving massaging, manipulating and pressuring the body, shiatsu is based on the ancient Chinese notion of the body's 'meridians', also used in ACUPUNCTURE and REFLEXOLOGY. The word itself is Japanese, meaning 'finger-pressure'. Virtually the same as acupressure, it can be practised on one's own body. It was originally developed in China as a sort of family first aid and refined in the 20th century in Japan.

SHINEHEADS

See SKINHEADS.

SHOE-GAZING

A categorization invented by the British music newspaper the *NME* (formerly *New Musical Express*), Shoe-gazing was applied to members of some INDIE POP bands at the end of the 1980s. It referred to the fact that, whilst playing their guitars, these introverted and amateurish musicians would stare at the stage floor, where lyric sheets and chord changes were stuck on pieces of paper. The word also carries overtones of their 'navel-gazing' and deliberately reticent general pose.

- *It doesn't really bother me that the shoe-gazers are posh-oes – alright it bothers me that Slowdive's parents bought them cars. And guitars. But it doesn't bother me that they're middle class, what bothers me is the fact that they make really dull music.*
  NME, 4 January 1992

SICK HUMOUR

A vogue for sick humour swept the USA at the very end of the 1950s. Word-of-mouth jokes were enshrined in published anthologies and a magazine entitled *Sick* was launched to rival the established parody magazine *Mad*. The fashion for morbid or sadistic comedy probably originally sprang from sardonic strains of Jewish humour, but more immediately from the SATIRE boom as manifested by stand-up nightclub comedians such as Mort Sahl, cabaret performers such as Tom Lehrer (whose records were passed around among British Bohemians) and the writer and cartoonist Jules Feiffer, who popularized the adjective itself. The cult cartoonist Charles Addams probably also influenced the fad. The taste for the macabre – a daring and sophisticated release for unwholesome thoughts, and a legitimized form of oblique social comment – appealed particularly to 'corporate man' and to college students. When the craze spread to Britain it accompanied a revival of earlier exercises in black humour including Harry Graham's *Ruthless Rhymes*, Hilaire Belloc's 'Matilda' and Stanley Holloway's hit recital 'Albert and the Lion'. Sick humour subsided as a nationwide craze very rapidly, but subsisted as a mainstay of student rag magazines. Deliberate bad taste was also an important feature of much ALTERNATIVE COMEDY of the 1980s.

SIMULATIONISM
See APPROPRIATIONISM.

SITUATIONISTS
One of the most subversively influential and least-known libertarian groups since the Second World War, the Situationist International grew from an earlier cell, active in the Left Bank café society of late 1940s Paris, which styled itself the Lettrist International. Led by Isidore Isou (born Ion-Isidore Goldstein in Romania), the Lettrists practised a kind of militant post-Dada CONCRETE POETRY (with overtones of Alfred Jarry's PATAPHYSICS) and proclaimed a new society, to be founded by revolutionary youth and based on creativity. In 1957 this small coterie regrouped, now calling itself the Situationist International, drawing upon ideas from early Marx, Hegel, Freud and Dada, and declaring in their 1960 manifesto that capitalism should be transcended by '*Homo ludens*', the personification of play. Over the next few years the leading Situationists Guy Debord and Raoul Vaneigem developed the idea of the Society of the Spectacle. This was the notion, touched on

by MCLUHANISM and much later refined by POST-MODERNISTS, that modern bourgeois society enslaves by dazzling the individual with the attractions of CONSUMERISM and hypnotizes with an empty display of entertaining images. As strategies to confront the Establishment's overwhelming power they conceived artistic tactics such as *détournement* ('hijacking' or 're-routing'), the taking of ready-made texts and images and adapting them to communicate subversive messages, and *la dérive* ('the drift'), a free-wheeling trip without a goal involving a series of acts, gestures and encounters.

After making contacts with radical student groups and a network of like-minded agitators, the Situationists had their only moment of real power when students following their lead took over the University of Strasbourg in 1966. In the student unrest of 1968, the Situationists played an important submerged role when most of the memorable slogans expressed in wall GRAFFITI and chanting during the Paris disturbances were coined by them, including 'Be Reasonable – Demand the Impossible!' and 'Beneath the Paving Stones – the Beach'. In 1969 their comic-strip tracts were circulated in London and their ideas began to influence the libertarian avant-garde there and in the United States.

Among themselves the Situationists operated an absolutist regime, with leaders – usually Debord – regularly expelling heretics, some of whom formed the London organization King Mob. Situationist concepts of fighting the system by staging anarchist provocations also influenced the PROVOS and the ANGRY BRIGADE at the time, as well as planting ideas that would later be realized in PUNK ROCK. The group, which never numbered more that seventy, rejected celebrity, refused to expand or collaborate with sympathizers and disapproved of the mystical and drug-influenced COUNTERCULTURE. Long before Francis Fukuyama popularized the idea, they declared that they had come to the end of history, and dissolved themselves in 1974. It was not until the late 1980s that the Situationists were celebrated in the English-speaking world, in an exhibition of pamphlets, posters and texts entitled 'Leaving the Twentieth Century', and in the book *Lipstick Traces* by the American Rock critic Greil Marcus.

- *The spectacle presents itself simultaneously in all society, as part of a society, and as instrument of unification. As a part of society it is specifically the sector which concentrates all gazing and all consciousness.*

Guy Debord, La société du spectacle, 1967

● *The more the consuming machine gobbles up the producing machine, the more we are governed by seduction, the less by force . . . We live in times when the ideology of consuming has consumed all ideologies.*

Raoul Vaneigem, Traité de savoir-vivre à l'usage des jeunes générations, 1967

SKA

A light, fast and fluid version of the intensely rhythmic Jamaican dance music that immediately preceded REGGAE. Coexisting during the late 1960s with BLUEBEAT and ROCKSTEADY, it was performed by such groups as Prince Buster and the Allstars, the Skatalites and the Ethiopians. The titles and lyrics of songs reflected the Kingston dance hall and street culture's identification with gangsters and movie heroes. In Britain Ska was popular with the white MOD subculture, and re-emerged around 1980 as the inspiration for the post-PUNK TWO TONE movement, which included the Specials and Madness. Displaced by Reggae, RAGGA and RAP in the black youth community, Ska remained a minority genre through the mid-1980s, promoted by a handful of groups, including the Potato 5 and the Deltones, and appealing particularly to white metropolitan leftists. In the early Nineties echoes of Ska were incorporated into some British HIP HOP records. Ska music was characterized by the kind of hissing voice percussion that probably gave it its name, as well as by saxophone solos and chugging accompaniment.

SKATEBOARDING

Skateboarding began in the USA in the 1950s as a children's game improvised from roller-skates fastened to trays or pieces of wood. In the Sixties children in Rio de Janeiro held downhill races on planks with truck wheel bearings attached. The new contraption was adopted by experienced or would-be SURFERS in order to practise or imitate less complex surfing manoeuvres. This 'sidewalk surfing' – celebrated in Jan and Dean's hit record of 1964 – became an integral part of surfing subculture and was adopted in Australia in the mid-1960s. In Britain the small, élitist surfing fraternity of Devon and Cornwall introduced the skateboard, which was a brief fad among MODS in 1966.

Skateboarding in the Sixties was limited by the essential clumsiness of the devices themselves. In the middle of the 1970s, however, young enthusiasts in Venice and Santa Monica, California, incorporated the new softer methane wheels that had been rejected by roller-skaters with a lighter, more aerodynamic 'deck'. The sport took off for a second time. This time purpose-built ramps were constructed, and knee-pads, helmets and other accessories were merchandised to support the now acrobatic craze. Teenage and pre-teen enthusiasts saw themselves as a heroic band of rebels, celebrated in FANZINES, although the mainstream media and local authorities were eager to cater for their needs. In the early 1980s skateboarding temporarily went into decline as ROLLER DISCO and BMX biking became fashionable, but by 1986 there was a third wave of skateboarding in California, which within two years had spread worldwide, helped by the film *Back to the Future*. Devotees – known as 'muties', from mutants – had evolved their own jargon, OP ART, neo-PSYCHEDELIC and BAGGY clothing and a pose that formed part of an urban street youth culture overlapping with HIP HOP.

- *The skate boards of London rust forlorn and forgotten in their appropriate dustbins . . .*
  Ark, *the Royal College of Art magazine, 1967*

SKIFFLE

A style of pop music that swept Britain from 1956 to 1960, Skiffle was the fast, jaunty singing of lightweight American Country, FOLK and early ROCKABILLY songs accompanied by acoustic guitars, banjos and home-made or amateur instruments such as washboards, kazoos, one-string broomhandle-and-box basses and jew's harps. The name is probably derived from an approximation of its sound, although there could be a connection with the archaic dialect 'skiffle', meaning a hurry. From the beginning a kind of parody, particularly in the nasal pseudo-cowboy singing style, Skiffle started as a means of entertaining audiences between performances at Dixieland jazz concerts. It had the advantage of appealing to all age groups and of being very easy to play; it was also a less subversive cousin of ROCK 'N' ROLL, then a fashionable but controversial novelty. It began to be played by teenagers in coffee bars whence some, including Tommy Steele and Cliff Richard, graduated to become the first British pop stars. Older performers turned it into a commercial success by blending with it elements of the British music-hall tradition: Lonnie Donegan had hits with the American 'Cumberland Gap' and 'Rock Island Line', and then with 'Does Your Chewing Gum Lose its Flavour (on the Bedpost Overnight)' and subsequently 'My Old Man's a Dustman'. The Skiffle of that period has never been revived, although the Rockabilly fad of the early 1980s was mocked by some as nothing but neo-Skiffle.

- *Other products of the Skiffle world were recruited, re-styled, renamed and launched by [John] Kennedy and his partner Larry Parnes: among them Marty Wilde (really Reg Smith), Adam Faith (Terry Nelhams) and Cliff Richard (Harry Webb).*
  Peter Lewis, The Fifties, *1978*

SKINHEADS
Skinhead was originally a slang term for a bald person, and in Britain was characteristically shouted at passers-by by members of street gangs. The word was also used contemptuously by HIPPIES and sophisticates of the remnants of the MOD movement, who in 1967 had evolved into a conformist, reactionary, working-class youth cult wearing a uniform of American Oxford button-down shirts (or their cheaper British Ben Sherman and Brutus imitations), Levi jeans and loafers, worn with a CREW CUT. The most 'lumpen' elements of the late Mod tendency added army boots and braces to this ensemble and fostered a cult of gang violence, directed particularly against long-haired middle-class students, Asians and gays. During 1968 and 1969 these youths further simplified their clothing into a quasi-military look: bleached jeans were worn above the ankle; the original army-issue BOVVER BOOTS (some wearers had been in the armed services, others just wanted the increased kicking power) were replaced by more flexible DMS, and hair was shaved even shorter. Girls wore more or less the same clothes, although their crops were often modified with long feathered hair at the back and sides.

For the first year or so of its existence, this youth subculture had no name; adherents were variously known as 'brush-cuts', 'spikeys', 'peanuts' (a ROCKER name for earlier Mods) and Boot or Bovver Boys, from their use of the slang euphemism 'bother', meaning extreme violence. By 1969 Skinhead was the epithet that had stuck. The style survived through the 1970s and Skinhead anti-culture spread from London to other cities around the UK. During the middle of the decade the movement began to be associated with the National Front and other extreme right-wing organizations; at more or less the same time it became the driving force behind organized football hooliganism. Like all youth cults, it had its musical accompaniment: in this case allegiances switched abruptly in the early 1970s from black SOUL music to the rabble-rousing ROCK anthems of Slade. After 1977 an overlap in musical tastes between the Skinhead and PUNK subcultures created the OI phenomenon of the early 1980s, while non-racist Skinheads identified more with TWO TONE.

During the early Eighties, the Skinhead appearance and values were picked up in France, Germany and, to a lesser extent, in the USA; after the collapse of Communism in Eastern Europe they also spread to eastern Germany, Czechoslovakia and Hungary. Confusingly to outsiders, there were also leftist and libertarian Skinheads, including the RANTING poet Seething Wells and the Redskins Rock group of the early 1980s. Moderate Skinheads referred to their extremist and even shorter-haired counterparts as Boneheads. By the end of the 1980s hard-core Skinhead culture seemed to be in decline in the UK itself, partly due to the effect of the hedonist ACID HOUSE and RAVE movements in seducing former football fans and troublemakers. The short-cropped or completely shaved head had meanwhile become fashionable in gay, progressive and avant-garde circles among designers and musicians, for example, in some cases in order to disguise incipient baldness, in others as a radical – but quite apolitical – style gesture. Exponents of this BALD LOOK were sometimes known as Shineheads and Chrome-domes.

- *The spikeys or brushcuts are summer's new dumb terrorists in jeans, braces and thick leather boots. With sharpened aluminium combs and hair to match they have already wrecked one major free concert.*

  Oz magazine, July 1969

- *A group were beaten up by skinheads outside a London pub on Wednesday night. They were the Nasties, led by ex-Nice guitarist Dave O'List.*

  Melody Maker, 2 January 1971

- *The summer of 92 will go down as the year when the skinhead haircut came to represent fashion and not fascism.*
  Guardian, 8 June 1992

SKIRMISH

See COMBAT GAMES.

SLAM-DANCING

A form of dancing, flourishing around 1980 and associated with HARD-CORE post-PUNK music, in which devotees literally hurled themselves bodily at each other, or at walls, stages and other fixtures. Like the POGO, it originated with the first Punks in 1977 as a form of ecstatic ritualized violence that was cathartic rather than genuinely aggressive. During the mid-Eighties it evolved into MOSHING and stage-diving.

SLAP-ITS

A novelty wristband that was a fad with schoolchildren in 1990 and 1991. It consisted of a swatch of plastic covered with brightly coloured material; when slapped against the wrist it wound round it. The Slap-It combined the gimmicks of CLACKERS and FRIENDSHIP BRACELETS.

SLOANE RANGERS

A term used to refer to young upper-middle- or upper-class people educated at public school and affecting certain well-defined modes of dress and behaviour. It was applied to a recognizable subcategory of British youth displaying the characteristics of what used to be known as the 'County Set', i.e. conservative and patrician values, coupled with a fondness for riding, hunting, social rituals and etiquette, and a strict but anti-fashion dress code. The equivalent of the North American PREPPIES and the Parisian BCBGs (*bon chic/bon genre*) and NAPs (Neuilly/Auteuil/Passy), Sloanes were defined and described by the journalist Peter York and, later, Ann Barr in *Harpers & Queen* magazine and publications such as the *Official Sloane Ranger's Handbook* (1982). The words first appeared in print in 1975, but were originally used by bar-room wits during the early 1970s to refer to would-be 'men-about-town' frequenting Chelsea pubs; only some of these 'Hooray Henries' and 'Debs' Delights', as they were then known, were the upper-class youths later so described. The term was of course a play on 'Lone Ranger', the dashing cowboy hero of a 1950s TV series, and Sloane Square, the epicentre of the smart Central London districts of Chelsea and Knightsbridge. The celebration of the Sloane was one of the first signs of the new conservatism, the return to traditional tastes and heritage-obsession that affected most Western societies throughout the Eighties. The more overtly materialist and socially mobile YUPPIE supplanted the Sloane Ranger in the public and media attention around 1984, and the term fell into disuse, although the social group continued to exist with a much lower profile. In the summer of 1992, the London *Evening Standard* claimed to have identified a new generation of Sloanes, recognizable by a 'curvy but slim figure, perfect complexion and shoulder-length straight blonde hair'. It dubbed this new subculture the 'Stepford Sloanes' after *The Stepford Wives*, an American film describing identikit Zombie suburban wives.

- *The appalling Sloane Ranger look. Worn by strapping, horsey girls aged 20 going on 53. Other components: striped shirts, a tame string of pearls, impenetrable pleated skirt, blue tights and prissy shoes. Printed headscarves optional. Thick ankles mandatory.*
  Judy Rumbold, Guardian, December 1989

SMART DRUGS

Also known as 'psychoactive cocktails', 'cognitive enhancers' and 'think-drinks', smart drugs take their name from the fact that they are supposed to improve intelligence, memory and mood – as opposed to so-called 'dumb' or 'stupid' drugs such as alcohol, caffeine, tobacco, amphetamines and cocaine, for example. These formulations are the designer drugs of the early 1990s, emanating from the USA, where they had become a staple accessory in fashionable bars, DISCOS and parties for hedonists and self-improvers alike. The (legal) drugs are mixed with fruit juices and drunk, or are available in pill form, carrying names such as Fast Blast, Clear Thought, Gusto, Rise and Shine and the Memory Martini. Their supposedly active ingredients are nutrients, amino-acids and chemicals spun off from research into the prevention of Aids and Alzheimer's Disease and the treatment of strokes and alcoholism; some of their properties are unknown, unproven, or even dangerous. With substances such as Vasopressin, Choline, Hydergine, Dilantin and the rest not being readily available in the US, American users were importing them from the UK and Switzerland. By 1991 British YUPPIES and ACID HOUSE devotees were also sampling smart drugs, now packaged and marketed professionally, but reactions were mixed given the high prices charged and the very low level of mood alteration resulting in most cases. Smart drugs represent the sanitizing of drug culture and its merging with health-conscious 'aspirational' lifestyles and NEW AGE experimentation.

- Dr McGaugh points to the danger of unsupervised chemical use. Dilantin, used originally to treat epilepsy, is used by smart-drug advocates to regulate the brain. It may cause foetal damage.
  Gareth Pownall, Evening Standard, September 1991

SMURFS
Smurfs were elf-like cartoon creatures invented in Holland in the mid-1970s and marketed originally as a children's craze and subsequently as a mascot for a petrol company's promotion campaign. Like GONK, MUPPET and WOMBLE before it, the name Smurf was appropriated in Britain to refer derisively to an ugly or otherwise unfortunate individual. In the US it was used in business jargon to describe a courier of illegal documents, but in France the translation 'Schtroumpf' was an anti-Semitic epithet.

SNOW SURFING
A fad among ski enthusiasts that was later adopted by some non-skiers, snow surfing consists of riding downhill on a single wide ski. Also known as monoboarding, this novelty sport combines the agility of skiing with the balancing and manoeuvring skills of SURFING and the risk of tobogganing. It began as an improvised game in alpine resorts in 1987.

SNUFF-DIPPING
A short-lived craze involving the chewing of sachets of tobacco,

snuff-dipping originated in the USA in 1985 among young people, particularly in rural areas. Manufacturers were ready to promote the practice as a 'tough' alternative to smoking until the high risk of oral and throat cancer became clear, whereupon the fad collapsed. Snuff-dipping was merely a repackaging – literally – of the long-established tradition of tobacco-chewing by an older generation of rural workers.

SNUFF MOVIES

The term appeared in the late 1970s denoting hard-core pornographic films supposedly featuring the actual death of one or more of the participants, 'snuff' being an American slang euphemism for kill. Despite many rumours of their existence, which often also suggest an origin in Latin America, there has never been confirmation that a snuff movie – as opposed to home-made films of the atrocities of serial killers and others – has ever been made for commercial purposes. *Cannibal Feast*, a notorious 'documentary' of the early 1980s, said to show explorers being murdered by tribespeople, was a fake. The term snuff movie has occasionally·been extended to encompass the obviously fictitious SPLATTER genre.

SOAP-DODGERS

A fairly obscure use of the rather dated humorous colloquial term, Soap-Dodger was used to categorize scruffy youths belonging to the ACID HOUSE, INDIE POP, RAVE and CRUSTY subcultures from around 1990. The epithet had a female equivalent, the so-called RAVE GRANNIE.

SOAP OPERAS

An obsession with TV soap operas was a long-time fixation among mainly working-class women in Latin cultures, where photo-novel magazines supplemented the low-budget sentimental and melodramatic television series. In Britain long-running daytime radio and lightweight TV dramas were known as serials until the mid-1970s, when the concept and term soap opera became fashionable as a newly discovered social phenomenon (the 'soap' reference recalled the detergent companies who sponsored pre-Second World War US programmes). The worldwide popularity of *Dallas* and *Dynasty* prompted journalists, sociologists and, in particular, FEMINISTS to analyse the values and mesmeric power of the soaps. The general taste for these programmes, and the vogue among intellectuals and the style-conscious for revelling in their triviality, was an early form of the flamboyant passivity and 'consumer-collaboration' with the commercial media that was characterized in the late 1980s by the COUCH POTATO and Jean Baudrillard's theories concerning HYPERREALITY. In the 1980s the sophisticated British TV viewer was catered for with soap operas imported from Latin America and Europe, whilst the family consumer was served by the new Australian imports, *Neighbours* in particular, which attracted a more fanatical following than in their country of origin, perhaps because they portrayed an English-speaking world that looked familiar, yet was classless, optimistic and sunlit. In contrast to the reassurance built into traditional soap operas, *EastEnders* and *Brookside* introduced a social realism that focused on social issues as well as emotional problems.

- *I am addicted to* Crossroads *not for its virtues, which escape me at the moment, but for its faults. I love it because of its warts, as it were.*
  Nancy Banks-Smith, Guardian, 8 August 1972

- *It is partly a ritual pleasure, which offers reassurance in its familiarity and regularity . . . And it is surely the predictable familiarity of the life represented which pulls us in.*
  Charlotte Brunsdon, Television Mythologies, 1984

SOCA

A musical form from Trinidad also popular elsewhere in the English-speaking Caribbean. Soca is an updated SOUL-tinged version of the 1950s Calypso, whose topical song performed over a rhythmic steel band and/or acoustic guitar backing was the first West Indian genre to become popular with white Bohemians in Britain in the 1950s. Soca combines carnival-style music with references to current social and political issues in its lyrics. There were signs in the mid-1980s that Soca was moving from a local to an international hip audience, and it did catch on in black communities in New York and to a lesser extent in London and among some white WORLD MUSIC aficionados. Soca's biggest stars were the Trinidadians David Rudder and Mighty

Sparrow, but in the early Nineties Barbados began to rival its traditional home for 'leadership'.

● *To a good tune and meaningful words, add the other essential soca ingredient – a gimmick. Everyone has to get something and wave – flags, hankies, shirts, or in the case of one woman captured on the island's national TV network, a pair of knickers.*
   Peter Mason, Independent, 22 August 1991

SOFT ROCK

See HARD ROCK.

SOUKOUS

A variety of SOUL-influenced dance music from Zaire that has flourished since the 1970s. It has been picked up, particularly in Paris, by WORLD MUSIC enthusiasts since the 1980s.

SOUL

A genre of black American music evolved from gospel singing and influenced by country and urban blues. The word 'soul' was originally used in the gospel milieu in a religious sense, but subsequently took on connotations of black pride, solidarity and depth of feeling, which were reflected in the emotional histrionics of the music. Ray Charles pioneered this style during the early 1960s, but it was in the second half of that decade that the Soul label started to describe a distinct movement represented on the Tamla Motown and Stax record labels, and featuring stars such as James Brown, Aretha Franklin, Stevie Wonder and Marvin Gaye, although confusingly, it also continued to be referred to as R & B. From 1965 to 1967 singers such as Sam and Dave, Percy Sledge, Solomon Burke and, most spectacularly, Otis Redding, produced a more mannered, rhythmic version of Soul that also appealed to white audiences. This was imitated in Britain by local black singers – notably Geno Washington and the Ram Jam Band – and established white singers such as Eric Burdon and Chris Farlowe. During the MOD era, Soul joined SKA and BLUEBEAT as the fashionable dance sound.

Soul gave black America a huge stake in the music and entertainment industry, but it came increasingly to represent a showbiz

version of black culture. By the end of the 1970s it was no longer in
touch with the street or the ghetto, having become middle-class and
middle-aged like its original performers and devotees. The music
had always tended towards sophisticated orchestration and lavish
production techniques; these, added to the synthesizer sound of
the mid-Seventies and the ambience of the gay discothèque created
DISCO, a genre that stressed danceability over musical or lyrical
content. Meanwhile in the UK, Soul, especially in its earlier forms,
formed the basis of an underground dance culture among working-
class teenagers and young adults: NORTHERN SOUL, beginning in the
late 1960s, and the SOUL BOYS, a subculture originating in the London
suburbs around 1974. By the 1980s Soul music in Europe had been
swallowed up by the confusion of poses, fads and sub-genres that
made up DANCEFLOOR culture.

- *Outside of reggae, which it resembles in some superficial aspects,
  Soul music is possibly the most unfashionable of all music forms –
  at least to the great mass of 'progressive' fans.*
  Melody Maker, 12 September 1970

SOUL BOYS

Soul Boys and Girls were a mainly working-class subculture
which coexisted with the PUNK movement of the mid-1970s.
Beginning around 1974 and continuing until the end of the decade,
the suburban Soul Boy movement had no ideology beyond an
identification with SOUL music. In contrast to the high-visibility
Punk stance of ritualized anger, it reacted to the uneasy climate of
Royal Jubilee Britain by emphasizing stylishness and dance. The
phenomenon, which to some extent paralleled the earlier NORTHERN
SOUL movement, was based on local clubs and discothèques in a
band of London suburbs from Catford to Bromley in the south round
to Ilford in Essex. Many Soul Boys were former fans of GLAM ROCK,
following their idol David Bowie when he moved from sci-fi GLITTER
to an American-influenced, mannered DISCO image. The fans also
to some extent continued the sexual ambivalence of Glam, the Soul
Boy uniform of white socks, pumps and tinted WEDGE hairstyle
owing something to gay styles, and in turn influenced the NEW
ROMANTIC look of the early Eighties. In the Seventies it was Punk
and later TWO TONE that attracted the attention of the press. The Soul

Boys had to wait to be mythologized until the mid-1980s, when journalists such as Robert Elms celebrated them as the pioneers of the new DANCEFLOOR culture. In 1990 they were featured in the award-winning film *Young Soul Rebels* by the young black director Isaac Julien. The underground Soul tendency continued in a different form during the early 1980s, now in a uniform of shorts and T-shirts, with accompanying whistle to be blown at mass dance parties and weekend excursions to resorts like Bognor and Great Yarmouth.

SPACE HOPPER

The Space Hopper was a cult toy of 1970 and 1971 that continued as a toyshop staple into the 1990s, often adapted to match successive fads (there has been a TEENAGE MUTANT NINJA TURTLE Space Hopper, for example). It consisted of an egg-shaped, hollow plastic body representing a cartoon extraterrestrial being, and on its head had two short antennae serving as handles. The object could be ridden by sitting astride it and bouncing up and down.

SPEEDCORE

See HARD CORE; THRASH METAL.

SPIKE-TOP

Spike-top was the name given to the standard PUNK haircut (the MOHICAN was worn only by a minority of adherents). It consisted, as the name suggests, of short, uneven clumps of hair greased or teased into vertical spikes. The look originated among the proto-Punks of the USA and has been ascribed to Richard Hell, the singer of Television and later of the Voidoids, who affected a Rimbaud-like image of teenage angst and bedraggled urban street style. The anti-fashion do-it-yourself spike-top also served the first Punks' anti-HIPPIE stance by being vertical and short, as opposed to the long, hanging hair that had dominated the previous decade. It became the emblematic hairstyle of the movement in 1977, worn by both sexes. By about 1981 it was outmoded, giving way to neater FLAT-TOPS and CREW CUTS.

SPIVS

During the postwar period in Britain, the spiv was a folk anti-hero, typically a disreputable, flashy male who lived by shady dealing rather than by honest work. The term had existed in the jargon of racetrack devotees and petty criminals since the late 19th century, but came into its own with rationing during the years following the Second World War, when it was adopted by the press and public to designate the touts, black-marketeers and 'wide-boys' who flourished until the early Fifties. Spivs pioneered the ZOOT SUIT in the UK and established a raffish dandy identity incorporating fedora hats, overcoats and wide, colourful ties even before the first TEDDY BOYS, whose subculture overlapped with that of the spiv. 'Spiv' has been facetiously derived from the initials of 'suspicious itinerant vagrant', but it is much more likely to be an alteration of 'spiff', an archaic dialect word for dandy that also gave rise to the colloquial adjectives 'spiffing' and 'spiffy'. The original strain of spiv disappeared towards the end of the 1950s but the word continued to be heard. The actor George Cole who portrayed the archetypal spiv 'Flash Harry' in the St Trinian films, later played an older incarnation in his role as Arthur Daley in the TV series *Minder*.

- *Max Kidd was an ex-plumber made good; a total spiv down to the last camel hair on his coat.*

  Kate Saunders, Evening Standard, *17 May 1989*

SPLATTER MOVIES

The graphic nickname applied in the early 1980s to a genre of explicit horror films that use special effects to portray details of violent death, and which were popular at the cinema and subsequently on video. These films, in which many characters are typically killed off for the entertainment of the audience rather than for the furtherance of the plot, began with the low-budget, cult *Texas Chainsaw Massacre* of 1974, continued with John Carpenter's *Halloween* in 1978, the films of David Cronenberg and Wes Craven, and the *Friday the Thirteenth* and *Nightmare on Elm Street* series. By the late 1980s splatter movies had become a teenage joke, as reflected by their alternative nickname of 'slice-and-dice', a phrase originally used for advertising food processors. Their near-relative the

VIDEO NASTY usually denoted a more extreme depiction of violence.
Noted examples were *Driller Killer* and *Nightmares in a Damaged
Brain*, which were refused a certificate for cinema release, but were
circulated privately for video viewing. Commentators lamented
the effect of all these genres on children and younger teenagers.
Continuing the horror-comic tradition of the 1950s, they undoubtedly
influenced the DEATH METAL vogue of the 1990s.

SQUATTING

In both the UK – where squatters' rights still survived in law –
and Holland, squatting was one of the most widespread and most
successful activities of the libertarian COUNTERCULTURE of the late
1960s. In Britain, squatting was coordinated by the high-profile
London Street Commune and the DIGGERS before being adopted in
1969 as a strategy for a variety of left-wing and anarchist groups.
In Amsterdam, highly organized squatting was associated with the
PROVOS and KABOUTERS, who occupied whole quarters of the city;
their tactics were later emulated in Copenhagen. British squatting
was legitimized by some local councils, who allowed homeless
people to occupy unused property.

- *Squatting is a delicate legal hassle and does not stand any further
  complications. IF YOU SQUAT DON'T SMOKE!*
  > IT, 28 March 1969

- *Mr Lewis and his family had gone into the house on June 28th
  and expected, like most squatters, at least three months unharassed
  possession before the complicated legal process of eviction could be
  completed by the house's owners.*
  > Private Eye, 14 August 1970

STAGE-DIVING

See MOSHING.

STEAMING

A criminal fad that arose among black gangs in London during 1985,
steaming involves moving into a shop, street, or train compartment
en masse and overwhelming victims in order to steal from them. The

technique is to move fast and cut off all means of escape, but to avoid one-to-one violence in favour of generalized pressure and the chance to mug while concealed by a crowd. The nickname of the activity comes from the colloquial use of 'to steam (in)' meaning to move forcefully and irresistibly.

- *Steaming is very modern, a term for mob-handed theft often by joeys, young criminals.*

  Independent, *23 December 1988*

STEPPING

A new form of AEROBIC exercise in vogue in 1991, stepping, as the name suggests, substituted rhythmic climbing on the spot for the standard dance movements.

STREAKING

The practice of running naked across a public place, streaking began during the HIPPIE era in the USA and spread quickly to other areas where the libertarian values of the COUNTERCULTURE prevailed. It could be done merely as a result of spontaneous exuberance or intoxication, or alternatively as a spectacular form of public protest. Group streaks were carried out in North America and Australia, particularly by students demonstrating against campus issues or the Vietnam War. In Britain a few politically inspired streaks took place in 1973 and 1974 before the fad subsided into occasional exhibitionism at cricket test matches and rugby games, for instance. A variation on the streak observed in Holland and Denmark was a swarm of naked cyclists. The craze was celebrated in Ray Stevens' novelty hit record, 'The Streak'.

- *. . . the biggest star of the era was Erika Roe, whose 40-inch breasts bounced across the Twickenham turf over 10 years ago . . . She was last heard of making sausages for a butcher in Petersfield.*

  Options, *May 1991*

STREET HOCKEY

A home-made team sport appearing in the early 1980s, street hockey
was played with roller-skates, ice-hockey sticks and a plastic ball.
The game appeared almost simultaneously in London and the USA,
probably originated by ROLLER DISCO devotees. By 1987 it had been
transferred from local streets to indoor halls and a league table
and sponsorship had been organized. An early example of amateur
minority sports using new technology, street hockey was followed by
ICEBALL and ROLLERBLADING.

STRUCTURALISM

A quasi-scientific methodology for the interpretation of cultural
expressions from tribal customs and rituals to literary texts and
movies. Structuralist theory was developed in France from the late
1940s by the anthropologist and ethnologist Claude Lévi-Strauss,
who adopted the insights of the Swiss-French linguist Ferdinand de
Saussure. In lectures delivered between 1906 and 1911, Saussure had
proposed a dramatic change of perspective in looking at language,
which he saw as a self-contained system of mutual relationships
– principally contrasts or 'binary opposites' – rather than as a
collection of words each representing a 'real' object or fact in the
world. Lévi-Strauss transferred Saussure's ideas about language to
his studies of social groups and discerned deep underlying structures
that existed regardless of local conditions and which generated the
surface 'signs' of a culture. These constants were held to be generated
by the fundamental workings of the human mind, and to exist in all
societies independently of time or place.

Lévi-Strauss's mentor in the field of linguistics was Roman
Jakobson, who belonged to a Russian and East European school
of thought known as Formalism, which had put forward proto-
Structuralist ideas developing V. I. Propp's analysis of the
constituents of folk tales (published in 1928). In the USA early
in the century the philosopher C. S. Peirce had paralleled – or
perhaps anticipated – these European theories in his Semiotics (see
SEMIOLOGY). Lévi-Strauss's writings appealed to French intellectuals
of the late Fifties and early Sixties, many of whom were Marxists
and most of whom were sympathetic to a universal critical theory
that could be applied to all the manifestations of bourgeois society

(and which in the process also incidentally elevated the status of the critic). Roland Barthes took Saussure's suggestion of a 'science of signs' to create a Structuralist interpretation of popular culture in Semiology. Others, including Lacan, Foucault and Althusser, applied Structuralist approaches in the worlds of psychology and politics.

In the Anglo-Saxon world Structuralism was disseminated much more slowly, and against the deep suspicions of empiricists and positivists alike. Saussure's work was not translated until 1954. The contributions of the later French critics triggered an intellectual fad in some circles in the 1970s, but as late as the early Eighties Structuralism was being condemned in some British universities as an avant-garde and bogus discipline. It was not necessary to 'believe' in Structuralism to make use of its methods of analysis, however, and many English social scientists and teachers of literature did so. An important spin-off was the further opening-up of cultural and media studies as a respectable field of investigation. There is debate as to when, how and why Structuralism gave way to POST-STRUCTURALISM, but it is generally agreed that it was the notion of DECONSTRUCTION introduced by Jacques Derrida that moved the discussion beyond Saussure's sign/signifier relationship and towards POST-MODERNISM.

- *. . . the ultimate quarry of structuralist thinking will be the permanent structures into which individual human acts, perceptions, stances, fit, and from which they derive their final nature.*
  Terence Hawkes, Structuralism and Semiology, *1977*

- *Lionel Jackson's thesis is that Structuralism is discredited as a literary theory and that in any case it has rested on a false interpretation of what Saussure actually taught.*
  English Today, *April 1992*

SUEDEHEADS

While the basic SKINHEAD visual repertoire of cropped hair, jeans and boots remained virtually unchanged from the late 1960s to the early 1990s, an early offshoot faction grew their hair and adapted some of the Skinheads' secondary accoutrements into a uniform. These were the Suedeheads, and the clothes they annexed were the Crombie overcoat, the button-down cotton shirt, and narrow mohair or Terylene trousers. Similar ensembles were worn by both sexes, usually with moccasin or polished lace-up shoes and accessories such as pocket handkerchiefs, cravats, ties and umbrellas. This more suave elaboration of the working-class gang style was the forerunner of the PRINGLE and CASUAL movements that arose at the end of the 1970s.

- *By 1970, it [the Skinhead look] was changing into the less stark Suedehead look: more detail and decoration on the clothing, more luxuriant hair – long back and sides, short top and fringe.*
  Jon Savage, The Face, February 1988

SURFING

The sport of surf-riding spread from Hawaii to California in the 1950s, achieving cult status in 1962 when the songs of Jan and Dean and the Beach Boys turned a local obsession into an international fad. In the USA its subculture overlapped with the HOT-RODDING fraternity and originated the SKATEBOARDING craze. Already established in Australia, it was also picked up in South Africa. In Britain during the 1960s it remained centred on Newquay in Cornwall, where the first native board-builders, Bilbo, opened in 1962. Biarritz on the Atlantic coast of France became the next focus around 1970. Surfing appealed to males in their teens and early twenties and quickly developed a technical jargon – 'hang ten', 'wipeout', etc. – and exclusive argot – 'gnarly', 'wimp' – that slowly filtered into mainstream slang during the 1970s and 1980s, contributing to VALLEY GIRL talk, for instance. By the end of the 1970s surfing had evolved, via a mystic HIPPIE phase, from a minority, highly athletic, élitist activity into a major summer pastime, spawning an industry of beach accessories and a graphic style based on Hawaiian and PSYCHEDELIC images which in the late 1980s merged with the ACID HOUSE look.

- *There's big money in the sport. In Newquay, for example, the surf industry – operating from more than 40 equipment shops, clothing stores and board factories – is estimated to make more than £4m profit a year.*
  Sunday Times, August 1990

SURREY GIRL
An alternative version of KNIGHTSBRIDGE GIRL, herself the stereotypical
spoilt middle-class counterpart of the fictional sluttish ESSEX GIRL.
All were the subject of a spate of vulgar jokes circulating in 1991 and
1992 and taken up by the UK media.

SURVIVALISM
In the mid-1970s a number of Vietnam veterans in the USA decided
to use their military training in order to live outside society, typically
in the wilderness areas of California and Oregon. This individualist
dropping-out was often prompted by psychological disturbance or
political disaffection, or both. The idea of living rough in a state of
constant armed readiness also attracted devotees of military regalia,
firearms and hunting, as well as right-wing extremists planning to
survive in the aftermath of some future apocalypse. These various
strains, reminiscent of Charles Manson's 'dune-buggy army', plus
benign HIPPIE retreats and earlier vigilante groups, coalesced into
the Survivalist movement, a recognizable subculture with its own
magazines, literature and retail and mail-order outlets. Hard-core
drop-outs were joined by weekending family men, as well as by a
few women, and by the end of the decade their activities, bolstered
by the popularity of the *Rambo* movies, had influenced such popular
phenomena as CB RADIO, FIGHTING DOGS, COMBAT GAMES and the first
stirrings of masculinism (see the MEN'S MOVEMENT). Survivalism's
attractions were not limited to the USA; the cult spread to Canada,
Britain and Australia. Several North American serial killers were
adherents of the Survivalist ethos, as was Michael Ryan, the
perpetrator of the 1987 Hungerford shooting massacre in Britain.

SUSHI
A Japanese delicacy consisting of various preparations of raw fish,
sushi first became fashionable in California in the mid-1970s. By
the early 1980s sushi bars were widespread in the United States and
were strongly identified with the YUPPIE and FOODIE lifestyles. The
food, with its suggestion of ZEN minimalism (visual presentation
being considered as important as flavour in Japanese tradition),
chimed both with the tastes of design-conscious Westerners and the

associated ritual meal-time meetings as practised in the business community. In fact, in the UK where it caught on in a small way, Sushi reflected the importation of US business culture as much as Japanese culinary style. Sushi bars, along with black-and-white decor and quasi-Oriental austerity, went out of fashion with the arrival of recession at the end of 1989.

T

TALKOVER

An earlier term for TOASTING, the Jamaican forerunner of RAP, talkover
consisted of a DJ or MC improvising a monologue over a background
of REGGAE music.

TAROT

A method of divination based on an original set of twenty-two
picture cards, although in modern fortune-telling a full pack of
seventy-eight cards is sometimes used. The pictures include one fool,
or joker, and twenty-one depictions of archetypes, elemental forces,
vices and virtues. The cards are cast for a client by an experienced
reader: the spread reveals the client's destiny and also acts as
a psychic trigger enabling the reader to empathize and interpret.
Originally known as tarok or tarocco (tarot is a later French variant),
the game seems to have originated in Italy in the 14th century, based
on the *arcana*, or secret symbolism of earlier would-be magicians.
Tarot had always formed part of the repertoire of European dabblers
in the occult, but it was not until the HIPPIE era that it became a
best-selling accessory. Like the I CHING and RUNES, it proved popular
with the NEW AGE movement of the Eighties and Nineties.

TATTOOING

Tattooing has been practised by adherents of nearly all the postwar
youth subcultures in Western society and its popularity has also
persisted in the armed services, in prisons and among the traditional
working class and new underclass, although its appeal to women
is relatively new, beginning in earnest at the end of the 1960s. The
TEDDY BOYS and ROCKERS of the 1950s and early 1960s favoured
traditional dedication motifs or expressions of bravado, as did HELL'S

ANGELS. In the HIPPIE era tattooing was a minority taste, and it was at this time that the discreet or hidden tattoo with purely decorative or erotic overtones was introduced to the middle classes. SKINHEADS used the tattoo to express patriotism, allegiance or aggression, in some cases indelibly decorating the head and face, a practice shared by extremist PUNKS. In parts of the gay (see GAY LIBERATION) community and among some avant-garde artists there was a vogue for tattooing the genitals at the end of the 1970s.

By the early 1980s tattooing had become a widespread, if controversial, form of fashion statement by affluent 'style victims' as well as post-Punks and GOTHS. Despite laws in the UK and in some American states against the tattooing of those under eighteen years of age, some tattooed celebrities, including the singer Cher, have encouraged their teenage children to emulate them. The quasi-tribal and sado-masochistic overtones of tattooing have been noted by many commentators, including the German Stephan Ottermann in his 1979 masterwork, *Zeichen auf der Haut: Die Geschichte der Tätowierung in Europa*. The tattoo parlour as the point where primitivism meets fashion flourished in the West in the mid-Eighties in particular, turning the romantic backstreet studio into a place where the home-made ink-and-razor-blade expressions of blood brother- and sisterhood and love and hate became a consumer durable.

TECHNO

One of the many subsets of DANCEFLOOR DISCO music flourishing in the late 1980s and early 1990s. Techno, in the ascendant in 1991, was characterized by a frenzied rhythm (124–135 beats per minute, as opposed to the 120 BPM of HOUSE and Disco) and futuristic noises (particularly 'bleeps') over machine-like bass lines and 'break-beats' (sampled drum loops). The genre originated in Detroit, where club DJs and musicians such as Derrick May, Juan Atkins and Kevin Saunderson, some of them fascinated by robot technology and cybernetic visions of the future, blended the progressive synthesizer ROCK of mid-1970s German groups such as Kraftwerk and Tangerine Dream with black American FUNK. Other influences were REPETITIVE MUSIC, the INDUSTRIAL MUSIC of the early 1980s, the futuristic pop of Gary Numan, Orchestral Manoeuvres in the Dark, Dépêche Mode and the Human League, and ELECTRO, the New York dance craze of 1982.

More than other strains of 'underground' club music, Techno succeeded in the UK in joining the mainstream of pop, as manifested by record sales and exposure in the mass media. British exponents of the style, mainly based in the industrial Midlands and North, re-exported Techno sounds to the US from 1990; Belgium was the other major source of hits. Aficionados would further subdivide Techno into categories such as the lightweight 'Techno pop' or 'playground Techno', and the extremist 'HARD-CORE Techno'. Unlike its rival sub-genres, and in spite of its use in hedonistic and physical RAVES, Techno taps into a tradition of progressive electronic music and has a cerebral – some devotees even claim a spiritual – dimension allied to CYBERPUNK.

- *Techno's interest in scientific advances is misleading. The irony is that most of the music is made on the most outdated analogue equipment. This came about initially through necessity (lack of cash).*
  John McCready, The Face, December 1991

- *Techno is the definition of what I find unappealing about contemporary music in that it lacks a voice, it lacks a character and it lacks poetry and passion . . .*
  Chris Roberts of Catwalk, NME, January 1992

TEDDY BOYS

The first recognizable British youth cult, Teddy Boys were initially known as 'Edwardians' after the frock-coats and ornamental waistcoats they wore with stovepipe (later 'drainpipe') trousers. They were identified by their flamboyant clothing and hairstyles, which combined a number of influences. Upper-class young adults and Savile Row tailors had briefly revived the Edwardian dandy look in the late 1940s. Working-class emulators, rebelling against the drab austerity of postwar Britain, added a hairdo – the DA – borrowed from American ZOOT-SUITERS and JITTERBUGGERS, and adapted and embellished the velvet-trimmed frock-coat, influenced by the drape jackets of their SPIV predecessors and the Mississippi gambler outfits – including the bootlace or 'slim-jim' tie – seen in Western movies. This ensemble, with minor mutations – highly polished lace-up shoes gave way to thick, crêpe-soled brothel creepers and later to WINKLE-PICKERS; the DA, which could be substituted by the QUIFF or

ELEPHANT'S TRUNK — appeared around 1950 and dominated teenage fashions until the beginning of the 1960s. Female counterparts — Teddy Girls — imitated the American BOBBYSOXER look of PONYTAIL, wide skirt or blue jeans and flat shoes, the latter replaced around 1960 with stilettos.

When the first wave of Teddy Boy culture waned in Britain, it left behind a hard core of devotees who continued to dress and dance accordingly. There were revivals in the early 1970s as part of the pop-GLAM visuals promoted by the Mr Freedom store, in 1976 and 1977 by a new generation of authentically violent Teds wearing simplified and highly coloured versions of the old uniform and opposing PUNK, and again in 1979 in the form of the ROCKABILLY craze. The Teds of the early 1950s — also known as CORNERBOYS — were generally viewed as inarticulate and loutish, gaining a reputation for gang violence that was played up by the press following a murder in 1953 and confirmed by their part in the Notting Hill race riots of 1958. Their main contribution to postwar popular culture in Britain was their espousal of ROCK 'N' ROLL in 1956, and the fact that they were the first 'teenagers' identified as such. They influenced other youth cults, particularly the ROCKERS, but attempts to see them as subversive or progressive foundered on reality: in all their incarnations they remained lumpen and conservative. Abroad the Teddy Boys were imitated in Australia by BODGIES and WIDGIES in the 1950s, and by the self-styled Teds of Paris and Tokyo during the 1970s and 1980s.

TEENAGE MUTANT NINJA TURTLES

The Turtles began when the American freelance illustrators Peter Laird and Kevin Eastman met in 1982 and in the following year collaborated in sketching a cartoon strip. The heroes of the cartoon were inspired by the urban folk-tale that the sewers of American cities are inhabited by unwanted pet terrapins, flushed away by their owners. Laird and Eastman imagined the turtles mutating under the influence of pollution into a 'posse' of teenage martial-arts enthusiasts emerging to fight evil. (The 'ninja' reference is to the Japanese assassin cult based on ninjitsu; in the UK the word was substituted by the more innocuous 'hero'.) Having combined three current preoccupations, the cartoonists added a rodent guru/mentor, some slang and catch phrases and a diet of marshmallow pizzas. The parody was run in an adult comic book, whence it was adapted by a Hollywood animation studio and by Playmate Toys of Hong Kong. From 1987 the Turtles featured in over 100 TV episodes and two feature films, as well as lending their images for the merchandising of games, toys, clothing, etc. In 1988 the craze spread to the UK, where it continued to flourish for the next three years. The multi-million-dollar worldwide success of the Turtles took many adults by surprise: in spite of their differentiation by name – Donatello, Raphael, Leonardo and Michaelangelo (sic) – they seemed to lack character or charm. Nevertheless children identified with their outlaw status and cheerful heroism, and helped by an industry now geared to sophisticated promotion they outlived all imitators.

- *The only ones clearly out of pocket are the parents. But at least they know that in 10 years' time there will be a whole generation of school-leavers able to name at least four Renaissance artists.*
  Business *magazine, December 1990*

TEPEE PEOPLE
See TRAVELLERS.

TEX-MEX
As its name implies, Tex-Mex is a blend of Texan Country music and Mexican melodies and lyrics, typically sung to an accompaniment of electric guitars and accordion. The genre was briefly fashionable in the UK in 1984 in the wake of the ROCKABILLY fad; its best-known exponent, Flaco Jimenez, a Mexican based in San Antonio, Texas, toured Europe several times with his band in the early and mid-1980s.

THATCHERISM
While the expression 'Thatcherite' was being applied (often pejoratively) from 1979 to followers of the Conservative Prime Minister, the term Thatcherism only began to be heard after the British General Election of 1983. In June of that year the administration of Margaret Thatcher, which had already been in power for four years, was re-elected with a sufficient majority to allow it to impose its radical anti-consensus policies. After her

ousting in 1990, Mrs (later Baroness) Thatcher herself began to use the word when referring to the ideology and practices of her years in power. In 1991 the Thatcher Foundation was set up with the express aim of propagating these ideas, especially in the post-socialist economies of Middle and Eastern Europe. Margaret Thatcher's political philosophy was based on a combination of MONETARIST belief in the necessity of controlling the money supply and a personal belief in the need to return to (supposedly) 19th-century virtues of thrift, enterprise and family values. In practice, Thatcherism consisted of strict controls on government spending on welfare and in subsidies; the limiting of government intervention in the economy and business so as to allow free rein to market forces; a wholesale programme of privatization of public utilities; the curbing of trade-union power; and a vigorously pro-American, anti-Communist and anti-socialist foreign policy.

Mrs Thatcher's stances chimed with the mood of large sections of the population, in particular the skilled working and lower middle classes, also appealing to frustrated executives and entrepreneurs and to those with right-wing views in general. Thatcherism was thus able to bring about the sort of radical shifts in attitudes and practices that had always been expected from the Left. During the mid-1980s, the Prime Minister presided over the boom in retailing and service industries, largely fuelled by her deregulation of the City and the lowering of interest rates. Her autocratic style and strength of purpose in defeating the miners' strike and ignoring social unrest helped rather than damaged her popularity. It was the combination of recession, the universally unpopular poll tax and her antipathy to Europe that dislodged her. After her removal she upbraided her successor, John Major, for abandoning the tenets of Thatcherism in favour of mild interventionism, but only two years later Thatcherism had become for many a pejorative buzz word denoting an uncaring, ruthlessly acquisitive short-termism that had left the country divided and again impoverished. Only a few loyalists, including her economic guru Sir Alan Walters, still proclaimed the Thatcherist message.

THEATRE OF THE ABSURD

An extremely influential avant-garde movement during the 1950s
and 1960s, the so-called Theatre of the Absurd included the austere
work of the Irish exile Samuel Beckett and the farcical satires of the
Romanian exile Eugène Ionesco, both of whom were based in Paris.
Rejecting naturalism and using paradoxes of language and illogical
juxtapositions, this type of drama presents human existence as
meaningless within an indifferent universe. The works of Beckett and
Ionesco were first performed in the early 1950s, but the genre was not
named until 1961 by the critic Martin Esslin in 1961. The absurdist
tendency owed something to earlier progenitors including Alfred
Jarry, the inventor of PATAPHYSICS, the Czechs Franz Kafka and Karel
Čapek, and the Surrealists and EXISTENTIALISTS. In Britain absurdist
drama has been represented by the work of N. F. Simpson, which
contains elements of farce and whimsy, and by Harold Pinter's more
mannered and sardonic MINIMALISM. Echoes of the Theatre of the
Absurd can be found in other areas of entertainment in the UK over
the last thirty years, notably in the broadcast humour of the *Goon
Show* and *Monty Python's Flying Circus*, but these probably owed
more to the existing tradition of whimsy and surrealism in British
humour than to the self-conscious European vein.

THEME DISCOS

A feature of the club and DANCEFLOOR culture of the early 1990s,
theme discos were an extension of the theme fancy-dress parties
beloved of students and socialites for at least two decades. In most
cases particular nights would be given over to the celebration of
landmarks of KITSCH culture. Among these, revivals of PSYCHEDELIA,
cult TV programmes and parodies of fashion and movie stereotypes
were common. During one night in London in 1992 there was a camp
restaging of *Jesus Christ Superstar*, an evocation of the Costa del Sol,
a party in which revellers impersonated characters from the sitcom
Are You Being Served?, female 'divas' wrestling in cream cakes,
and the hosting of an 'adult games session' by the Ultra-Vixens.
Theme discos took their immediate inspiration from the gay (see
GAY LIBERATION) underground of the 1970s and events such as the
transvestite Alternative Miss World contest, staged by the sculptor
Andrew Logan. Increasingly from 1990 the themes in question

involved eroticism and sexual titillation, with the militant hedonist
female Pussy Posse group hosting events in various venues,
and the Kinky Gerlinky, Love Ranch and Milk Bar clubs, among
many others, light-heartedly promoting 'pussy-power' (guilt-free
feminine sexuality, glamour and safe sex) as well as cross-dressing
(see GENDER-BENDERS), fetishism, lesbianism and heterosexual
flirting.

- *Records were played by the Cleavage Sisters, who painted their
  nails between tracks as a dig at the current cult of the DJ, while
  the crowd were organised to play games – men did the ironing or
  fertility chants, while women did press-ups or arm wrestling.*
  The Face, *July 1992*

THERAPY

A buzz word of the late 1960s, therapy – from the Greek *therapeia*
meaning treatment – referred to the treatment of disorders
without drugs, and was usually shorthand for group therapy or
psychotherapy, although it was later extended to include NEW AGE
healing techniques from AROMATHERAPY to the high-profile PRIMAL
SCREAM. The gaming, simulations, role-playing and transactional
approaches pioneered by therapists, many of them working within
or on the fringes of the COUNTERCULTURE, permeated other disciplines
such as language teaching, management training, social work and
drama during the 1970s, taking with them the 'psychobabble' with
which they were sometimes promoted.

THRASH METAL

A music journalists' categorization, Thrash Metal describes a crude,
speeded-up version of HEAVY METAL, heavily influenced by PUNK.
The style, which arose in the USA in 1986, was epitomized by
groups such as Anthrax, Metallica, Napalm Death, Extreme Noise
Terror and Slayer; it was a scarcely distinguishable variant of the
slightly earlier HARD CORE and Speedcore and was also known as
Thrashcore and Speedmetal. In Britain, Thrash, as it became known,
was championed by the radio disc jockey John Peel and rivalled ACID
HOUSE for popularity in 1988. A later generation of bands continued
in the same vein under the GRUNGE banner.

- *Peel, in the face of an initially wary press, somehow managed to give credence to the new hardcore hybrid when for nearly a decade it had been seen as indiedom's foul relative.*

  Steve Lamacq, NME, *December 1988*

TICKETS

See MODS.

TM

See TRANSCENDENTAL MEDITATION.

TOAD-LICKING

A fad among drug-users in Australia and North America during
the late 1980s, toad-licking came about through the discovery
that the giant cane toad secretes through its skin a milky-white
hallucinogenic chemical known as bufotenine. This is the toad's
protection against predators and whilst it can produce hallucinations
in humans who lick the toads' heads, it can also provoke sweating,
vomiting, involuntary defecation, palpitations and sometimes death.
Aside from its toxic properties, the cane toad, which overran
Queensland, had already become the focus of a cult in Australia,
where it was the subject of a TV documentary later shown worldwide.

- *Vancouver police want the Canadian government to ban the import of Giant Cane Toads from Australia following the deaths of several Australian drug-users.*

  Independent, *July 1991*

TOASTING

A Jamaican music fad in which lyrics were chanted over a REGGAE
or DUB backing by a performer who was as much disc jockey or MC
as singer. Now largely forgotten, it was the immediate forerunner of
SCRATCHING, RAP and HIP HOP. The term was inspired by 'toast', as
in inviting to drink or participate in a celebration. The technique as
practised by exponents such as I-Roy was first known as TALKOVER
and consisted of a monologue, often containing cultural, political
and RASTAFARIAN references, jokes and wordplay in patois, which

was improvised over a backing track with or without its own pre-recorded lyrics, and played on a home-made sound system. Toasting introduced the concept of interfering with a ready-made recorded product, and began the trend that established the supremacy of the DJ or producer, rather than the musician, in DANCEFLOOR culture.

● *Power . . . hung on the air – invisible, electric – channelled through a battery of home-made speakers. It was present in every 'toasted' incantation.*
Dick Hebdige, Subculture: The Meaning of Style, *1979*

TON-UP BOYS

See ROCKERS.

TRAD

The nickname is short for 'traditional jazz' and describes a British fad which lasted roughly from 1959 to 1961, beginning as a purist revival and ending as a bland element of mainstream show business. Since the late 1940s jazz in Britain had been associated with white middle-class Bohemia, as exemplified by Humphrey Lyttleton and London's 100 Club, home of the original 'Hooray Henries' (see SLOANE RANGERS), and the ANGRY YOUNG MEN. The preferred style of playing was New Orleans revivalism, as opposed to either the 'debased' Bebop, or modern JAZZ, an austere avant-garde mode for a minority. In the middle of the Fifties ROCK 'N' ROLL eclipsed jazz as the music of the fashionable young, although older devotees, usually male and often students or teachers and vaguely left-wing, continued to patronize jazz clubs. The hiatus between the end of Rock's novelty and the appearance of the new pop of the Beatles coincided with a radicalizing of the educated young, based on Beatnik (see BEAT MOVEMENT) culture and the CND movement. Earnest, duffel-coated students were in the ascendant, and their music was FOLK or Trad.

This second wave of Trad popularity, led by musicians such as Chris Barber and Ken Colyer, quickly spread from the small groups of expert (often antiquarian) purists to a larger public who were attracted by the Dixieland rhythms of the banjo. Flamboyant showmanship and rowdy, stamping audiences (sometimes anticipating later IDIOT DANCING and POGOING) became the norm, and the mass media paid attention. Trad swept the country, with performances in clubs, pubs and open-air festivals, even on Thames riverboats. A film, *Its Trad Dad*, was released and records by the popularizer Acker Bilk entered the hit parade. The Trad boom triggered a strain of novelty-nostalgia in British pop culture that encompassed the camp syncopations of the Temperance Seven and the musical comedy of the Bonzo Dog Doodah and New Vaudeville bands and the taste for Victoriana and imperial regalia that characterized the mid-1960s. Trad was essentially regressive and conservative; in popularizing itself it abandoned any remains of the original energy or feeling of black jazz. It never fully crossed over into the working-class teenage market (although TEDDY BOY fans of Acker Bilk rioted at the 1961 Beaulieu Jazz Festival) and was quickly swamped by the beginnings of the MERSEY BOOM in 1962. On the jazz circuit, modern and free styles became increasingly popular.

TRAINERS

By the 1980s the training shoe had achieved the unprecedented status of a cult fashion object that was also a mass-market consumer product. This came about at the end of the 1970s with a convergence of the ghetto chic of nascent black HIP HOP culture and the jogging/AEROBIC fads of the white middle classes. In black and Hispanic American youth subculture trainers were first worn as a cheap successor to the ubiquitous basketball boots and sneakers (usually 'Chuck Taylor Allstars') of the Fifties and Sixties until one-upmanship and the idolizing of sports stars created a hierarchy of styles and labels. The Adidas sports shoe, developed by Adolf Dassler in Germany in the 1930s, was already seeking endorsement by US athletes in the 1960s; Puma, an Adidas offshoot, was briefly the favourite brand in the 1970s. Meanwhile, the Nike shoe was being developed at the University of Oregon. In the 1980s, the campaign of sponsorship, endorsement, aggressive marketing and merchandising and constant technical innovation resulted in the five major brands (the others were Reebok, Avia and Converse) fighting for a market worth $2 billion per year in the USA alone. It was estimated that in the early 1990s 98 per cent of the North American population, irrespective of age, race or class, owned at least one pair of trainers.

Sportswear also became the encoded youth uniform of American street gangs, triggering the so-called 'trainer war' phenomenon of the late Eighties whereby in Los Angeles the rival gangs of the Crips and the Bloods identified their enemies by their brand of footwear. In South Chicago alone, 100 young people died in muggings and shootings associated with sportswear.

In the UK traditional plimsolls and sand shoes had always been regarded as deeply unfashionable, although the MODS of the late 1960s had adopted heavy tennis shoes – 'bumpers' – and basketball boots as part of their repertoire for a time. Trainers arrived from the US with the teenage SKATEBOARDING and BMX fads, as well as via the music-based BREAK DANCING fashion. From the early 1980s brands went in and out of fashion, shoes were CUSTOMIZED with coloured or extra-fat laces, paint, etc., and worn with tongues inside or outside, with and without laces, according to the dictates of mysterious underground trends. The first New York YUPPIES had been identified by their habit of wearing athletic shoes with business suits; their successors later practised their own code of brand loyalty in trainer ownership, generally favouring Reeboks over more flamboyant alternatives.

TRAIN-SURFING

See URBAN SURFING.

TRAMPOLINING

The HI-TECH miniature trampoline was a fad among YUPPIES and NEW AGE health enthusiasts at the end of the 1980s. In addition to their decorative function, the circular or rectangular contraptions in steel and black rubber were said to focus the body's energy flow and to help in reaching a state of serenity. They were thus promoted as a combination of stress-reducer, executive toy (see NEWTON'S CRADLE) and AEROBIC exercise.

TRANSACTIONAL ANALYSIS

A genre of alternative THERAPY developed by the American psychologist Eric Berne in his 1964 book *Games People Play*, transactional analysis examines the motives behind human interactions. Berne posited three basic 'ego states' from which people may operate when communicating with each other; the 'parent'

– responsible, authoritative and protective; the 'adult' – rational, analytical and decisive; and the 'child' – emotional, playful and creative. TA concentrates on the roles and strategies conditioned into human agents and encourages patients to go beyond stock moves and responses to a new autonomy. It has had a lasting influence on the teaching of communication skills and on aspects of business training and drama, as well as in the field of psychotherapy. Critics have noted that, like other Western techniques, it has tended to bolster individual assertion and strengthen the 'bourgeois' ego.

TRANSCENDENTAL MEDITATION

In the 1950s the Maharishi ('Great Seer') Mahesh Yogi took the prehistoric Indian tradition of Ayur Veda ('science of life'), a Hindu collection of folk remedies and religious insights, and used it as the basis for a new system of universal enlightenment. Access to this enlightenment would be through meditation accompanied by the repetition of a secret, personalized mantra (a sacred word or sound). The Maharishi's transcendental meditation programme achieved great success in the USA and subsequently in Europe during the HIPPIE era; this was crowned by the highly publicized visit of the Beatles, their wives and other BEAUTIFUL PEOPLE to the Rishikesh ashram in 1968. Unlike other gurus of the Sixties who were exposed as charlatans, condemned for unscrupulous methods or indicted for financial transgressions, the Maharishi continued to flourish through the 1970s, skilfully employing Western marketing and merchandising techniques while refining the packaging of consciousness-raising and world peace. Among other innovations were the training of adepts in 'flying', supposedly a form of levitation, but described by cynics as 'bottom-hopping'.

In the 1980s, the Transcendental Movement – now generally shortened to TM in keeping with the de-emphasizing of its Hindu aspects in favour of a YUPPIE image – was a multinational commercial organization. By the end of the decade it had headquarters in New Delhi, Germany (where, the Maharishi claimed, its prayers brought down the Berlin Wall) and Washington, DC, from which the TM group withdrew in 1992 to move to the countryside, having failed to control the spiritual degeneration of that city by meditation. At that time TM was estimated to have 3.5 million practitioners worldwide, together with assets calculated at

$1.5 billion. Like the less benign MOONIE empire, the Maharishi's organization conceived of itself as introducing a global Utopia based on mobilizing spiritual energy, developing a higher consciousness, restoring 'natural law' and at the same time encouraging commercial enterprise and affluence. Again adapting to the times, the TM ideology of the Nineties emphasized GREEN issues and embraced the speculations of the NEW SCIENCE, linking modern physics to Eastern mysticism. In 1992 TM candidates stood in the British General Election under the Natural Law Party banner. Their massive investment in the campaign did not pay off in this instance.

TRANSFORMERS

Transformers were plastic toys that combined futuristic science-fiction and fantasy images with the build-it-yourself principle. They could be transformed into a number of identities by fitting their components together in different configurations: a rocket could become a robot which could mutate into a car, for instance. Transformers were a craze of 1984 in the 'promotional toy' (i.e. manufactured fad) market.

TRANSISTOR RADIO

Like the later GHETTO-BLASTER, the transistor radio has had a symbolic cultural significance in addition to its importance as a technological advance. The development of transistorized circuitry at the end of the 1950s meant that radio sets could be miniaturized, mass-produced and sold cheaply. Young people who vied to own the smallest radios (often masterpieces of early Sixties design in aerodynamic coloured plastic and chrome) could listen to music in public places, much to the disgust of the older generation, who protested to the press and pressurized authorities to ban the devices (British by-laws were quickly amended to prevent transistors being played in parks amongst other places). Known by the end of the decade as 'trannies', transistor radios became a combination of fashion accessory and symbol of youth rebellion, although radio music programming restricted the actual enjoyment to be derived from listening until the advent of PIRATE BROADCASTING in the late 1960s. The cassette recorder was the next piece of technology to appear in portable form after 1969, but the radio continued to evolve and in the early 1970s novelty radios were a brief fad, one being the futuristic bracelet wrist-radio, a forerunner of the Walkman. The indistinctness of the medium-wave signal meant further difficulties for outdoor listeners, and it was not until FM and the advent of the ghetto-blaster that enthusiasts could be assured of a truly portable music source.

TRAVELLERS

As the HIPPIE philosophy receded as a fashionable element of popular culture after about 1972, the remaining exponents of the drop-out lifestyle retrenched, congregating in inner-city squats (see SQUATTING) and in countryside communes, including the short-lived tepee villages and GEODESIC DOMES of north Devon and mid-Wales. In Britain the main move was towards Wales and the West Country, where a more equable climate could be combined with the attractions of legendary sites, in particular Glastonbury, the location of mythical Avalon, and Stonehenge, and the cultural focuses of Bath and Bristol. This alternative subculture organized itself around a network of open-air festivals – 'festies' – at which adherents, still known in the Seventies as Hippies, gathered during the summer. In June 1972 the first Glastonbury free festival was held; in 1974 the first solstice festival at 'Henge'. After spending a summer on the road moving from one festival to another, some decided to adopt a mobile existence for the rest of the year, living in vans, converted buses and caravans; like Romanies and tinkers before them they referred to themselves as Travellers. Some, such as the tepee people, the Wallies and the Rainbow Village, formed tribal groupings.

During the late Seventies the number of people living on the road in the UK grew, as did the number of impromptu camps, celebrations and entertainments catering for them, despite harassment by the police, hostility from local residents and criticism in the press. By 1984 there were an estimated minimum of 15,000 vehicles moving around the summer circuit and the press began to refer to the phenomenon as the Hippie Convoy, although the Travellers preferred the description Peace Convoy. Attempts to set up longer-term winter settlements, such as the Rainbow Fields Village at Molesworth in early 1985, were thwarted by police and local authorities, although some farmers made smaller sites available. In June 1985 police attacked a group of Travellers attempting to reach Stonehenge for the midsummer festivities in what became known as the 'Battle

of the Beanfield', injuring women and children and destroying
or incapaciting vehicles. As a result of this and similar incidents,
some Travellers relocated to Spain and Portugal; others became
more militant and better organized. In 1989 the police applied an
exclusion order under Section 13 of the 1986 Public Order Act to
prevent anyone from approaching Stonehenge; in 1992 a 15-mile
exclusion zone was created around Glastonbury.

The phenomenon took on a new aspect at the end of the 1980s
as the traditional spectrum of ecologically conscious drop-outs
– now often known as New Age Travellers – and their messier,
less scrupulous companions were joined by members of the
urban-beggar CRUSTY fraternity and by devotees of ACID HOUSE
and RAVE culture, who brought a new level of entrepreneurship
and efficiency, including the use of mobile phones and faxes, as
well as a sophisticated drug economy. The tightening of the rules
for social-security signing-on and for access to bed-and-breakfast
accommodation for the homeless also encouraged many young
unemployed to go on the road for the summer months, thereby
swelling the numbers of Travellers.

● *Following the break-up of the 20,000-strong 'New Age' camp in the
shadow of the Malvern Hills, police were last night considering a
nationwide intelligence network to curb the joining forces of hippies
and 'rave' revellers.*

Observer, 31 May 1992

TREE-SNIFFING

An obscure form of NEW AGE THERAPY that consists of contemplating
a tree at close quarters while inhaling the resinous fumes given off by
its bark and leaves. Identification with trees has been a long-standing
mystical component of occult and HIPPIE belief systems, and the
ritualized contemplation of nature, particularly of rock, snow and
blossom, has been a staple of Japanese custom and Chinese folk
tradition. In tree-sniffing (also known as forest therapy) these two
strains combine, supported by the scientific claim that certain
evergreens give off soothing vapours. Tree-sniffing overlaps with the
more purely mystic concept of invoking pre-Christian tree spirits and
forest gods practised by some devotees of New Age philosophies and
some participants in the outdoor SHAMANISTIC rituals of the MEN'S
MOVEMENT.

TREPANNING

A fad of the 1960s more talked about than indulged in was trepanning (also known as trepanation), the cutting of a hole into the human skull. In 1962, Dr Bart Huges, a Dutch mystic, decided that a person's ability to reach a higher state of consciousness depended on increasing the flow of blood through the brain. The brain's normal capacity was limited by our upright posture, he claimed, a situation that could be temporarily remedied by PSYCHEDELIC drugs, but permanently altered by drilling a hole through the cranium. Huges experimented on himself and having survived (trepanning has been safely practised by surgeons since prehistoric times to relieve pressure on the brain) he recommended the technique as a universal panacea. His ideas attracted the interest of the authorities, who committed him to a psychiatric hospital, and to members of the early COUNTERCULTURE, who saw his method as a way of opening the 'third eye' of wisdom referred to in Oriental mysticism. Trepanning caused a stir in UNDERGROUND circles after Huges's visit to London in 1966. Two British disciples of Huges, Joey Mellen and Amanda Feilding, carried out the operation on themselves in 1970 and campaigned for its legalization without success. Their mentor had meanwhile been banned from Britain as an undesirable alien.

- *Animals keep their brain functions optimal by holding their necks in a horizontal position. But since his origin man has been searching for the means to replace the lost blood in his brain.*
  From H. B. Huges' manifesto, reprinted in Bamn, *1971*

- *Among those impressed was Heathcote Williams, who published a dialogue between Joey and Bart in the literary* Transatlantic Review *and made a trepanation scene the climax of his award-winning play, AC-DC. An important convert was Julie Felix . . . an American singer in the style of Joan Baez.*
  John Michell, Eccentric Lives and Peculiar Notions, *1984*

TRIBUTE ACTS
See ROCK DOUBLES.

TRICKLE-DOWN THEORY

The so-called trickle-down theory holds that by liberating the successful sectors of a society to enrich themselves further, the increased economic activity, prosperity and competitive ethos will permeate and stimulate the less successful areas of the economy. In crude terms, it states that more wealth for the rich will eventually bring benefits to the poor. This notion was used as a rationale by the Reagan administration for cutting welfare payments to the unproductive levels of society while cutting taxes for higher income groups and for industry. As well as providing the basis of REAGANOMICS, the theory was much quoted by the NEW RIGHT and YUPPIES in the early 1980s. By the end of the decade, however, many commentators had concluded that the idea of wealth soaking down through a porous economy was simplistic and misleading, and the actual benefits to the poor of top-down, as opposed to bottom-up, wealth creation were negligible or short-lived.

TRIMBALL

See LOLOBAL.

TRIP GOGGLES

Goggles with multifaceted glass lenses were invented by LSD enthusiasts in the late 1960s as part of the paraphernalia used to simulate a PSYCHEDELIC experience. Unfortunately, the prismatic visions and disorientation produced also tended to cause physical injury in wearers, who collided with unnoticed obstacles. Such devices fell into disuse in the 1970s and early 1980s, but reappeared with the advent of ACID HOUSE, the NEW AGE movement and VIRTUAL REALITY; one such was the DAYDREAMER, sold in 1991.

TRIVIAL PURSUIT

A general-knowledge quiz in the form of a board game, promoted by Parker, a subsidiary of the Tonka toy manufacturer. Originating in Canada in 1979, the game was a hit first in YUPPIE circles and then, in the mid-1980s, worldwide. Later it was also adapted as a TV show and VIDEO GAME. Trivial Pursuit (the name was previously a deprecatory cliché) coincided with a boom in interest in reference books and general knowledge, as well as a vogue for one-upmanship at dinner parties among the upwardly mobile.

TROLLS

The fashion for Swedish teak and pine furniture and glassware that was a feature of the early 1960s brought with it exposure to other Scandinavian decorations and accessories. Among these were corn dolls, candelabra and, most importantly, trolls, the dwarfish or giant hobgoblins of Nordic folklore. These objects, made in wood trimmed with fur and leather or in stuffed felt, became popular fetish toys for schoolchildren and some adults. The fad was reinforced by the 'Moomin' cartoons of Tove Jansson, which were run in the national press. Trolls were the forerunners of a series of homunculus crazes that included GONKS, WOMBLES and MUPPETS.

TRUSTAFARIANS

A compound of RASTAFARIAN and 'trust fund', the nickname Trustafarian was coined by the *Sunday Times* Style File in August 1992 in a belated attempt to categorize a stratum of London society that had been observable in the Notting Hill district since the early 1980s. These were the sons and daughters of wealthy, generally liberal families who frequented the now chic ghetto areas of London W10 and W11. It was this clique that gentrified the bars and cafés of the Portobello Road in the mid-Eighties and turned the former 'front-line' no-go area of All Saints Road into a fashionable site for restaurants and shops.

- *But though they seem irredeemably boho, Trustafarians are closely related to the dying breed of Sloanes who used to rip it up on the opposite side of Hyde Park . . . 'They've thrown out the Alice bands and got in the crystals,' says Guinness heiress-and-author Tania Kindersley . . .*

  Sunday Times, *30 August 1992*

TWIST, THE

Among many dance crazes of the 1960s, the twist was the first, the most popular and the least transient. Its vogue among the fashionable young was short-lived, but unlike the shake, the jerk and the watusi, for instance, the twist was adopted by all age groups and quickly spread beyond the discothèques (themselves a brand-new phenomenon of the time) where it had first been established. The dance had an universal appeal, largely because it was extremely easy to perform: dancers were instructed to imagine that they were stubbing out cigarettes on the floor with both feet while drying their backs with an imaginary towel. It was also energetic and even mildly risqué; wits resurrected the description previously applied to the tango: 'a vertical expression of a horizontal desire'.

In early 1960, the song 'The Twist' was a minor hit in the USA for Hank Ballard and the Midnighters. Re-recorded by Chubby Checker later in the year, it became a worldwide success, selling over three million copies. (In 1989 a new version of the song, but not the dance, was a hit for Chubby Checker recording with the American cult group the Fat Boys.) Twist marathons were held in public and in private and the instantly forgettable films *Hey, Let's Twist* and *Don't Knock the Twist* were released in 1961 and 1962 respectively. Between 1960 and 1965 a rash of ephemeral dance crazes was exported from the USA, including the hully-gully, the mashed potato, the pony and the locomotion; Europe countered with the let-kiss from Scandinavia, and the bostella from Paris, but none of them outlasted the twist. Dance crazes, a feature of JITTERBUG and BOBBYSOXER lifestyles in the USA, were embraced in Britain by the MODS, but the twist's significance was not so much as a dance fad but as the first sign of mainstream and commercial exploitation of the then élitist DISCO culture.

- *When the record ['Let's Twist Again'] made the chart, Mecca suddenly caught on and they asked a team of Arthur Murray dancers to come down to the Lyceum and demonstrate the Twist. Can you imagine how obscene that was!*
  Jeff Dexter, reminiscing in Melody Maker, *12 September 1970*

TWO TONE

The Two-Tone movement was the most significant phenomenon in British youth culture between the demise of PUNK and the rise of ROCKABILLY and HIP HOP. It flourished between 1979 and 1982, although two of its representatives, the groups Madness and UB40, continued to make hit records throughout the Eighties. Two Tone resurrected the rhythms of late 1960s SKA and early REGGAE and added a NEW WAVE energy. Two Tone devotees of both sexes adopted a uniform derived by late Sixties MODS from the US and Jamaica: dark mohair suits, snap-brim hats, CREW CUTS and loafers. The name of the new movement enshrined its self-conscious anti-racism and also as played on references to the two-tone shoes and cars featured in mid-Sixties American street chic, and the two sounds of black dance music and white pop. The Punk subculture had approved of REGGAE, but had never adopted its sound; Punk had been non-racist, but its exponents were nearly all white. It had been nihilist rather than politically committed, and it was to redress these shortcomings that the Two-Tone movement with its own '2-Tone' record label and logo and its anti-Thatcher message was conceived. Some of its leading bands, including the Specials (from Coventry, where the movement originated), the Selecter and UB40, contained both black and white musicians; others, including the all-girl Bodysnatchers and Modettes, were white. Most of the groups, who often toured and performed together, were associated with ROCK AGAINST RACISM. Ironically, at one end of the audience spectrum Two Tone's following merged with the racist working-class SKINHEAD and OI factions, notably so in the case of the fans of Bad Manners and, to a lesser extent, of Madness. In its original form, Two Tone ran out of steam by the middle of the decade. Some of its exponents moved towards experimental and jazz styles, theatre and deeper political commitment; others like Madness into pop vaudeville.

UFOs

See CROP CIRCLES.

UHBs

An ephemeral attempt to invent another social category on the lines of PREPPIES and YUPPIES, UHB stood for 'urban haute bourgeois(ie)' and was applied by some journalists to a fashionable section of the *jeunesse dorée* of New York in 1990. Social commentators in London subsequently imported the initials, but the appellation did not catch on.

- *There may be a UHB living in your street; the signs are all too familiar: several trips to the dry-cleaner to have black ties or ballgowns cleaned; remarks such as 'Mummy was* right *to say that they shouldn't have allowed divorced people into Ascot after the War . . .'*

    Sunday Times, *November 1991*

UNCERTAINTY PRINCIPLE

Like CHAOS THEORY and the ANTHROPIC PRINCIPLE, the uncertainty principle of the German physicist Werner Heisenberg has been one of the rare concepts in physics and cosmology to excite the interest of non-specialist progressives. A principle in quantum mechanics, it states that it is impossible to measure accurately and simultaneously both the momentum and the position of a particle, and the more certain our value for its position, the less certain our value for its momentum. Heisenberg propounded the theory before the Second World War, but its implications for other areas of human activity took until the 1980s to filter down to popular consciousness and to intrigue some commentators. Put very crudely, the principle seems to support the notion that observation of a process necessarily interferes with that process and that relative, not absolute, values are the outcome. Despite its age the uncertainty principle figures largely in the spectrum of thinking loosely referred to as the NEW SCIENCE.

● *According to Heisenberg's Uncertainty Principle I must be lost.*
Lapel badge by BIFF Products, London, 1985

UNDERGROUND

Taken from its use to describe resistance networks during the Second World War, the underground became in the late 1960s a near synonym for the COUNTERCULTURE and the ALTERNATIVE SOCIETY. With its implications of repression, defiance and 'submerged' activity, it may be a more accurate description of the HIPPIE milieu than the other terms with their optimistic suggestion of a coherent antithesis to 'straight' society.

UNICORN

A male hairstyle consisting of a cropped or shaved head with an exaggeratedly pointed widow's peak at the front. The style was worn in the 1980s by some gay (see GAY LIBERATION) CLONES, progressive pop musicians and artists. It was probably a blend of two earlier influences, the ROCKABILLY QUIFF and the kiss-curl, as worn by the pioneer ROCK 'N' ROLLER Bill Haley and Hergé's cartoon character, Tintin.

UNISEX

The unisex look of the early 1970s was a mass-market consequence of the blurring of sexual stereotypes during the preceding five years. Feather-cut hair, tank tops and baggy flared trousers, sometimes worn with CLOGS, became a basic uniform for both females and males. At the progressive end of the fashion spectrum, genders were more flamboyantly confused during the subsequent GLAM period (see GENDER-BENDERS). Unisex was a journalistic and commercial term coined to describe an existing phenomenon that had come from the streets.

- *It [the feather-cut] had taken the social-sexual revolutionary deviations of the Sixties, teased them out, blow-dried away the unwashed associations, and welded a unisex helmet on the world and his family.*

   Ian Penman, The Face, *February 1988*

URBAN SURFING

A do-it-yourself dangerous sport of the urban teenage underclass, urban surfing (also known as roof-riding) consisted of riding illegally on the outside of underground and surface trains (train-surfing), buses or cars. The craze began in earnest in the USA during the early 1980s, spreading to Latin America shortly after and to the UK in 1988. The film *Teenwolf*, in which Michael J. Fox rides on the roof of a moving van, helped to boost the craze in Middle America. After a number of deaths the fad subsided around 1990.

URINE-DRINKING

A yoga discipline that received generally incredulous press comment during the early 1980s. Urine-drinking (either neat or diluted by fruit juice) was purported to have nutritional as well as spiritual benefits. Several international celebrities were said to indulge under the guidance of personal health advisers, and Indian politicians also subscribed to the practice. Urine therapy is an important part of the ancient Indian Ayur Veda medical techniques (which have strongly influenced the TRANSCENDENTAL MEDITATION movement). In the West, the actress Sarah Miles has endorsed urine-drinking, as has the British osteopath Arthur Lincoln Pauls, who has drunk his own urine every day for twenty years. A study carried out at the University of Newcastle, New South Wales, in the early 1990s suggested that urine-drinking could cure jet lag and relieve insomnia, due to the presence of the hormone melatonin, which affects circadian rhythms. British experts have disagreed, pointing out that melatonin in urine is present in only minute quantities and is in any case inactive.

V

VALLEY GIRLS

Valley Girl – subsequently shortened to 'Val' – was the generic nickname given during the mid-1970s to the teenage daughters of affluent parents living in and around the San Fernando Valley in outer Los Angeles. These females formed a distinctive subculture that became famous around 1981 for pioneering RECREATIONAL SHOPPING, and also for its own variety of slang. Often the offspring of Sixties-generation parents working in the media, the music industry or the professions, Vals evolved a sybaritic lifestyle in which CONSUMERISM and leisure were elevated into a social code. The phenomenon was articulated in the American press by Moon Unit Zappa, daughter of the ROCK musician Frank Zappa; later publicity came in the form of *The Valley Girl's Guide to Life* by Mimi Pond, published in 1982, and in an article in the British fashion magazine *Harpers & Queen* in 1983. Valspeak, the Valley Girls' scathing and hyperbolic vocabulary spoken in a self-conscious whine, was partly invented and partly adapted from the argot of SURFING, college students and other sources. Many of their favourite expressions – 'gag me with a spoon!', 'grody', 'gnarly' and 'to the max' are examples – became teenage vogue terms on a wider scale during the mid-1980s.

● *The greatest creative work that any Val does is trying to think of a slogan for her [personalized car number-] plate.'*

Harpers & Queen, 1983

VAPORUB

A fad in British discothèques and ACID HOUSE gatherings during 1991 was the use of Vick's aromatic ointment, VapoRub, which was smeared or mutually massaged on to the skin of revellers. The purpose of this was to increase tactile and olfactory stimulation in conjunction with frenzied dancing and, in many instances, the effects of the euphoric hallucinogenic drug ECSTASY. Jars of VapoRub became a fashionable accessory, and references to ointment use – on T-shirts, for example – helped to reinforce subculture identity. The manufacturers issued a public disapproval of the practice.

● *Although one clubber on the dancefloor boasts he has bought two tablets of Ecstasy inside Shelleys, the search team outside is finding more VapoRub than anything else. Sometimes it finds a little Ralgex Deep Heat. It allows it through.*

Independent on Sunday, *8 December 1991*

VEGANS

Vegans are strict vegetarians who refrain from consuming any products derived from animals. They therefore refuse dairy produce as well as meat and will not wear fur or leather. Taking its name from a shortening of the word 'vegetarian', the vegan movement began in the 1940s, inspired by Indian principles of non-violence to all living things. Some vegans involve themselves in ANIMAL RIGHTS movements and SABBING; conversely, some members of those factions subsequently become vegans. Critics draw attention to the dangers of inadequate nutrition inherent in a vegan diet, but the Vegan Society issues guidelines that they claim will prevent this.

VIDEO GAMES

During the 1980s, video games moved from the arcade to the television and the home computer. By the end of the decade they had been miniaturized to fit the small, hand-held consoles manufactured by firms such as Nintendo and Sega. By 1991 these games machines, particularly the Nintendo Gameboy, had become *de rigueur* for fashionable youngsters, regardless of age, sex or class. Critics questioned the value of the technically and graphically sophisticated but intellectually and ethically suspect software; fans claimed that the games increased concentration skills. By 1992 an underground games culture had grown up wherein handsets could be CUSTOMIZED and games were pirated or imported illegally. At the same time in the USA, support groups were set up to counsel parents whose children either craved computer games or overindulged in their use. In the early 1990s one in three households in America owned a Gameboy, but only 20 per cent of users were female. The next phase was to develop female-oriented software.

- *For some the latest imported games have the same hip aura as import 12-inch dance tunes. Certainly shops like Micro-Byte, the UK's biggest chain of independents, have the same clued-up, anti-mainstream feel as specialist record shops.*
  Jim McLellan, The Face, January 1992

VIDEO NASTIES
See SPLATTER MOVIES.

VIRTUAL REALITY
In 1990 computer graphics and animation made the transition from on-screen simulations of three-dimensions to a more sophisticated representation of a synthetic 'reality', using mobile headsets and glove handsets. Computer-generated hologram imagery based on processed photographs or mathematical modelling now allows the participant to move within and interact with an artificial landscape. In addition to their applications in architecture, engineering, film special effects and game-playing, the increased power of computer systems and the increased sensitivity possible in the rendering of shape and texture have allowed virtual-reality techniques to approximate 'fine art' for the first time. Virtual reality – now abbreviated to VR – became a buzz word in progressive circles in 1991, particularly appealing to fans of CYBERPUNK and CYBERPORN.

- *Already you can walk through a four-dimensional hyperbolic dodecahedron, a shape that should only exist as a mathematical formula. But VR is really still at the wonderful toy stage . . .*
  Sheila Hayman, Independent on Sunday, August 1991

VOGUEING
A fad originating in gay (see GAY LIBERATION) discos in Manhattan during the late 1980s, vogueing (from the name of the magazine) consists of simulating the show-off mannerisms of the modelling catwalk while dancing to HOUSE music. This flamboyant successor

to earlier acrobatic styles such as BODY POPPING first involved black and Hispanic dancers competing, often in groups known as 'houses' controlled by 'house mothers' or 'fathers'. Many of the original participants in this craze, who called their gatherings 'balls' and favoured semi-transvestite feathered and sequinned outfits, were active in the fashion and clothing industry. The craze was promoted by the cult entrepreneur Malcolm McLaren and was imitated by black and white DANCEFLOOR devotees in London, but was short-lived. The singing star Madonna later organized her dance troupe along vogueing lines.

W

WALLPAPER MUSIC
See REPETITIVE MUSIC.

WANNABES
Wannabe (also spelt Wannabee) is a humorous slang term – perhaps
suggesting an exotic creature, on the basis of 'wallaby' – meaning
an aspirant or imitator. A fashionable Americanism of 1986 and
1987, it was quickly adopted in the UK and Australia, and by the
early 1990s was in regular usage in the print media. The original
wannabe, typically a teenager or young adult, exhibited an envious
or ambitious desire, characterized by such phrases as 'I wanna be
like Madonna', 'I wanna be thin', 'I wanna be in Palm Beach'. In
the USA the word subsequently took on more specialized senses. It
became associated with black American culture in which it signified
an 'Uncle Tom', or an OREO, a black imitator of white values or styles
(Oreos are biscuits that are dark on the outside, white inside; the
British and Caribbean equivalent is 'coconut'). In the young black
American director Spike Lee's 1988 film *School Daze*, set in an
all-black college campus, the wannabes – party-loving conformist
hedonists – are contrasted with the ethnically aware, politically
active JIGABOOS. In police parlance in American inner cities
wannabes are white youths who form or join street gangs in imitation
of blacks, while in the business world the word is used for junior
staff who are desperate to move up the promotion ladder at any price.

● *There are two kinds of Wannabe. The first kind are the clones – the
stagedoor [Boy] Georges, the Cindy Lauperettes, the Apple scruffs,
the Madonna Wannabes (aka Madonnabes) – the devoted fans who
ape their idols as closely as possible. The other kind are the young
urban upstarts with a desperate lust for fame.*
i-D, *November 1987*

WAREHOUSING

The practice of organizing or attending ACID HOUSE parties or orbital RAVES. This was a particular phenomenon of 1988 and 1989, when Rave culture was arranged on the basis of mobile underground networks illegally holding mass gatherings, and before it returned to the environment of clubs and open-air festivals. The mass gatherings in question required meticulous planning, being held in such venues as hangars, warehouses and disused factories. Entrepreneurs used mobile telephones and advertised on PIRATE radio and computer networks; revellers usually paid to attend.

- *The philologically-inclined will note that in Tony's world the word 'warehouse' has turned into a verb. 'Yea,' says Tony. 'I warehouse, you warehouse . . . we was warehoused . . . Essentially what it means is this: to overwhelmingly swamp with people.'*
  Evening Standard, *9 October 1989*

WEATHERMEN

The Weathermen, or Weather Underground, as they later referred to themselves, were a revolutionary group active in the United States at the end of the 1960s and the beginning of the 1970s. These former student activists, almost all from white, middle-class backgrounds, took their name from the line in Bob Dylan's 1965 song 'Subterranean Homesick Blues': '. . . you don't need a weatherman to tell which way the wind blows'. It was the Weathermen's self-appointed task to tell the American Establishment where it was going wrong: communiqués praised the government of North Vietnam, urged the end of the Vietnam War, and argued for social justice and equality within the USA. After the Chicago riots of 1969, the libertarian Left moved from provocative pranks towards violent struggle. The Weathermen went underground, emerging to free from jail Timothy Leary, the guru of PSYCHEDELIA, meanwhile establishing links with European and Third World terrorist movements and preparing to arm themselves. Three members of the organization were killed in 1970 when their bomb factory blew up. From then on the remainder of the small group went on the run, pursued by the FBI. Most were later imprisoned, their cause having been forgotten.

● *Weatherman was an astonishing development. For the first time the sons and daughters of white middle-class Amerika, indeed of the very captains of industry whose corporations they bombed, were ready to die rather than be forced to take part in the Amerikan bad dream.*
   Bamn, *edited by Peter Stansill and David Zane Mairowitz, 1971*

WEDGE

The wedge was the standard vogue hairstyle during the second half of the 1970s for young British DISCO habitués, particularly the SOUL BOYS and their female counterparts in the south of England. The hair was worn fairly long and flopping to one side on top, but shaved at the neck and above the ears; it was commonly dyed blond on top, or streaked. The look was often identified with the singer David Bowie, who in 1975 adopted a camp SOUL image after his GLAM ROCK phase, but style commentators of the 1980s, to whom the wedge was an important icon, trace it to a female hairdo created by Trevor Sorbie at the Vidal Sassoon salon in London in 1974. In fact a similar hairstyle had been worn by male gays in New York City since 1971. In Britain the wedge of the late Seventies became part of the smart apolitical uniform of club and discothèque culture, lasting through the eras of PUNK and TWO TONE to reappear in the repertoire of the BLITZ KIDS.

WELLIE-WANGING

A do-it-yourself competitive sport practised typically in British pub gardens and at village fêtes and other fund-raising events, wellie-wanging consists of tossing a rubber wellington boot as far as possible. It probably started as an improvisation by rural revellers. 'Wellie' – the word and the object – became a household joke of the later 1970s, perpetuated by comedians and disc jockeys. The 'wanging' element presumably echoes the sound of the boot rebounding against turf or concrete, or else is an invention influenced by words such as 'fling' and 'wing'.

WEREWOLVES

See MOTHERFUCKERS.

WESSEX MAN

A tongue-in-cheek social category invented by the *Sunday Times* in 1992 in response to the earlier incarnation of the philistine ESSEX MAN and ESSEX GIRL. Wessex Man belonged to the burgeoning NEW AGE movement involving consciousness-raising, HOLISTIC MEDICINE and an interest in exotic or pseudo-archaic rituals. Interest in these things was shared by middle-class progressives, fans of CYBERPUNK and VIRTUAL REALITY, as well as by the TRAVELLERS who had been propagating them since the demise of the original HIPPIE movement in the early 1970s. 'Wessex' refers to the fact that since the late 1960s drop-out and alternative lifestyles had focused on the West Country and Wales, with their equable climate and clusters of ancient holy places.

- *Essentially white and middle-class, with an average age of 35, modern Wessex Man chucked in his first career and marriage in London or the Midlands – surprisingly few Wessex men were actually born in Wessex – and now lives with three other ATs (Alternative Types – he hates the term New Age Man) under the Glastonbury Tor.*

Sunday Times, *3 May 1992*

WHITE PANTHERS

Founded in imitation of the BLACK PANTHERS, the White Panthers of Detroit were radical activists who rejected the love philosophy of the HIPPIE COUNTERCULTURE in favour of theatrical provocations and revolutionary rhetoric. The group was formed by John Sinclair out of the Detroit Artists workshop in 1968 and consisted mainly of his protégés, the ROCK band the MC5. The Panthers used slogans – 'Power to the People!' was a favourite – and threatened to outrage straight society by such gestures as burning the American flag (they did not in fact carry it out). Like their contemporaries the YIPPIES and the WEATHERMEN, the hard core of this quasi-political party were eventually forced to go into hiding, disowning the MC5 for espousing Rock-star greed (they wanted sports cars). In Britain, Mick Farren, underground journalist, singer with the Deviants Rock group and self-publicist, founded a London chapter of the White Panthers based on a small clique living around Ladbroke Grove. The British White Panthers dedicated themselves to the cause of free music festivals and, helped by French and Algerian radicals, tore down the perimeter fences at the Isle of White pop festival in 1970. After squabbling arose between rival chapters of the Panthers, the British venture collapsed in 1972.

- *The White Panther Party is a revolutionary organization dedicated to building a new man, new woman and new world.*
  Announcement in Oz magazine, August 1972

WICCA

The name adopted by practitioners of NEW AGE witchcraft or occultism in the late 1980s and early 1990s. The word is Anglo-Saxon ('wicca' is actually a masculine form meaning wizard or warlock, the feminine forerunner of witch being 'wicce'), giving an antiquarian tone to a modern vogue that embraces 'white' and sympathetic magic, spiritual healing and worship of the supposed pre-Christian 'Great Goddess', together with the mystic black-magic hedonism promoted by covens and followers of the prewar 'Great Beast', Aleister Crowley. The witchcraft movement of today is unlikely to be a lineal descendant of prehistoric or even medieval folk customs, but rather a reformulation based on a jumble of historical texts and suppositions and given its impetus by 19th-century theosophy and spiritualism, Californian revivalisms of the late 1960s, and the activities of the writer Geraldine Gardner. Gardner was the most influential figure in moving witchcraft away from élitist sorcery towards neo-pagan nature worship. In the 1970s the feminine principle inherent in Wicca attracted many FEMINISTS, as well as those of both sexes who wished to reject Judaeo-Christian orthodoxies. In the 1980s, Wicca meshed with New Age concerns including divination, herbalism, psychic healing and identification with myth. The American Church of Wicca and the New Wiccan Craft are two of the current incarnations of a loosely connected network of like-minded enthusiasts.

- *Neopagan witchcraft and its rites provide a great deal of room for poetry, dance, music, laughter and whatever the moment and the tradition inspire. Witchcraft encourages an openness to the awe of the natural world and reverence and love of the cosmos.*
  Jeffrey B. Russell, A History of Witchcraft, 1980

WIDGIES

The female counterparts of BODGIES, Australia's Widgies were the
equivalents of the British TEDDY GIRLS. Typically wearing PONYTAILS,
long skirts or blue jeans, they were a less respectable version of the
American BOBBYSOXER and flourished in milk bars, dance halls and
cinemas between 1952 and 1960. The word is probably a diminutive
of 'widgeon', used as a term of endearment to young women.

WILDING

A black American slang term meaning to go on the rampage or run
amok, wilding was given front-page prominence on 22 April 1989
in the *New York Times* and thereafter worldwide, when a group of
black youths were tried for the rape and assault of a young white
woman. The case became a cause célèbre in the racial politics of
North America, and the new word entered the media's lexicon. In
origin it was either a mishearing, or shortened version, of the phrase
'doing the wild thing', probably distantly inspired by the Troggs' hit
record of that name.

- *A beautiful woman jogger viciously gang-raped and left in a coma
  by a mob of 'wilding' youths in New York's Central Park has
  woken from the dead.*
  People *magazine, 14 May 1989*

WINKLE-PICKERS

The British nickname given to (men's) shoes with sharply pointed
toes, 'winkle-picker' reflected the views of an older working-class
generation who had used pins to extract the shellfish delicacy.
Pointed shoes had been popular since the 1920s in France and Italy,
particularly in showbiz, proletarian and louche circles, but were
considered outlandish in a 1950s Britain dominated by military-
inspired anti-fashion. Bohemian stylists, some of whom later became
the first MODS, imported the style from Italy around the end of 1958.
It was then adopted by the TEDDY BOY and ROCKER subcultures. By
the time the Mod movement was underway in 1964, the winkle-
picker, once a shocking symbol of aggression and flamboyance, was
associated with an outdated look. In 1975 the pointed toe again

appeared in Italy, probably influenced by Western boots; it was taken up in Britain and the USA as part of the PUNK repertoire, but the nickname was no longer heard.

WOMBLES

The children's stories by Elisabeth Beresford describing rodent-like creatures living on London's Wimbledon Common were made into a television series that at the beginning of the 1970s caught the imagination of a family audience. The Wombles supposedly disposed of litter left by humans, and this early environmental awareness helped their popularity. A merchandising drive accompanied by Mike Batt's catchy pop songs and a group in Womble costumes playing concerts confirmed the craze. Wombles belong in the tradition of fetish toys that encompasses TROLLS, GONKS, MUPPETS and SMURFS. Like the first three terms, Womble also entered British slang as a synonym for a foolish, clumsy or unfortunate individual.

WOMEN'S LIBERATION

See FEMINISM.

WORLD MUSIC

The origins of the term World Music are, perhaps surprisingly, the subject of heated debate. Some claim that it originated from a meeting of music industry independents and journalists in an upstairs room at the Empress of Russia pub in Islington; others point to the phrases *sono mondiale* and *son mondial* coined by Italian and French magazine writers respectively. It was in any case a logical choice for a marketing label conjured up in the early 1980s to cover a multitude of sounds previously referred to as ethnic music. During the 1960s and 1970s, apart from a brief flirtation with Indian music by HIPPIES, musical forms from outside the developed world had remained largely a minority taste. American avant-garde jazz musicians and experimenters in REPETITIVE MUSIC had incorporated African and Asian elements in their work; music connoisseurs such as the British DJ John Peel had given radio airtime to authentic archive recordings of exotic music; and at the end of the Seventies the WOMAD festival gathered together pan-ethnic

FOLK music. But it was in the Eighties that the exhaustion of ROCK and pop modes, coupled with the new cosmopolitanism of NEW AGE MUSIC aficionados and dance-music devotees, prompted an upsurge of interest in Latin American, Oriental and Arab music. Later in the decade the imported and fusion styles were joined on the record retailers' shelves by émigré music such as BHANGRA and RAI.

- *Fashions change in the taste for World Music as if a music that has more substance than pop were a mere convenience for the selling.*
  David Toop, The Face, *February 1988*

WRIST RADIO

See TRANSISTOR RADIO.

X

X
See ECSTASY.

X-ers
See GENERATION X.

YIPPIES

In 1968 HIPPIE activists Abbie Hoffman – author of *Revolution for the Hell of It* – and Jerry Rubin, supported by Marshall Bloom, Paul Krassner and Allen Ginsberg, founded the Youth International Party to agitate against the American political and military Establishment. The short-lived Yippie movement was a loose coalition of radicals, anarchists, libertarians, artists and musicians concerned with SITUATIONIST tactics and confrontational political gestures; their best-known stunt was probably their putting forward a pig as presidential candidate at the 1968 Democratic Party convention in Chicago. After the violent attacks on anti-war demonstrations by Mayor Daley's police, Hoffman and others – the so-called 'Chicago Seven' – were put on trial. While Yippie came to be used as a catch-all, often pejorative, term for a politically involved member of the COUNTERCULTURE, the original activists were treated with suspicion by many, particularly in the UK, who found their militant posturing incompatible with HIP hedonism. At the Woodstock Festival in 1970, Pete Townshend of the Who ROCK group battered Abbie Hoffman from the stage when he attempted to harangue the crowd. With the exception of the little-known Paul Krassner, many Yippies recanted or conformed during the later 1970s; Jerry Rubin, for instance, became a management consultant. Hoffman, on the other hand, was forced to go underground and remained on the FBI's 'Most Wanted' list until shortly before his death in 1989. Publication of his collected writings in 1990 did much to rehabilitate his reputation, if not that of the Yippie movement.

- *The life of the American spirit is being torn asunder by the forces of violence, decay and the napalm cancer-fiend. We demand the politics of Ecstasy!*

  YIP manifesto, 1968

● *. . . many people have shared my disappointment . . . the entrances and exits of yippie heavies drooling enthusiastically about [Timothy] Leary's fiftieth birthday present, a gun . . .*
Richard Neville, Oz magazine, November 1970

YOUNG FOGEYS

A British phenomenon of the mid-1980s, Young Fogeys (a journalistic categorization by humorous analogy with the colloquial 'old fogey') were youngish males of self-consciously traditionalist attitudes, manners and aesthetic ideals. The best-known exemplars of Young Fogeydom (although they themselves rejected the label) were the fastidious and conservative novelist A. N. Wilson; Charles Moore, editor of the *Spectator*, and the architectural critic Gavin Stamp. These and other members of, or aspirers to, the upper middle classes attempted to re-create in their lifestyles (they overlapped with the so-called NEW GEORGIANS) and outlook the more refined values of pre-1960 Englishness, while at the same time admiring Margaret Thatcher (see THATCHERISM). High Anglicanism, literary dabbling, a liking for traditional cooking and clothing and an antipathy to 'progressive' attitudes and popular culture were some of their characteristics; older inspirations included P. G. Wodehouse and John Betjeman and the journalists William Deedes, Peregrine Worsthorne, Auberon Waugh and Richard Ingrams. In their nostalgic priggishness the Young Fogeys were the cerebral wing of the NEW RIGHT tendency, in the ascendant from 1983 to 1988. In keeping with their supposed status as a cult or subculture (in fact they would be better described as a coterie), a *Young Fogey Handbook*, on the lines of those celebrating PREPPIES, JAPS and SLOANE RANGERS, was published in 1985.

● *Few young fogeys perhaps can afford to pose as the squire or the lord of the manor, but they can so easily take on the aspect of a younger son, the kind who took Holy Orders, lived in the Glebe House and pursued knowledge and foxes while preaching a simple morality and enjoying social esteem all his days.*
Suzanne Lowry, The Young Fogey Handbook, 1985

YUPPIES

The 1970s cliché of the 'dynamic young executive' gave way at the
end of that decade to a new categorization. Variously defined as
the YAP (Young Aspiring Professional), Yumpie (Young Upwardly
Mobile Professional) and Yuppie (Young Urban Professional), the
males and females in question could be identified by their uniform
of business suit and running shoes and their attitude of unashamed
careerism. Of the three acronyms, Yuppie (the '-ie' was added on on
the lines of HIPPIE, YIPPIE and PREPPIE) came to predominate, and
by 1984, when the *Yuppie Handbook* was published in New York,
was in currency throughout the English-speaking world. For the next
seven years similar coinages were attempted by lifestyle journalists –
'guppie', 'buppie', 'grumpie', etc. – but failed to catch on.

The Yuppie was the symbol of success in the enterprise culture of
the 1980s and epitomized the new glamour of money, materialism
and conspicuous consumption (see CONSUMERISM). Significantly in
Britain the Yuppie, unlike the earlier SLOANE RANGER or the coeval
YOUNG FOGEY, was defined by aspiration and wealth, not by class.
The chance of 'telephone-number salaries' in the City of London
brought the ESSEX BOY into the same world as the middle-class
professional. Yuppies – who never acknowledged the term, 'the
Y-word' being a taboo – were celebrated in the press, in the cinema
by the American movie *Wall Street* and a host of lesser films; in
the theatre in Caryl Churchill's *Serious Money*, and belatedly on
television, notably in Thames Television's *Capital City* SOAP OPERA.
Their tastes and habits revolved around a number of key accessories,
in particular the FILOFAX, the Porsche and the mobile phone, as well
as around such venues as wine bars, fashionable FOODIE haunts and
HIGH TECH or NEOCLASSICAL offices and homes. The high point of the
London Yuppie was the BIG BANG of October 1986, but the stock-
market crash of 'Black Monday' one year later marked the beginning
of the subsequent recession. The image of the financier was tarnished
by trials for insider dealing and fraud in New York – 'Yuppiegate' –
and London, and by 1990 the term Yuppie was rarely heard except as
a pejorative reference to the excesses of the previous decade.

● *Yuppie scum fuck off . . . Kill a yuppie today.*
> *Wall graffiti protesting against the gentrification of the*
> *East End, London, 1988*

YUPPIES

- *Design yuppies had their preppie classics, their vintage Forties ties, their big spectacles, their hip briefcases and bulging Filofaxes, and the new soft unstructured suits that Italian designers had been refining since the Seventies. City yups had their revamped pinstripes, their braces and mobile phones.*

Arena, November 1991